Give a Man a Fish

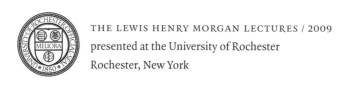 THE LEWIS HENRY MORGAN LECTURES / 2009
Presented at the University of Rochester
Rochester, New York

Duke University Press   Durham and London   2015

GIVE A MAN A FISH

A FISH

Reflections on the New Politics of Distribution

JAMES FERGUSON   Foreword by Thomas Gibson

Printed in the United States of America on acid-free paper ∞
Designed by Natalie F. Smith
Typeset in Quadraat Pro by Westchester Publishing Services

Library of Congress Cataloging-in-Publication Data
Ferguson, James, 1959–
Give a man a fish : reflections on the new politics of distribution / James Ferguson.
pages cm—(The Lewis Henry Morgan lectures)
Includes bibliographical references and index.
ISBN 978-0-8223-5895-4 (hardcover : alk. paper)
ISBN 978-0-8223-5886-2 (pbk. : alk. paper)
ISBN 978-0-8223-7552-4 (e-book)
1. Economic assistance, Domestic—Africa.   2. Public welfare—Africa.
3. Africa—Economic policy.   4. Africa—Social policy.   5. Neoliberalism—
Africa.   6. Capitalism.   7. Poverty—Africa.   I. Title.   II. Series:
Lewis Henry Morgan lectures.
HC800.Z9P63 2015
361.96—dc23
2014037998

Cover photo: © Oliver Asselin / Alamy. A man counts money he has
just received from a social cash transfer program in the village of
Julijuah, Bomi County, Liberia, 2012.

Contents

Foreword

The Lewis Henry Morgan Lectures were originally conceived in 1961 by Bernard Cohn, who was then chair of the Department of Anthropology and Sociology at the University of Rochester. A founder of modern cultural anthropology, Morgan was one of Rochester's most famous intellectual figures and a patron of the university; he left a substantial bequest to the university for the founding of a women's college. The lectures named in his honor have now been presented annually for over fifty years and constitute the longest-running such series in North America.

The first three sets of lectures commemorated Morgan's contributions to the study of kinship (Meyer Fortes in 1963), native North Americans (Fred Eggan in 1964), and cultural evolution (Robert M. Adams in 1965). They were originally delivered to public audiences on Tuesday and Thursday evenings over a period of two to three weeks and published as book-length monographs. A public lecture is now delivered on a single evening, followed by a day-long workshop in which a draft of the planned monograph is discussed by members of the Department of Anthropology and by commentators invited from other institutions. But the public lecture and the monograph are still intended to present an example of current anthropological thinking to a general audience.

The present volume is based on the Lewis Henry Morgan Lecture that Professor James Ferguson delivered at the University of Rochester in October 2009. The formal discussants who participated in the workshop that followed the lecture included Marina Welker (Cornell), John Western (Syracuse), Dunbar Moodie (Hobart and William Smith), Mary Moran (Colgate), Douglas Holmes (Binghamton), and Daniel Reichman (Rochester). Ferguson's argument touches on many of Morgan's key interests, including the development and transformation of communal and individual forms of property, the role that kinship and the state play alongside the market in the distribution of economic resources, and the way that non-capitalist societies around the world can serve as "concrete forms of political inspiration" for the future.

Ferguson's primary concern is with new forms of distribution that are emerging across the global South in nations like South Africa, Namibia, Mexico, Brazil, and India. In view of the fact that the current phase of global capitalism has rendered a growing proportion of the population in these nations chronically unemployed, many political activists have begun to question the assumption shared by both capitalists and Marxists that only waged workers have a right to a share of the social product. Ferguson notes that many figures in the radical democratic tradition, such as Tom Paine and Peter Kropotkin, argued that value is produced by society as a whole, that all members of society should be regarded as shareholders in a collective enterprise, and that everyone thus has a right to a share of the total social product. Others, such as Marcel Mauss and Julius Nyerere, developed different arguments about the just distribution of the collective social product without basing it on the labor of individuals.

One of the most radical proposals circulating in South Africa and Namibia today is that every member of society should receive a basic income grant without reference to their age, gender, employment, or family configuration. Ferguson notes that such a grant would help undermine the value system associated with industrial capitalism in which it is socially demeaning for adult men to be dependent on anyone but themselves while it is socially acceptable for women, children, and the aged to be dependent on male kinsmen or on state benefits. This value system perpetuates both gender inequality and the criminalization of the long-term unemployed. By contrast, in the kinship-based societies and subcultures traditionally studied by anthropologists, the cultivation of economic and moral interdependence within a network of effective kin is one of the main goals of social life. Proposals like the basic income grant seek to scale this sort of morality up to the level of the nation-state and beyond.

Just as previous studies by anthropologists of actually existing forms rather than of ideal models of capitalism and socialism provoked political economists to think about the role of markets and planning in a new way, Ferguson's study of the actually existing forms of mutuality that are emerging across the global South should provoke political activists to think about social justice in a new way. The book seeks to go beyond the now-familiar critiques of neoliberal capitalism and open up a new debate about what a better future might look like for us all. In doing so, it remains true to the radical spirit of anthropology that Lewis Henry Morgan himself practiced.

Thomas Gibson
Editor, Lewis Henry Morgan Monograph Series

Preface and Acknowledgments

In the course of doing critical studies of "development" over a period of many years starting in the early 1980s, I was often asked by would-be "developers" some version of the question "Well, then, what should we do?" I felt this was in important ways the wrong question (see epilogue to Ferguson 1990). But seeing the way money was being poured into project after project with little positive effect on the lives of the supposed beneficiaries, I was sometimes tempted to answer the question by suggesting that better results could be obtained if the project funds, instead of being spent on Land Cruisers and foreign consultants, were simply handed over directly to the "target population." Over the years, several other anthropologists have confessed to me having had the same impulse. I remember one who even proposed, half-seriously, that the money spent on development projects be simply scattered out of helicopters, so that local people could harvest it.

The fact that such thoughts could only take the form of suppressed impulses or cynical humor reflects the power of a long-standing anxiety about simply "giving" money directly to poor people. From the time of its birth, a key imperative for capitalism has been to drive people into labor, and any plans to directly distribute resources to those who lack them have been met by powerful worries about undermining what is politely called "the incentive to work." Such considerations have long made it self-evident that development projects should prepare people for such work, not provide them with sources of livelihood independent of it. Handing out cash was simply not in the cards, and proposing such a thing could only be understood as some sort of joke.

It is no longer a joke. I began to notice this as I watched the steady expansion in recent years of a system of paying cash grants to the poor in South Africa. As I puzzled over the apparent paradox of a "neoliberal" regime sending monthly checks to a steadily expanding roster of citizens that now exceeds 30 percent of the population, I gradually realized that the new willingness to "just give money to the poor" (as the title of a recent book has it [Hanlon, Barrientos, and Hulme 2010]) was not a South African peculiarity but an emerging reality across much of the world. As this book details, recent years have seen the spread of major programs of direct distribution of cash to the poor (so-called cash transfers) all across the global South, often with the support of established development institutions (such as the World Bank) that would not long ago have recoiled in horror at the very idea. This has happened at the same time that increasingly large populations find that they have no access to wage labor— the form of livelihood that has long been understood both as a historical telos of economic development and as an anchor of progressive politics.

How are we to understand this new situation? And what is the significance of the global trend toward cash transfers to the poor, in southern Africa and beyond? This book is, in the first instance, an attempt to answer these questions, and to propose at least some preliminary ideas about how we might think about the emergence of what I call a new politics of distribution. The argument that unfolds in the following chapters is that the current conjuncture is pregnant with both new political possibilities and new dangers. At the same time, I suggest that a sustained reflection upon certain practical puzzles and impasses of the present political moment reveals that some of the foundational assumptions that have guided critical social theory for generations are in significant ways out of step with our new realities. Moving the question of distribution from the periphery of our theoretical concerns to the center, I will argue, both opens up new political possibilities and sheds new light on a host of analytical issues ranging from labor and livelihoods to markets and money to dependence and personhood.

I approach these questions through a long engagement with a specific regional history. While the empirical cases that will be most fully explored here are those of South Africa and Namibia, the account I seek to provide of distributive processes extends to much of the wider southern African region and has involved pursuing lines of investigation I have worked on for years while revisiting (and in some cases reinterpreting) some of my own earlier ethnographic research in Lesotho and Zambia. But far more important than my own work here has been the work of countless others. The book is, in no small measure, an attempt to review and synthesize that work in hopes of bringing the insights of an exceptionally important and high-quality regional literature into a wider circle of discussion. Studies of the southern African region (especially the detailed and richly empirical accounts that feature in the best of its ethnographic research) are, I suggest, of broader significance and import than has sometimes been recognized. And if, as I will argue, our ability to conceive of real political alternatives in these neoliberal times has suffered from a certain poverty of the political imagination, this rich ethnographic archive may contain resources that might be of some use as we seek to find new ways both of understanding the present and of envisioning possible futures.

Beyond my intellectual debt to this outstanding body of literature, I also have personal debts to many of the scholars who have produced it, scholars who have in one way or another inspired or assisted my work over the years. Some I have known for decades now, and many have been directly supportive of me and my work. Especially helpful have been Patrick Bond, Jean and John Comaroff, Ben Cousins, Donald Donham, Andries du Toit, Harri Englund, Gillian Hart, Achille Mbembe, Donald Moore, Nicoli Nattrass, David Neves, Francis Nyamnjoh, Stephen Robins, Jeremy Seekings, Andrew Spiegel, and Eric Worby. I am very pleased to have held honorary appointments in recent years at both the Department of Social Anthropology at the University of Cape Town and the Department of Sociology and Social Anthropology at the University of Stellenbosch, and I am grateful for my wonderful colleagues at both institutions.

In the course of this project, I also came to realize how much can be learned from the people I came to think of as "policy intellectuals"— sophisticated thinkers engaged with pragmatic issues of social policy in settings as various as NGOs, think tanks, universities, government departments, trade unions, and political parties. I have interviewed many of these people, formally and informally, over the last decade. For the most part, they are not named in the text, either because they were promised anonymity or simply to avoid causing them embarrassment. But I am grateful to all of them. In South Africa, I am especially grateful to the busy officials at the Department of Social Development who so generously took the time to share their perspectives with me, while in Namibia I have special debts to Dirk and Claudia Haarmann and Uhuru Dempers of the Basic Income Grant Campaign for their kind assistance and generosity.

The heart of this book was originally presented as the Lewis Henry Morgan Lectures at the University of Rochester in October of 2009. I am grateful to the Department of Anthropology at Rochester, and especially to Tom Gibson and Bob Foster for inviting me and providing warm hospitality during my visit, as well as to Dan Reichman and Eleana Kim. I am also indebted to the discussants for the lectures—Douglas Holmes, Dunbar Moodie, Mary Moran, Marina Welker, and John Western—who provided a host of valuable suggestions and questions. In developing this volume for publication, I have tried to keep the feel of a series of lectures. As its subtitle suggests, the book is intended less as an authoritative report on research than as a series of "reflections," whose goal is less to explain the new distributive programs I describe than to reflect on their meaning and significance. The chapters are envisaged as an ordered sequence of independent essays. While they are meant to fit together into an integrated whole when read in sequence, my intention is that each chapter can also be intelligible if read separately. My hope is that the reader will forgive a certain amount of redundancy that must inevitably accompany this strategy.

Support for this project was provided by the Stanford Humanities Center, where I held the Ellen Andrew Wright Fellowship in 2010–11, as well as by the Stellenbosch Institute for Advanced Study, where I was a fellow in the spring of 2011. I am grateful for the intellectual stimulation of the colleagues with whom I shared fellowship time at both institutions, and especially to members of the research group with which I worked at Stellenbosch: Ben Cousins, Henry Bernstein, Bridget O'Laughlin, and Pauline Peters. I am also grateful to the Vrije Universiteit of Amsterdam, where I had the opportunity to serve as international fellow from 2008 to 2010. Of those colleagues who generously hosted me while helping me to refine my ideas, I would especially like to thank Freek Colombijn, Marjo de Theije, Birgit Meyer, and Oscar Salemink. I also benefited from being part of the seminar "Markets and Moralities" at the School for Advanced Research, Santa Fe, New Mexico, which was held in May 2009. I am grateful to all of the seminar participants, who pushed my thinking forward in important ways, and especially to the seminar organizers, Ted Fischer and Peter Benson. A version of chapter 4 appeared in the volume that emerged from this seminar, *Cash on the Table: Markets, Values, and Moral Economies*, edited by Edward Fischer (Santa Fe: School of Advanced Research Press). A version of chapter 2 appeared in *Registration and Recognition: Documenting the Person in World History* (*Proceedings of the British Academy* 182, 495–516), while a version of chapter 5 appeared in the *Journal of the Royal Anthropological Institute* 19 (2): 223–42.

Tania Li has been a wonderful source of ideas and questions for many years now, and I have greatly benefited from her comparative thoughts about distribution and what she once called "worlds without work." Liisa Malkki, as always, has been a font of insightful questions, inspired suggestions, and new ideas. I have received very valuable comments from many other readers of sections of the book, including Keith Breckenridge, Jean and John Comaroff, Harri Englund, and Hylton White. I also benefited from an extensive discussion with Lawrence Cohen, Stephen Collier, and Tobias Rees. Austin Zeiderman and Sarah Ives both did very valuable work as research assistants and have my thanks.

I continue to benefit from being in the intellectual company of a stellar group of scholars in the Department of Anthropology at Stanford. I am grateful to them for providing such a supportive and intellectually engaging home base from which to work, and especially to Thomas Blom Hansen and Lynn Meskell for their stimulating reflections on the South African scene. In the wider Bay Area, a group of colleagues was kind enough to read the entire manuscript at a late stage: Don Donham, Gill Hart, Donald Moore, Lisa Rofel, Anna Tsing, and Sylvia Yanagisako. I am deeply grateful for their insights and encouragement. As always, Ken Wissoker has been the best of editors, whose good judgment and unflagging support have been assets I could count on throughout the process.

Finally, I wish to observe that, like any human production, this book has only been possible thanks to a long series of prior enactments of material distribution and social and emotional care. I therefore dedicate it to all those who have supported and nurtured me through the different stages of my life, and especially to my parents, Jane and Jim Ferguson.

Introduction.
Cash Transfers and
the New Welfare States

From Neoliberalism to
the Politics of Distribution

Something unexpected has happened in the last two decades. We have become used to a debate pitting triumphalist accounts of the global spread of "free-market" capitalism (decreeing the end of history, or telling us the world is flat) against critical accounts of that same ascendancy that tell a formally similar story but with the moral polarity inverted.[1] But both sides of this great debate seem to agree on the story's fundamental plotline: unfettered, "free-market" capitalism is regnant, and "neoliberal," market-based systems of economy and governance are everywhere on the march, while the welfare state is embattled, in retreat, or barely hanging on. In this context, it has been profoundly surprising to see that recent years, in a host of different sites across the global South, have in fact yielded something quite different: the creation and expansion of extensive social welfare programs targeting the poor anchored in schemes that directly transfer small amounts of cash to large numbers of low-income people.

The ideological narratives of market triumph (pro or con) made it easy to miss this development, since the narratives seemed agreed that neoliberalism is (as sociologist Peter Evans [2008, 217] put it) "congenitally blind to the need for social protection" and that "the poor" therefore must, in these market-friendly and state-slashing times, receive less attention (not more) from national states. But they also made it easy to suppose that whatever interventions or innovations *were* occurring in the world of development and poverty policy must be those that fit the narratives, leading to a burst of scholarly attention to such paradigmatically "neoliberal" things as microcredit and microfinance schemes. But now that the smoke has cleared, it is plain to see that the really big "development" story of the last twenty years is, in fact, not microcredit but (as a recent policy review put it) "the rise and rise of social protection" (Roelen and Devereux 2013, 1).[2] And the central mechanism of the new anti-poverty programs is not credit, securitization, or any other sort of neoliberal predation but the startlingly simple device of handing out small amounts of money to people deemed to need it. As the title of one volume of full-throated advocacy for such cash transfers recently put it, *Just Give Money to the Poor*.[3]

Whatever one may think of this outcome, it is decidedly *not* where dominant narratives of marketization and neoliberalism expected us to end up. And it is a turn of events that implies some quite different sorts of political possibilities and dangers than those suggested by the usual neoliberalism story. This book, then, is a sustained reflection on these new worldwide developments and their political and social significance, with southern Africa (a region I have studied for more than three decades) as its key point of focus. The book's goal is less to explain these developments than to reflect on what they might mean and how they may be transforming the field of political limits and possibilities, both within the region and beyond it.

Neoliberal Welfare States? The Surprising Outcome of Political and Economic Restructuring in Southern Africa

The disjuncture between certain influential scholarly stories about neoliberalism and concrete developments at the level of social policy is especially pronounced in southern Africa. Here, narratives about neoliberalism have been central to most critical understandings of the massive political and economic changes of the last few decades, as I will describe below. But at the same time the region has been a widely hailed pioneer in the expansion in social protection that has swept the globe. South Africa here has led the way, with an extensive national system of social payments anchored by old age pensions, child care grants, and disability payments. But others in the region have followed suit, and there are now similar major nationwide programs in Botswana and Namibia, along with smaller ones in Lesotho, Swaziland, and Mozambique, as well as pilot and regional programs (intended to soon be scaled up to the nationwide level) in Malawi, Zambia, and Zimbabwe.[5]

Southern Africa (and especially South Africa) has sometimes been seen not only as an instance of neoliberalism but even as a paradigmatic case of it (see, e.g., Klein 2008). And if neoliberalism is, as some accounts have (rather Eurocentrically) tended to suggest, first and foremost a worldwide project centered on the erosion, rollback, or downsizing of the Keynesian "social" states that dominated the post–World War II (Western) world (see, e.g., Harvey 2007), it seems clear enough in what direction "neoliberal" southern Africa must be headed: toward the heartless world of neoliberal capitalism, in which the welfare state withers while the poor are ever more exposed to the depredations of "the market." With the issues framed in this way, even the most astute of the region's many critical observers have sometimes paid less attention than they should have to a remarkable set of events in the region, events that have in fact led to sustained *expansions* (rather than reductions) in programs of social assistance and indeed to the emergence of what could reasonably be described as a new kind of welfare state. And while many influential accounts of neoliberalism have seen only ever-growing social exclusion, we here must also take stock of a new kind of inclusion as millions of poor citizens previously ignored or worse by the state have become direct beneficiaries of cash payments.[6]

The most influential critical accounts of neoliberalism in southern Africa center on the region's economic core, South Africa, so it is important briefly to review how such accounts understand South Africa's post-apartheid transition and the economic changes that came in its wake. As the story is generally told, the African National Congress (ANC) party that took the reins of government after the 1994 transition, having abandoned its old commitments to socialist economic transformation, opted for what Patrick Bond (2005, 6) has termed a "homegrown" structural adjustment program, yielding without much of a fight to the World Bank/ IMF orthodoxy of the time that called for the opening up of markets (via deregulation and privatization), in the hopes of making the new South Africa an attractive destination for international capital investment. Following a brief and transitional commitment to a "Reconstruction and

Development Plan" (RDP) that articulated a broad if vague social democratic commitment to a "mixed economy," 1996 saw an official shift to
a new, more "neoliberal" approach, the "Growth with Employment and
Redistribution" (GEAR) program. At the heart of the plan was the claim
that a business-friendly, "growth-led" strategy would generate sufficient
economic growth to secure substantial employment growth and in the
end to lift all boats.[7] But moves to "open up" the economy to "the market"
yielded only limited economic growth, disappointingly failing to come
close to the optimistic early projections. Even more dramatic was the failure to generate much employment. Not only was there no burst of new
employment; old standbys like agriculture and mining actually shed huge
numbers of jobs—just the sorts of jobs that had formerly allowed low-
skilled and low-waged workers to sustain urban and rural livelihoods and
communities all across the region. The result was a rapid acceleration of
a shift that had begun already in the 1970s, from a labor-shortage economy to one of massive labor surplus (Seekings and Nattrass 2005; Marais
2011). With persistent mass unemployment (official figures stuck near 25
percent and broader measures generally much higher[8]), many of those at
the bottom of the economic heap seemed to have little to show for their
supposed liberation. New wealth was certainly being generated, some of
it now conspicuously accumulated by black South Africans (often well-
connected ANC elites), but inequality rose to levels exceeding even those
seen under apartheid. This led to a society whose superficial prosperity
disguised formidable underlying ills, including inequality, mass unemployment, and lack of full social inclusion.

This critique, in its broad strokes, gets a lot right. Both its account of
economic liberalization and its diagnosis of the social ills that followed
in its wake are broadly correct. But there are two gaps in such accounts
that make them of only limited value in understanding the region's new
welfare states.[9] First, the critiques are inevitably most articulate about
what they are *against* ("neoliberalism") and have often struggled to lay out
convincing and realistic alternatives and strategies. Too often, in fact,
critical accounts of neoliberalism have settled into a politics of denunciation (what I have elsewhere [Ferguson 2010] analyzed as "the politics of
the anti-") in which political identities are constituted or consolidated
less by concrete programs of government or political mobilization than
by a declaration of opposition to a malevolent and polymorphic "other"

named "neoliberalism." The result is a strange state of affairs in which nearly every intellectual and politician in South Africa today condemns "neoliberalism" but no major political parties have emerged advocating any very substantially different policy path (at least until very recently).[10] The second problem is not unrelated. It is that the now-standard critical accounts of South Africa's "neoliberalism" fail to attend to the very substantial ways in which that country (pioneering a path for many of its neighbors) has taken a turn that, in some respects at least, seems almost the opposite of the standard neoliberal model: that is, by elaborating an enormous system of non-contributory social benefits that today transfers 3.4 percent of the nation's GDP directly to "the poor" via non-market cash payments that are now received by more than 30 percent of the entire population (National Treasury 2013, 84–86).

It seems clear that this development was the product of a quite particular conjuncture. For it was at just the moment that the post-apartheid ANC regime came to power, with a mandate to transform the economic conditions of the poor and working-class people who made up its political base, that a worldwide economic restructuring undermined the low-wage employment that had long provided the entire region with its economic core. (On the brutally abrupt collapse of labor markets for low-wage and low-skilled labor, see Seekings and Nattrass 2005; Marais 2011.) Facing the pressing political need to deliver concrete changes to the new black political majority, and with "pro-market" economic policies failing to yield the rapid economic growth that had been supposed to "lift all boats," social protection became a key domain of policy innovation. South Africa and several of its neighbors had long had quite well-developed social welfare systems for whites, but provisioning for blacks was rudimentary at best (see chapter 2). As part of the transition to the new, post-apartheid regime, pension rates were equalized across racial groups, and social assistance rapidly became of much greater economic value for the majority populations. At the same time, a decision was made to implement a substantial new nationwide cash benefit for those caring for small children. Similar programs were soon taken up by neighboring countries Namibia and (to a lesser extent) Botswana, and the range of beneficiaries was rapidly expanded (in South Africa, the age limit for a child's eligibility was gradually raised from seven in 1998 to the current age limit of eighteen).[11] The rapid growth of such programs responded not only to post-apartheid political expectations but also to another conjunctural feature of the regional moment: the emergence in the 1990s of a massive HIV epidemic that was creating huge numbers of orphans even as it left many elderly caring for the ill.

The result of this complex conjuncture has been the emergence of a very extensive set of state commitments to provide monthly cash payments to a wide range of beneficiaries. In South Africa, grants are paid to more than sixteen million individuals (some 30 percent of the total population), in the context of a doubling (in real terms) of overall social spending between 2002–3 and 2011–12 (National Treasury 2012, 78). Nearly three million South Africans aged sixty and over receive old age pensions (each with a 2013 value of R1260 [~US$125] per month), with another eleven million receiving child support grants (now set at R300 [~US$30] per child).[12] These benefits are non-contributory (i.e., not based on any payments previously made by recipients) and are paid directly from the state treasury. They are nominally conditional on an income test, and in principle school attendance is required for child support grants. But such strictures have in practice been only loosely applied (if at all), meaning that for the most part the grants do not have the strong "conditions" that have often been attached to cash transfers in Latin America and other regions (indeed, the Ministry of Social Development is currently planning to phase out even the means test for old age pensions). And it must be noted that the benefits (while, of course, tiny when compared in absolute terms with those of Northern welfare states) are, in the context of the lives of low-income people in the region, quite substantial; indeed, as one recent study has pointed out (Garcia and Moore 2012, 311), the South African old age pension as of 2010 amounted to 1.75 times the median per capita income. The grants reach a huge swath of the population, with some 44 percent of all households nationwide receiving at least one grant, a figure that rises to nearly 60 percent in the predominantly poor and rural provinces of Eastern Cape and Limpopo (Statistics South Africa 2013, 19–20).

Namibia has expanded its old age pension scheme along lines very similar to those of the South African program. It has also introduced the Child Maintenance Grant, modeled on the South African Child Support Grant, as well as a number of other, smaller programs. Due to a less flexible implementation and poor administration, the child care grants are not as widely distributed (yet) as in South Africa, but here too both expenditures and the number of recipients have expanded rapidly in recent years. As of 2008, some 12 percent of Namibia's total population were receiving social grants (Levine, Van der Berg, and Yu 2009; Garcia and Moore 2012, 287–90). Botswana also has a comprehensive non-contributory old age pension system as well as a major program providing cash payments to those caring for orphaned children—no small thing in a country where some 15 percent of all children are reckoned to be orphans (Dahl 2009). Social protection schemes are less developed in other southern African countries, but the successes of the South African model have inspired even the poorest states in the region to attempt to emulate it, albeit with much lower levels of benefits. Swaziland, for instance, now has a universal old age pension, and even Lesotho (long widely regarded as lacking the financial means to attempt any sort of social protection) introduced a modest old age pension in 2004 and is now developing a program of child care grants (Garcia and Moore 2012, 264).

It is now well documented that these programs, in their own terms, "work." For South Africa, where the programs have been studied most intensively and for the longest time, a robust consensus now exists that, as one recent evaluation study put it, "South Africa's social grants have been extremely successful at reducing poverty" (DSD, SASSA, and UNICEF 2012, 3; see also the authoritative overview of the evidence in Neves et al. 2009). According to a recent national survey, the percentage of households that reported experiencing hunger decreased from 29.3 percent to 12.6 percent between 2002 and 2012 (Statistics South Africa 2012, 4). A recent comprehensive evaluation of the Child Support Grant program concluded that it clearly yielded "positive developmental impact" not only in nutrition but also in educational and health outcomes while at the same time providing some protection to adolescent recipients from "risky behaviors" in the context of the high HIV prevalence. A recent survey of living standards (based not on reported income but on concrete lifestyle markers such as the presence of running water or flush toilets and ownership of key goods and appliances) found that the proportion of South African adults falling into the lowest of ten categories for living standards had fallen from 11 percent of the population in 2001 to just 1 percent in 2011.[13] Major declines were also found in the other lowest categories, along with substantial rises in proportions occupying the middle rungs of the scale. One of the researchers (Georgina Alexander of the South African Institute of Race Relations) provided this explanation of the results:

The improvement can be attributed in part to the increase in the number of people receiving social payments, such as old age pensions and the child support grant. In particular, the number of recipients of the child grant increased by 1200% between 2001 and 2010/11. In 2001 some 8% of South Africans were beneficiaries of grants. This proportion increased to 29% in 2010/11 and accounted for 10% of government expenditure.[14]

It is not only quantitative surveys that attest to the efficacy and importance of the expanded programs of cash transfer. Among the scores of experts and ethnographic researchers whom I have consulted in the course of this project, many with very long and intimate familiarity with the social realities of the region's poverty, none doubted that social grants are playing an absolutely vital role in sustaining poor households and communities and in preventing the worst sorts of destitution. When I asked one such highly knowledgeable researcher what South Africa would be like without the grants, he paused before replying simply, "Apocalyptic. Off the chart."

In Namibia, social protection programs have been less well studied and assessed, but what data is available suggests that the effects of the programs have been broadly similar to those in South Africa. A recent overview found that these schemes are making "a substantial and growing contribution to poverty reduction" and concluded that social cash transfers have lowered the number of "poor" individuals by 10 percent and the "very poor" by 22 percent (Levine, Van der Berg, and Yu 2009, 49, 50). The report also finds the programs to be broadly sustainable in fiscal terms, projecting a gradual reduction in social grant expenditures (as a percentage of GDP), since GDP growth is expected to outpace the projected growth in number of recipients (Leving, Van der Berg, and Yu 2009, 42, 45).

Not surprisingly, these programs have been generally popular among those receiving the cash payments.[15] What is perhaps more surprising is that a broad acceptance of these programs appears to extend across nearly the whole range of society, with feelings about the legitimacy of public assistance quite widely shared across both class and race divides. Jeremy Seekings has shown that, when asked about both specific social assistance programs and a range of scenarios in which a person in a certain situation might or might not "deserve" government assistance, South Africans of different races proved to have surprisingly similar views (Seekings 2008c). At least in South Africa (and thanks to a history that I trace in chapter 2), it seems to be broadly accepted that it is a normal and proper part of the mission of the state to issue monthly cash payments to a wide range of people deemed to be in need. Indeed, despite their substantial size and cost, the programs of social grants that I have described here are not a particularly contentious or embattled feature of the political landscape in any of the countries I have reviewed here. To my knowledge, in fact, no major political party has ever proposed eliminating them, or even reducing their amounts.

How did this come about? In South Africa, especially, it is very clear that the original ambition of the post-apartheid regime was hardly to create a welfare state catering to those excluded from the world of wage labor. Its first political imperative, on the contrary, was to generate jobs and to improve the condition of workers. The ANC, of course, had its intellectual roots on the political Left, and it has governed from the start as part of a "tripartite alliance" linking it with the powerful trade union federation COSATU and the South African Communist Party. Partly for this reason, a high value has long been placed on labor as the central mode of social incorporation, and on "the workers" as the figuration of those to whom the government must answer (see Barchiesi 2011). But in the context of new economic realities, as the country went through a wrenching economic restructuring that shed jobs as much as it created them, more and more of the population looked to government as a direct provider and provisioner. "Service delivery" was the new slogan, and increasingly black South Africans sought their "liberation" in the form of direct state provision of such goods as housing, electricity, water, sanitation, and social services. "Service delivery protests," indeed, became a familiar feature of everyday life in poor and working-class neighborhoods across the country. In this context, a patchwork of older programs of social assistance (inherited from the apartheid regime and newly deracialized) provided the starting point for the development of a vast institutional apparatus that would make it possible for the new state to provide highly visible and very effective support, in the form of direct cash transfers, to its electoral base—a way of "delivering" something tangible and valuable, even in the absence of jobs.

This was a matter of practical politics and pragmatic policymaking.[16] But along with the political and institutional innovations I have described here, it is also possible to trace the emergence of new ways of thinking, new ways of reasoning about matters of poverty and distribution. As Michel Foucault once remarked, the work of governing always involves at least a certain amount of thinking (Foucault 1988, 152–56). I am interested, then, not only in the new programs of social assistance but also in the new ways of thinking that are growing up alongside them, new "rationalities" of poverty and social assistance that, I suggest, may be understood as both harbingers of, and intellectual resources for, an emergent politics. This is what I term a "politics of distribution," and it involves new ways of thinking about a range of things that includes labor, unemployment, the family, and the meaning of "social" payments. We will not get far, I suggest, by either simply condemning these new ways of thinking or simply celebrating them. Instead, I wish to think both about them and with them, hoping thereby to gain a better understanding of both the political possibilities and the dangers of the present moment.

An older way of thinking (shared, at some fundamental level, by both official apartheid planners and their most radical critics) saw the majority black population first of all as a source of labor. Black populations confined to rural "homelands" or "Bantustans" appeared principally as "labor reserves," providing a steady supply of low-wage migrant labor, most of all to big employers such as the mines. While a permanently settled workforce would have provoked both political demands and a need for higher wages (high enough, at least, to cover the costs of the work force's own reproduction), state control of black movement and residence attempted to solve both problems by forcing labor to remain "migrant." As Marxist critics pointed out, this was accomplished only by off-loading the costs of social reproduction (including raising children and caring for the sick and aged) onto already-impoverished rural communities, thus enabling a kind of "super-exploitation" that afflicted not only workers themselves but also their communities and regions of origin.[17] For those who would replace the nakedly exploitative and repressive system of apartheid with something better, the starting place was therefore the idea that it was not only those directly employed by capitalists who were exploited by capitalism. People from the poor rural peripheries of the southern African political economy, even if not directly employed, were not at all marginal to the production system. On the contrary, thanks to the role they played in the reproduction of labor, they were in fact central to the massive production of wealth that was occurring at the industrial centers of this regional system. This was an analytical claim (i.e., that even the region's most peripheral people and locales were in fact vital for capitalism, "reproducing the labor force") that contained embedded within it both a functional imperative ("social reproduction" could only take place via the provision of at least some minimal "social wage" enabling it) and an ethical claim (those who were helping to generate wealth were also entitled to share in it).

But the developments of recent years force us to question the logic that allowed an earlier generation of critics to link the productivity of the industrial economy to the entire society in such a direct and compelling way. In a labor-scarce political economy, even the most remote rural reaches of the southern African region could plausibly be understood as providing vitally needed labor reserves for a vast and encompassing system of production. Today, however, a restructured capitalism has ever less need for the ready supply of low-wage, low-skilled laborers that the migrant labor system generated. As Tania Li (2010) has argued in an Asian context, the marginalization and impoverishment of so many today cannot be regarded as "a strategy of global capital" but is instead, in her terms, "a sign of their very limited relevance to capital at any scale" (2010, 67). This point was made to me most dramatically in the comment of a South African social researcher with long experience working with poor rural communities. "I wish this weren't true," he said, "but the fact is that there are at least ten million people out there who could drop dead tomorrow and the JSE [Johannesburg Stock Exchange] wouldn't register so much as a ripple."[18]

Under such circumstances, it has become more and more difficult to argue that the value produced at the region's industrial centers is generated by the suffering of those at its periphery; instead, the suffering of the poor and marginalized appears as functionally isolated from a production system that simply no longer has any use for them. And if such people increasingly receive social payments, this cannot plausibly be understood as part of a vital and necessary functional logic of reproducing a workforce, for there is simply no demand for the kind of labor such payments might plausibly "reproduce." On the contrary, insofar as today's social protection programs do support a sort of social reproduction, it is the reproduction of precisely that class of people who have increasingly slim prospects of ever entering the labor market at all.

At the same time, people whose labor is no longer wanted have acquired other kinds of power—specifically, political rights within a democratic regime whose political base is precisely the impoverished and historically excluded masses of "the poor."[19] And this regime has felt the need to "deliver" a range of goods and services to people whose claims are increasingly based neither on labor nor its reproduction but instead on such things as citizenship and political pressure. In this context, a "neoliberal" program of selective privatization and marketization has been combined with a far-reaching expansion of programs of direct distribution that are increasingly decoupled from issues of labor and labor supply.

A Worldwide Shift: The Cash Transfer Revolution and Its Meaning

These developments are not unique to southern Africa. It is true that southern African programs, especially those providing old age pensions, have their own, quite specific, historical roots (reviewed in chapter 2). But as I suggested at the start, their recent rapid expansion is clearly part of a much larger, worldwide trend.

In fact, the last two decades have seen the rise of new kinds of welfare regimes all over the world. The programmatic element that has been at the heart of this transformation has been "cash transfers," most with at least nominal "conditions" (typically school attendance for children and clinic visits for improved health) attached to them (thus "conditional cash transfers" or CCTs). These programs, in their modern form, can be traced to Latin American roots, in particular the Opportunidades program in Mexico (Molyneux 2007a, 2007b; World Bank 2009), followed by the Bolsa Familia program in Brazil, both focused principally on families with children. The latter, in particular, has served as something of a global model and inspiration, delivering benefits as it does to more than eleven million families, with what has been claimed to be both a strong anti-poverty impact and the familiar Keynesian benefit of enabling consumption and thereby stimulating the economy (Soares et al. 2010; cf. Lo Vuolo 2013). But what was once largely a Latin American phenomenon has gone global. A 2009 World Bank report traced the growth of cash transfer programs across scores of countries worldwide, noting that "countries have been adopting or considering adopting CCT programs at a prodigious rate" (2009, 1). Hanlon, Barrientos, and Hulme (2010) have characterized this shift as a "development revolution from the global South" and pointed to "a wave of new thinking" rooted in the conviction that "it is better to give money to poor people directly so that they can find effective ways to escape from poverty" (2010, 1). A recent literature review done by the United Kingdom's official development aid agency identified the spread of cash transfers as a "quiet revolution" and noted that such programs are now estimated to reach between 0.75 and 1 billion people (DFID 2011, i).

Southern Africa, as I have noted, arrived at such programs via its own route, and due to a unique history. But beyond southern Africa, social protection schemes elsewhere on the continent were until recently rudimentary or nonexistent. In fact, only a few years ago, social assistance hardly seemed to be in the cards for a continent renowned for "weak states" characterized by feeble fiscal capacity, bureaucratic dysfunction, and widespread corruption. Yet in the wake of the much-touted success of cash transfer programs elsewhere (and especially the examples in nearby southern Africa), today there is an explosion of new programs for transferring cash to "the poor" across a number of African states (albeit at significantly lower levels of benefits than those seen in southern Africa). A recent World Bank review identified no fewer than 123 cash transfer programs in operation across the continent and provided detailed reviews of programs in 28 countries (Garcia and Moore 2012; see also Ellis, Devereux, and White 2009; World Bank 2009).

Most of the discussion about these programs has been in the public policy field—asking questions about whether or how well such programs "work," how they can be improved or scaled up, and so on. I have suggested that the empirical evidence (at least for southern Africa) strongly indicates that these programs do in fact yield powerful improvements to a range of measurable "development" goods (for reviews of similar evidence worldwide, see Hanlon, Barrientos, and Hulme 2010; DFID 2011). There is a strong case, that is, that these programs have amounted to good public policy. But I wish to argue that there is even more at stake here than pragmatic gains in ameliorating the worst forms of poverty. Instead, I want to suggest that these new modalities of distribution are associated with both new kinds of political claim-making and new possibilities for political mobilization, even as they are also bound up with new ways of thinking and new rationalities of poverty. These new developments point both to the exhaustion of older forms of politics and to vital possibilities for new ones. In this respect, both the new official willingness to "just give money to the poor" (Hanlon, Barrientos, and Hulme 2010) and the new kinds of distributive politics associated with it are of deep interest and, from the point of view of progressive politics,[20] simultaneously exciting and deserving of critical scrutiny. My aim, then, is to describe a certain sort of new thinking in the domains of social policy and distributive politics while at the same time attempting to think both about it, and along with it.

Perhaps the first question that must be answered is whether, for all the talk of a "development revolution," the programs and perspectives I have here pointed to are in fact as novel as they pretend. There is, after all, nothing new about welfare states giving money to the disadvantaged— indeed, "the dole" is perhaps the most widely known and discussed of the many "social" programs associated with the classic welfare states of the global North. And the idea that it might be beneficial, both for economic growth and for the well-being of the underconsuming "poor," to put money into the hands of those most likely to spend it is not some sort of new discovery but a standard element of the Keynesian common sense that supported the creation and growth of the classical Northern welfare states of the twentieth century. Is the "revolution," then, really just a matter of the South catching up, belatedly achieving the sorts of social assistance that were pioneered elsewhere more than a century ago? The answer to this question is no. As a number of authors have pointed out, the new regimes of social assistance in the South have a number of distinctive features that distinguish them from their older and better-studied Northern cousins.[21]

First of all, there is real novelty in the very idea that "less developed" countries could even consider having extensive nationwide welfare institutions. As detailed in chapter 2, the architects of the European welfare states assumed that such programs presupposed both a "developed" industrial economy and something approaching full employment, at least for male "heads of household." Where "welfare" institutions were developed in the colonial world (as in South Africa and a few other places in Africa), they were chiefly for whites and a few privileged others. In colonial settings in which huge proportions of the population were both impoverished and outside the wage economy, "informal" social security such as "the African extended family" was the only solution that could be imagined.

Then, too, the conditions under which payments are received in the new welfare states of the South look quite different from earlier Northern models. In the North, the central conception was typically of a "safety net" that could provide social support for a "breadwinner" (often presumed to be a male "head of household") and his "dependents" in conditions either of the worker's old age or death or those exceptional contingencies that might interrupt wage labor (accident, disability, temporary economic slumps). And the usual mechanism for ensuring such payments was a kind of insurance system, based on payments made into a "system" by those who might one day need to be caught by the "net."[22] But the southern African schemes I have reviewed here are non-contributory, meaning that they are paid out of general treasury funds and make no reference to prior "contributions" by beneficiaries.[23] Such payments are made with no reference to employment histories and are allocated instead based on such labor-independent criteria as absolute age (for pensions) or number of children being cared for (for child care grants). What is more, the large share of the population that has come to rely on such grants strains any notion of a "safety net" as an extraordinary measure for dealing with abnormal contingencies. In South Africa today, for instance, 44 percent of all households receive one or another sort of grant (Statistics South Africa 2013, 19–20), meaning that, across many of the country's regions and neighborhoods, being at least partially supported by social transfers is more the norm than it is the exception. In the poorest communities, in fact, the ability to access an income often depends less on one's ability to work than on the ability to claim a condition that might give one access to a monthly cash transfer. Anxieties that poor women might decide to have children simply for the income do not appear to be well founded (birth rates have in fact gone down or stabilized since the child care grant was introduced [Macleod and Tracey 2009, Neves et al. 2009]). And economists' worries that disability grants may perversely incentivize such things as contracting HIV tend to rest more on second-hand anecdotes than on convincing data. But while such worries may be ill-founded, they are a response to a very real, and rather startling, new fact, which is that conditions associated (in the "safety net" model) with losing a steady income (illness, old age, disability, needing to care for small children) are now, for many, more likely to appear as the only plausible way of obtaining one in the first place.

Yet the incomes thus obtained are, by design, not comparable to the sorts of incomes associated with full-time wage labor. While the traditional "dole" in the North was meant to replace the normal paycheck for an injured or temporarily unemployed worker, the much smaller cash transfers that are at the heart of the South's new welfare states are explicitly not intended to be a substitute for other economic activities but rather a catalyst—enabling, supporters claim, both "informal" livelihoods such as small businesses and sometimes even access to wage employment itself. A recent comprehensive literature review found very little evidence that cash transfers produce any negative effects on labor market participation, and noted, on the contrary, that many studies have found positive effects, as cash transfers cover costs associated with job seeking or create new employment opportunities by creating new markets in poor and remote areas (DFID 2011; cf. Neves et al. 2009). In this respect, cash payments are less about replacing income lost through inactivity than they are about the rendering active of people who (due to poverty, poor health, lack of transportation, and so on) have had their range of economic activity acutely restricted (cf. Ferguson 2007).

Also important is the way that new cash transfer programs (at least in southern Africa) have broken with the ambition (long central to Northern welfare states) to govern or police the structure of domestic life.[24] Since 1998, for instance, South Africa's huge program of child support grants has had no requirement that the recipients of the grants be in any prescribed familial relation, either conjugal or filial. The marital status of the recipient is not considered, nor is the question of whether or not they reside with a partner (of either gender). Indeed, the "primary caregiver" who receives the grant is not required to be a parent, or even a relative, of the supported child. Unlike traditional Northern systems that became notorious for seeking to apply moralizing familial norms via intrusive social workers, there is here no attempt to identify "real parents," to impose responsibilities on fathers, or to impose "proper" behavior or family forms.[25]

Most radically, some new thinking on social policy is beginning to break from the central conception of the classic welfare states—the conception that social payments are fundamentally a way of dealing with the interruption of a "normal" situation in which adult heads-of-households (most of all men) earn wages that support their dependents. Until now, social protection programs in the region have effectively ignored the fact of mass unemployment, supposing that "social" support is needed only for "dependent" categories such as the elderly, those caring for children, and the disabled. Working-age "able-bodied" men, in contrast, are all counterfactually presumed to be able to support themselves through their labor. Directly challenging such conceptions, a campaign in South Africa and Namibia has in recent years proposed a "basic income grant" (BIG) that would provide a small monthly cash payment to each and every individual citizen. The amount of the payment was initially set at R100 (N$100) per person (an amount that was, at the time of the initial proposal, worth about US$16). (The proposal is discussed at greater length in later chapters, especially chapter 6; see also DSD 2002; Standing and Samson 2003; Meth 2008; Haarmann et al. 2009.) In such a program, there would be no means testing of any kind, so all citizens would receive the grant (though the better-off would have their $16 and then some recouped through the tax system). In this conception, receipt of a social payment would make no reference to gender, age, employment status, or family configuration, and even "able-bodied" working-age men would be eligible. In this, the most innovative of the new social payment schemes recently envisaged or implemented in the region, cash transfers to citizens are completely divorced from calculations about wage labor and family structure alike.

As discussed in the next chapter, powerful criticisms can be leveled against most currently existing cash transfer programs precisely on the grounds that they do not go far enough toward the radical rethinking of the meaning of social payments that can be observed in the basic income grant campaign. Indeed, I will argue at some length that social policy across the region is in too many ways still trapped within the terms of the old European "social" state, as if that old imagined world of breadwinners and their dependents could be meaningfully mapped onto social settings more often characterized by mass structural unemployment, "informal" livelihoods, and highly fluid domestic groups. It is also noteworthy that existing programs, based as they are on national citizenship, have yet to find satisfactory solutions to the issues of migration and xenophobia that bedevil all welfare states, issues that reveal the conventionally nationalistic particularities that still lie beneath the surface of even the most ostensibly universal programs (this set of issues is discussed in the book's concluding chapter). But if one looks closely, it is possible to see that there is also some profound and sometimes very challenging new thinking going on in and around these new programs. And in the end, it is that new thinking, and not simply the presence of this or that concrete policy, that makes southern Africa such an interesting site for thinking about distribution today. Perhaps because of the region's dramatic political history as well as the extremity of its current inequalities, one is constantly struck by both the starkness, and sometimes the boldness, with which key issues are posed. With inequalities both extreme and (in large measure) color-coded, they are both especially visible and openly contested. And while many regions of the world have had to deal with the consequences of the decline of certain forms of low-wage labor, here the change has been so abrupt and wrenching as to open up space for thoughts that might elsewhere be unthinkable, or only furtively and hesitantly pondered in the safety of private musings or low-level policy conclaves. Here, the unthinkable is in fact being thought, quite publicly, and often with a very high level of intellectual rigor and critical self-consciousness. Thus, one might open up a leading South African business daily and read the following remarkable argument (by the well-known political and cultural analyst Jonny Steinberg):[26]

> "If we create enough jobs to keep the youth off the streets, we will be saved. If we cannot, South Africa will implode." I put the statement in quotation marks because it has become a gospel truth. Question it and you risk being declared insane.
>
> And yet it is wrong. If we are honest with ourselves, we have long ago given up trying to employ everyone, or even to halve unemployment. . . . South Africa started bleeding jobs in the mid-1970s, along with much of the rest of the world. We have been bleeding jobs ever since. . . . It hasn't mattered who has been in power or whether our

political system has been a racial dictatorship or a democracy, or whether our labour law has been rigid or flexible—we cannot employ everybody. We can't even come close. To think that we can is to indulge in millenarian thinking, as if Jesus will come and remake the world, as if there is a thing called magic.

Deep down, we know this. For while we talk about creating jobs, we have been doing something else—we have been handing out grants. Some say that it is a stopgap measure, just to tide us over until jobs are found. Others say that it is creating a culture of idleness from which there will be no return.

But if we are honest, it is what we do now and what we will keep doing forever. It is a substitute for work and it holds the country together; it has saved many millions from starvation and misery.

If we accept that welfare is permanent, we must go the whole hog; we must start giving grants to the one category of poor people entirely excluded from them—young men.

A whole series of taboos that govern thought and discourse around employment all across the world are here summarily discarded as so much superstition. While leaders in every nation promise jobs for all, Steinberg simply states it as a fact that, for a huge swath of the population, wage labor–based livelihoods are simply not going to return, and new forms of distribution are a permanent and necessary feature of the new world. Won't the expansion of grants create "dependency" and undermine the will to work? According to Steinberg, "that is dead thinking that made sense long ago, in a time when jobs were plentiful. There isn't sufficient demand to employ this country's young men. We will either give them grants or they will get nothing. They are our fellow citizens, after all. To put some money in their pockets to spend as they wish is to confer upon them some dignity" and to bring "life, not idleness" to the lives of the poor.[27] Indeed, he suggested in a companion column a few weeks later that in a context in which millions have inherited structural unemployment from their parents, where the promise of decent jobs is "not even a living memory," arguing that welfare will make people lazy "borders on madness."[28]

I will return to Steinberg's provocative arguments in the book's conclusion. For the time being, I offer this short excerpt only as an example of the openings that are today allowing bold thinking and heterodox ideas to emerge and to be articulated even in quite mainstream venues. It is this, the crisis-born opening up of possibilities for new thinking (over and above any specific program or policy), that makes the story of southern Africa's new welfare states such an interesting one. And we do not yet know how it ends.

Toward a Distributive Politics

Beyond the specifics of the new programs of social assistance, this book is also about a broader set of questions that they have provoked—questions about the general processes of distribution as they unfold in contemporary societies, and about the sorts of binding claims and counterclaims that can be made about these processes. It is this that I refer to as the politics of distribution, and this volume has the ambition of linking the recent rise of new sorts of welfare states in the global South to the possibilities and dangers of emergent forms of distributive politics that are unfolding in contexts where ever more "working-age" people are supported by means other than wage labor.

It is useful to start by considering the issue of distribution in its most general form. How are the goods we produce distributed? Which of them may I have access to? Differently organized societies, economic anthropologists have long pointed out, have provided a wide range of different institutional answers to that question, ranging from the obligatory rules for meat-sharing among hunter-gatherers to such famously elaborate ceremonial gifting institutions as the kula ring and the potlatch (Mauss [1924] 2000). But in modern capitalist societies, a standard account would point out that while I may access certain goods directly by producing them myself or receive others as gifts, the normal way that people access most of the goods and services they consume is via "the market." Which, then, of the vast quantity of goods produced each year, are distributed to me? In the simplest terms, I may have those goods which I can buy. And how is it that I have a certain quantity of funds to buy goods? The usual answer to this question is that I work for it. I exchange my labor (or its products) for money, and then can use the money to buy the quantity of goods that "the market" allows. Whether one reads neoclassical economists or their Marxist critics, it would be easy to arrive at the conclusion that distribution in capitalist societies is organized by "the market," that the exchange of labor is the source of most people's purchasing power, and that purchasing power in the market is both the fundamental mechanism of distribution and the underlying source of consumption.

Even some of the most articulate and insightful recent critics of the hegemony of work seem to accept the basic premise that, as Kathi Weeks (2011, 6–7) puts it, "Waged work . . . is, *of course*, the way most people acquire access to the necessities of food, clothing, and shelter" (emphasis added). But plainly that is simply not the case in much of Africa, where only small minorities participate in waged work and where a range of other activities and mechanism allow "most people" to obtain their livelihoods. And lest we write this off too quickly as a symptom of Africa's "underdeveloped" condition, let us linger for a moment on the supposedly "advanced capitalist" United States, generally taken as a country in which the wage labor form is especially dominant. Here, too, I want to suggest, paid labor may be less central to processes of distribution than is often imagined. Indeed, in the United States, as in the rest of the world, the question of how people actually gain access to the things they need turns out to be far more complicated than simply exchanging their labor.

We are used to tracking a very narrowly defined official "unemployment rate" (the percentage of the workforce that is, at any moment, actively seeking but failing to find employment). The fact that this rate is generally in the single digits (currently around 7 percent) might lead one to believe that the rest of the population (the ninety-odd percent who are *not* "unemployed") is in fact employed. But in fact, official labor force statistics for 2012 show that *only 58.6 percent of the adult population of the United States is actually in employment.*[29] In a total national population of 314 million, just 142 million were (as of 2012) employed.[30] Of the rest, only 12 million were officially "unemployed," while nearly 90 million adults[31] were reported as neither employed nor unemployed but simply "not in the labor force" (i.e., "those who have no job and are not looking for one").[32] These adults of course include traditional "dependent" categories such as retirees and stay-at-home mothers, but it includes many others, too. Indeed, a recent article by *New York Times* columnist David Leonhardt noted with alarm that even at the core of the classic "breadwinner" group (men aged 25 to 54), nearly one out of five were neither employed nor seeking employment but "managing to get by some other way."[33]

Such observations have led conservative ideologues to characterize the distributive economy of the contemporary United States in terms of a huge underclass of "takers" living on the productive virtue of their economic betters. Leonhardt's concern was directed specifically at the expanding rolls of the federal disability program, but he might just as well have pointed to the huge numbers of working-age adults living in households that receive nutritional support from the federal SNAP program (some forty-eight million Americans, or 15 percent of the population, currently receive so-called food stamps)[34] or, indeed, the astonishing number of working-age men incarcerated as prisoners (at any given time, one out of every forty-eight working-age men is in prison [Schmitt, Warner, and Gupta 2010, 1]).

But the importance of receiving a livelihood via direct distribution rather than as a market exchange for labor is not only something one finds in the lower reaches of the socioeconomic order. As Kimberly Morgan has recently pointed out, nearly all Americans are recipients of benefits from one or another government program (96 percent, according to her sources) and the receipt of such benefits in fact flows disproportionately to those in the middle and at the top of the income ladder (Morgan 2013). And let us remember that, for all the popular fantasies about welfare cheats and loafers on unemployment benefits, if one really wants to find idle non-workers nonetheless receiving generous cash incomes, the better-off end of the spectrum is surely the place to start. It is difficult to calculate the percentage who live on invested capital, but there is no doubt it numbers many millions—the super-rich, of course, but also many upper-middle-class people retired on private pension plans (including many who retire early in life), and young adults supported partly or wholly by trust funds. And, of course, there are uncounted young people who have reached adulthood but are still supported by parents or other kin as well as the millions of students (university, graduate, and professional) who are supported by some combination of parental largesse and institutional grants and scholarships. In fact, while a certain common sense tells us that "everybody" has to work for a living, the plain fact is that massive numbers of Americans (indeed, most of them, if one includes children) do not (at least not the sort of "work" that is counted by the U.S. Labor Bureau). Instead, they are supported not by exchanging their labor for its market value but by being granted distributive allocations from other individuals, institutions, or both.[35]

This is, of course, even more true in southern Africa, where massive unemployment is the norm and a myriad of distributive practices (from "informal" remittances and kinship-based sharing to state programs of grants and pensions) have long furnished livelihoods to a huge chunk of the populations (see chapter 3). Yet the distributive mechanisms through which so many Americans and Africans alike make their way in the world are widely disparaged. As discussed at some length in chapter 1, a kind of productivist common sense has too often rendered distribution subsidiary, invisible, or even contemptible.

This neglect and denigration of distributive modes of livelihood has continued, even as such livelihoods have become increasingly important across much of the world. As Mike Davis (2006) has pointed out, vast masses of poor people across the global South have left rural livelihoods for city living in recent decades. Yet instead of being swept up in an industrial revolution that would turn them into proletarians (as both modernization theory and Marxism might have predicted), they have more often been recruited into informal slums where they eke out a living via a complex range of livelihood strategies to which agriculture and formal-sector wage labor alike are often marginal (see chapter 3). The exclusion from wage labor of those exiting small-scale agriculture (whether they come to the city or remain in the countryside) is certainly not happening everywhere (as witnessed by the massive recruitment of rural peasants as industrial workers in some regions of very rapid economic growth, notably in China), and one should beware of the temptation to extrapolate current tendencies toward some inevitable global future of universal mass redundancy. But it is unmistakably the case that (for the present and for the foreseeable near future, and across much of the world) people lacking access both to land and to waged employment form an increasingly prominent part of our social and political reality. Equally important, those occupying such precarious and ill-defined social locations are both pioneering new modes of livelihood and making new kinds of political demands. It is in this context that distributive practices and distributive politics are acquiring a new centrality.

Distributive issues in the southern African region are probably most readily identifiable in the tense debates around land reform and the nationalization of mineral resources. Yet such explosive issues have sometimes taken the spotlight away from another distributive discussion—the discussion about the social payments that have come to form such an important part of the economic and social structure in the region. It has often been observed that the relative decline of wage labor as a basis of livelihood has produced a kind of crisis of masculinity, in which young men whose social power long rested on their ability to earn wages have found their position undercut and rendered more precarious. But at the same time, it is clear that new powers and possibilities have often opened up for those occupying other social positions (notably women and pensioners) who previously had far less social and economic power. This is partly due to the relative expansion of work in service industries that are more open to women than the old "blue-collar" industrial jobs of the past. But a rich literature also makes it clear that such transformations are also, at least in substantial part, a product of the expanded availability of social grants.[36]

Indeed, in a context of scarce and diminishing employment opportunities, distributive outcomes for those at the bottom of the economic heap are increasingly determined within the domain of social policy. Social protection has thus emerged as a key arena within which fundamental questions are addressed concerning how resources should be distributed, who is entitled to receive them, and why. The possibility to which this book is devoted is that the new regimes of social payments may be not just ameliorative, but that they may also open new possibilities for moving more fundamental issues of distribution to the center of our analytics and our politics.

The essays that compose this book therefore seek to document an emergent politics, and to offer a critical assessment of its dangers and possibilities. Chapter 1 reviews the ubiquity of anti-distributionist sentiment in the domains both of scholarship and of practical policymaking and explores the masculinist and misogynistic bases of such hostility toward distribution. It then notes certain reasons to believe that this state of affairs may be changing, introducing some of the book's key assertions about the growing role of distributive politics and the importance of distributive claims grounded in ideas not of need or charity but of a "rightful share." Chapter 2 provides historical contextualization for this story. It shows that earlier, mid-twentieth-century versions of "the social" never had much purchase in most of Africa, allowing for a common but mistaken view that "welfare states" simply bypassed the continent. But the welfare state had its own distinctive history in Africa, especially in the settler-colonial societies of southern Africa, and it is only out of that peculiar and highly racialized history that a new kind of social protection has emerged.

Chapter 3 reviews the way that new state programs of distribution intersect with long-established vernacular processes and practices of distribution. There is a vast and rich regional literature on the multiple livelihood practices that are utilized by low-income people across the region and on the social relationships that sustain and enable such practices. This chapter attempts to distill the key insights of this literature and to draw some lessons from it about how to understand the place of what I term "distributive labor" in the regional political economy. The fact that distribution and production are here (like the social and the economic) so intimately entangled requires us to bring together domains that are often kept separate. Chapter 4 follows up on this point by tracing the conceptual dualism that continues to plague thinking about market and society and the pernicious effect of such dualism on understanding distributive processes and distributive politics. It traces a persistent conceptual error found on the political Left (confusing money and markets with capitalism) and explores an alternative framework for understanding "cash payment" and the socialities with which it is associated. Here certain new thinking emerging in the domain of social policy provides both an object of analysis and a sophisticated inspiration.

The "mutualities of poverty" that bind poor southern Africans to both markets and each other are, of course, riddled with inequalities. In livelihoods that depend on distributive relations (whether with other persons or with institutions), distributive practices are typically bound up with relations of dependence that are unequal, hierarchical, and often exploitative or abusive. Chapter 5 explores the ironic fact that, in societies we like to think of as "liberated" and "postcolonial," many actively seek precisely such hierarchical and dependent relationships with well-placed others. Tracing a regional history in which social orders based on the scarcity and value of people were abruptly overturned by ones in which people came to be regarded as in surplus, it seeks to historicize both the contemporary hunger of many of "the poor" for social dependence and the evident eagerness of the propertied classes to evade such entanglements. Understood against this long history, the chapter argues, the desire for dependent relations with powerful others is not some archaic and reactionary remnant of the paternalistic past but a very up-to-date (and in at least some measure effective) response to current economic conditions. This has implications for contemporary debates around social policy in general and for discussions of "dependency" in particular.

Finally, the book concludes with a survey of the possibilities the current conjuncture raises for progressive politics. It suggests that emergent new forms of distributive politics, involving both cash transfers in specific and the broader ground of "service delivery" in general, are demonstrating the potency of new kinds of mobilization and claim-making. The social question today therefore is not simply a technical matter of whether certain sorts of social assistance can ameliorate certain sorts of poverty. More fundamentally, it involves the emergence of new understandings of what cash payments are, or could be, and of why and how distributive payments ought to be received by citizens. While thinking on questions of distribution has long been trapped within the conceptual opposition of gift (social assistance seen as a kind of generosity) and market (wages understood as a market exchange for labor), chapter 6 traces the emergence of other ways of understanding the meaning of social transfers, including the idea of cash payments as rightful shares that are due to owners. Distributive claims here are rooted in a conviction that citizens (and particularly poor and black citizens) are the *rightful owners* of a vast national wealth (including mineral wealth) of which they have been unjustly deprived through a historic process of racialized dispossession—a conception that provides a very different, and much more politicized, justification for cash payments than is available in the usual framework of "social assistance" as generous help for the needy. The concluding chapter provides a speculative look forward, noting a range of sites where new thinking is emerging around new kinds of distributive politics and seeking to assess the significance and promise of such thinking.

"Increase the Experiments Wherever Possible"

As I noted at the start, I have been drawn to this project by an impatience with the increasingly empty (as it seems to me) politics of "opposing neoliberalism." Critiques of neoliberalism have had an important and necessary place, but one reaches a point of diminishing returns when the same critiques are simply repeated over and over (as they today seem to be) in what I have elsewhere called a "politics of the anti-" (Ferguson 2010). In place of such denunciations, the more pressing issue seems to me to be the challenge of positive government, the need to develop real strategies and tactics that would enable one to mobilize around specific programs or initiatives that one might be for, not against.

In his 1979 lectures on neoliberalism (2008), Michel Foucault famously spoke of the "absence of a socialist art of government," and the historic failure of the Left to develop an "autonomous governmentality" comparable to liberalism. And he concluded his discussion of socialist governmentality by insisting that the answers to the Left's governmental problems require not yet another search through our sacred texts but a process of conceptual and institutional innovation. "If there is a really socialist governmentality, then it is not hidden within socialism and its texts. It cannot be deduced from them. It must be invented" (2008, 94).

Such invention will probably happen (if it does) not in the lectures of philosophers or anthropologists but in the push and shove of actual governing and actual politics. And my suggestion is that important elements of such invention may be emerging as we speak, in the working out of new forms of "social" governance and new modalities of distribution in the new welfare states of the global South.

That is not, of course, to say that the sorts of programs I analyze here are in any simple way socialist, or necessarily subversive of dominant capitalist forms of economic organization. On the contrary, the programs I analyze in the book are creatures of their time. In certain ways, they undoubtedly do partake of the neoliberal spirit of the age. As I have noted elsewhere (2007), even the proposals for the basic income grant (BIG) (which I have suggested is the most conceptually ambitious and interesting of the new cash transfer schemes on offer in the region) have relied on a number of characteristically neoliberal arguments.

One example of this is the common use of ideas of "investment" and "human capital" as justification for social grants, including the standard neoliberal move to treat the poor individual as a kind of micro-enterprise. The BIG would (as the BIG Coalition website once claimed) "enable working families to invest more of their incomes in nutrition, education and health care—with corresponding productivity gains" (Tilton 2005). Arguments for social transfers today in fact normally rely on language that recasts social spending as investing in a kind of capital (see Fine 2000 for a useful critique of "social capital" theory). Similarly, arguments for social payments sometimes draw on neoliberal valorizations of "informal" enterprise, seeing grants as catalysts for improvised livelihoods that might energize the inactive unemployed into entrepreneurial "activity" (Ferguson 2007).

Such compatibility with certain elements of neoliberalism has been central to many Left critiques of the new cash transfer programs. Patrick Bond, for instance, has recently characterized the South African social policy regime as a merely "tokenistic" complement to neoliberalism as usual, providing "talk left" ideological cover for the real "walk right" policies of the ANC regime (Bond 2014). Franco Barchiesi (2011), while recognizing that programs of direct distribution may hold out more radical possibilities, notes that existing programs are only too compatible with the expansion of "precarious" forms of casualized labor that has been characteristic of neoliberal restructuring. But as I have noted, these programs (and certainly the most progressive among them such as the basic income grant campaign) also include elements that seem to move in the opposite direction. Rather than turning everything over to "the market" (as we are told neoliberalism is determined to do), they grant unconditional claims to income rooted in national citizenship. Rather than transferring resources upward to the "1 percent," they rely on progressive taxation to impose real, if modest, income redistribution. Organizations like the International Labour Office (ILO), as I discuss in the conclusion, even see such social protection programs as the first stage in the development of international norms that would guarantee a right to a minimum income in the same way that we now expect states to provide basic education. As shown in chapter 6, contemporary demands for cash transfers may also involve claims to social payments as a "rightful share," received not as "aid" but as the share properly due to owners. This, as I will argue, raises the possibility that the new programs of direct distribution may become the terrain of a far more radical politics than is usually associated with social "assistance."

Is it, then, the case that substantively "pro poor" effects may be obtained even in the face of the presence of countervailing neoliberal elements? In fact, the situation is more interesting than this. For it is not only that such effects are obtained in spite of "neoliberal" program elements and modes of reasoning; it is also that formally "neoliberal" elements may themselves be put in service of those effects. For instance, while the standard neoliberal objection to social assistance points to the danger of "dependency" on the state, contemporary advocates for new social transfer programs use neoliberal reasoning to neatly reverse the argument. It is the *existing* "safety net," say promoters of a basic income grant, that breeds dependency, since any economically productive poor person, under the current system, is surrounded by dependents who must be supported. This dependency constitutes a "tax" on the productivity of the poor, which both creates a disincentive to work and degrades human capital. The "dependency" of absolute poverty is a drag on productivity, and it makes workers unable to be economically active, to search for better jobs, and so on. What is more, insecurity breeds passivity and inhibits entrepreneurship and risk-taking. A poor South African thinking of starting a small business under present circumstances, for instance, must consider the terrible risk of falling into destitution and hunger in the event of failure. The same person with a monthly BIG payment would be empowered to be much bolder. Providing basic income security for all, it is claimed, will enable the poor to behave as proper neoliberal subjects (i.e., as entrepreneurs and risk-takers); the status quo prevents it, and promotes "dependency" (see, e.g., DSD 2002, 61). In this conception, the BIG would provide not a "safety net" (the circus image of old-style welfare as protection against hazard) but a "springboard"—a facilitator of risky (but presumably empowering) neoliberal flight (Ferguson 2007).

A similarly ironic reversal can be observed around another characteristically neoliberal element: the valorization of transparency, evaluation, and measurable quantifiable outputs that is at the heart of what has been termed "audit culture" (Strathern 2000). These neoliberal elements have often been associated with Foucauldian ideas of "governmentality" and with objectionable forms of control and surveillance. But in the push for cash transfers, both in southern Africa and around the world, the "neoliberal" demand for transparent indicators and measurable results has often been used to argue precisely for "no-strings" cash grants—for the simple reason that such programs are relatively easily implemented, can be effectively evaluated, and generally produce (as most development projects do not) immediate and quantifiable gains in a range of "development" indicators of health, nutrition, education, and so on (World Bank 2009).

The relative simplicity and "transparency" of cash transfers is another point on which neoliberal reasoning is deployed toward a political end not usually associated with neoliberalism (i.e., expanding social protection). Neoliberal discourses on welfare have traditionally disparaged social assistance as a form of paternalism (as in the old Thatcherite complaint about the "nanny state" that tries to run everybody's life in the name of the needs of "society"). Yet advocates for new forms of social payments such as the BIG use these arguments not to argue against welfare but to argue for a new and expanded form of it. They point out that simple, universal, and unconditional cash transfers neither make moralizing judgments about "the deserving poor" nor require the surveillance, normalization, and so on that are normally associated with "social assistance." The BIG that they propose would be paid to everyone; citizens would access their funds (in the ideal scheme) by simply swiping their national identity cards in an ATM. They would use the funds in the way they saw best, knowing their own problems and their resources for addressing them better than any state agency could. There would be no policing of conduct, no stigmatizing labels, no social workers coming into homes—and no costly bureaucracy to sort out who does or doesn't qualify. While means-tested conditional cash transfer programs (and still more so public works schemes) inevitably require elaborate bureaucratic and informational apparatuses and spend much of their budgets on administrative costs, the relative simplicity of the unconditional cash transfer allows more of the money allocated to end up in the hands of the intended beneficiaries. Through the bold step of eliminating means testing (and, in some versions, replacing documents with biometric technology [see chapter 2]), it is proposed that even an extremely far-reaching transfer scheme need not require an overbearing or oppressive state presence. The state is here imagined as neoliberally "slim" (in the sense of eschewing costly and intrusive government programs for engineering the conduct of those under its care) while at the same time carrying out a very substantial economic intervention (both redistributing resources and acting as a kind of direct provider for each and every citizen).

Ideological lines often become blurred around programs of cash transfer, today as in the past. Critics on the Left, for instance, sometimes seek to discredit programs of direct distribution by pointing out that the arch-neoliberal Milton Friedman supported a "negative income tax" that had certain similarities to contemporary cash transfer programs. But they often fail to note that at the same time Martin Luther King Jr. (1967)

was advocating for a guaranteed income in terms very similar to those of today's advocates of basic income. At the same moment in history that Richard Nixon was proposing a "Family Assistance Plan" that would have provided a minimum income for all households with children, his ideological opponent on the Left wing of the U.S. mainstream, George McGovern, was campaigning on a platform that called for giving every U.S. citizen a redistributive cash payment of $1,000 per year. Such strange bedfellows are misunderstood if they are thought to reveal the sinister "neoliberal" essence lying beneath an only-apparently progressive policy proposal. What they reveal is only the radical political indeterminacy that always attends any specific governmental technique. As I have argued elsewhere (Ferguson 2010), specific institutional and intellectual mechanisms can be combined in a great variety of ways to accomplish quite different social and political ends. With social technologies as with any other sort, it is not the machines or the mechanisms that decide what they will be used to do.

Stephen Collier (2012, 188) has recently pointed out that those who see "neoliberal" elements as marking the necessary and nefarious presence of a sinister "big Leviathan" known as "neoliberalism" or "the neoliberal project" are ironically reproducing the reasoning of the original neoliberal, Friedrich von Hayek, who erroneously believed that there could be no such thing as a "mixed economy" since the presence of "socialist" elements of planning and redistribution could only lead to "serfdom" (i.e., totalitarian dictatorship). Just as Hayek could not imagine that (as Collier [2012, 188] puts it) "elements of the Marxist programme could function in systems that bear no resemblance to a dictatorship of the proletariat" so do contemporary "anti-neoliberalism" critics seem to struggle to imagine how ideas and techniques with "neoliberal" origins or affinities might contribute to quite different sorts of political and social systems than those imagined by the likes of Hayek and Friedman. Yet if history has shown us anything, it is that it has no respect for original intentions, promiscuously throwing together diverse institutional and conceptual elements with little regard for ideological purity. Just as socialist elements ended up mingled with liberal capitalism to yield what we today know as social democracy or the welfare state, so might apparently "neoliberal" elements today be in the process of becoming something else (cf. Ferguson 2010).

If we are willing to consider this possibility, then we will need to cultivate in our thinking certain virtues, first among which are an open mind and a willingness to be surprised. Our politics must become less deductive and more inductive, less judgmental and more experimental. Are cash transfers, for instance, bound to remain trapped within the limits of national citizenship and the chauvinistic xenophobia with which they are often associated (a question addressed in this book's conclusion)? Might they simply expand the domain of precarity (a danger of which Barchiesi [2011] has warned)? Or actually increase certain sorts of insecurity (as Dubbeld [2013] has recently suggested)? Are such payments really a device for demobilizing the poor (as some traditional Marxists claim)—effectively buying the political quiescence of those who have the most to gain from radical social change for a paltry token sum? Or do they, as many proponents of a politics grounded in demands for direct distributions such as basic income argue, help to open up a new space of mobilization and political demand by decoupling labor and consumption and opening a new domain of distributive politics? These are not the sorts of questions to be answered theoretically or ideologically; the only answer that really convinces is the empirical and experimental one: let's find out!

Such a stance, I suggest, allows us to begin to meet the challenge that Foucault posed to the Left, the challenge of inventing arts of government adequate to the times. For Foucault, government and politics alike were always more about experimentation than denunciation, puzzling out possible ways forward in concrete settings rather than deducing the correct path from a general political theory (cf. Koopman and Matza 2013). In an interview on social security, Foucault insisted that what was required for a progressive rethinking of social policy was not a theoretically derived "line" but, as he put it, "a certain empiricism," an approach that would be devoted less to critique than to experimentation. The whole field of social policy, he suggested, should be treated as "a vast experimental field, in such a way as to decide which taps need turning, which bolts need to be loosened here or there, to get the desired change." The goal, in his account, was less to arrive at a desired and known end state than, as he put it, "to increase the experiments wherever possible" (1988, 165).

What this implies is a form of politics that has less to do with critique and denunciation than with experimentation and assessment. If we are indeed to arrive at viable Left "arts of government," we will need to be open to the unexpected, ready to "increase the experiments wherever possible," and attentive to the ways that new conditions may be opening up new possibilities for politics and policy alike.

Where does such a politics lead? This book's conclusion briefly reviews a range of interesting and politically promising current "experiments" (institutional and intellectual), but this is nothing more than a beginning of what must be a long process of analysis, assessment, and reimagination involving a range of interested actors. In fact, there can be no deductive answer to the question of where distributive politics is going. Instead, this book is animated by Foucault's experimental and empirical sensibility, and by the conviction that a politics adequate to the times must be more than a set of normative certainties that one brings to bear on an issue. It must be a process of discovery and invention.

1. Give a Man a Fish

From Patriarchal Productionism to the Revalorization of Distribution

Anyone with even a passing familiarity with the world of development and global poverty policy has encountered what is perhaps the world's most widely circulated development cliché. It is the slogan (sometimes dubiously attributed as a Chinese proverb) that reads "Give a man a fish, and you feed him for a day. Teach a man to fish, and you feed him for a lifetime." It is often proclaimed (sometimes on posters) in "helping" agencies of various kinds—from Christian missions to development agency offices to NGO training facilities. The slogan encapsulates a certain development ethos, economically expressing a core belief that the object of development work is transformation, not charity, and that recipients of aid should get productive skills and the opportunity to work, not handouts and dependency.

Critical scholars have for many years now pointed out some of the problematic assumptions embedded in the "give a man a fish" cliché. Those attentive to issues of gender inequality have been quick to question the apparent assumption that the fisher is a man. Those more oriented to political economy have noticed instead the suggestion that poverty derives from a primordial ignorance on the part of the poor and have observed that poor people are in fact far more likely to lack the material *means* to enter an occupation like fishing (boats, motors, nets, and access and rights to waterways) than they are to be held back by a lack of knowledge. Students of "indigenous knowledge," on the other hand, are likely to be most disturbed by the proverb's apparent faith that the external development worker is the bringer of empowering expert knowledge to benighted locals, when the truth is that people who live in local ecosystems are typically far from ignorant about the practical arts of making a living there—and, indeed, usually can put foreign would-be "helpers" to shame when it comes to such locally grounded and practical knowledge as how to catch fish.[1]

There is, however, an even more fundamental problem with the slogan that generally goes less noticed. This more foundational issue is that the "teach a man to fish" refrain assumes that the problem of poverty is fundamentally a problem of production (not catching enough fish) and that the solution is to bring more people into productive labor (by adding, via training, more fisherfolk). It implicitly scoffs at the importance of distribution ("giving a man a fish") and implies that a durable solution must instead bring the hungry person into the world of production (by catching, and not just eating, fish).

This productionist premise (that "development" is, in essence, about catching more fish and putting more people to work) is located at a deeper epistemological level than the assumptions about knowledge and ignorance, and it is not challenged by the familiar critiques I cited above. Yet it is empirically dubious, even in the case of fishing.

Like much else in the contemporary world, fishing is not what it used to be. The growth area in today's fishing industry is aquaculture, which now contributes nearly half of the total amount of fish available for human consumption (FAO 2012, 26). Like the manufacturing industries that it increasingly resembles, the aquaculture industry is overwhelmingly located in a few countries in Asia (Asia produces some 89 percent of all world aquaculture production—and 69 percent of that is in China [FAO 2012, 27]). It is for this reason that an extraordinary 87 *percent* of the entire world's fishing employment (fishers and fish farmers) is located in Asia, along with fully 97 *percent* of the world's aquaculture employment (FAO 2012, 41). Meanwhile, in the most important fishing nations, "the share of employment in capture fisheries is stagnating or decreasing" (2012, 10). This is not because fewer fish are being caught but because it takes fewer workers to catch them when fishing is conducted, as it increasingly is, by highly capitalized private corporations (often on large specialized craft that have been termed "floating factories"). While such capital investment has led to increasing catch rates (and profits), labor demands have diminished even as production has expanded. Indeed, fishing employment in developed countries actually shrank by 11 percent from 1990 to 2008 (FAO 2010). Nor is Africa immune to these trends. The coastal towns and villages of southern Africa's Atlantic coast (for which fishing has historically been the economic mainstay) today swarm with unemployed fishermen. An allocation of quotas in one South African town (meant to increase the size of fishing enterprises to a "financially viable level") resulted in the allocation of permits to just 25 percent of the more than 4,000 applicants. The other 3,000 fishermen (who, let us remember, had followed the productionist advice of learning how to fish) remained, as one press account put it, "lounging about in the centre of [town] and at the harbor."[2]

Teaching a man to fish in these times, then, may be just a good way of creating an unemployed fisherman, or, at best, a marginal hanger-on in an already oversaturated competitive field. It is not obvious that being trained for a nonexistent job would benefit the man in any way, and it is certainly nonsense to suppose that he would, by virtue of that training, be fed for a lifetime. Nor is it at all clear that such training would be beneficial for the fishing industry, the global ecosystem, or, indeed, the fish.

Is the fishing industry really hungering for new armies of trained and ready labor? Or is the problem not, in reality, precisely the opposite—a massive oversupply of labor and an industry utterly unable to absorb it? A recent event in Zambia is illuminating on this point. A fishing company in the small town of Mpulungu on the shores of Lake Tanganyika let it be known that they would be hiring a small number of temporary casual workers. As the owner of the firm (Great Lakes Products, Limited) arrived in Mpulungu to do the hiring, the news spread, and before long more than 5,000 desperate job-seekers had gathered at the company gates (in a town whose total population is only 10,000). A frantic jostling for position resulted in a horrific stampede that killed nine people and injured another thirty-eight.[3]

The "teach a man to fish" slogan seems to come from a world where the labor of poor people was *needed* by the apparatuses of production and where the central problem was creating enough trained and willing workers to meet labor needs. That is not the world that we live in today. And do we really need to catch more fish? The world's fishing catch is now about 154 million tons per year. *Per capita* production for human food amounts to more than 41 pounds of fish per year for every man, woman, and child in the world (FAO 2012, 3). That does not sound like a shortage. We must look elsewhere, then, to understand why so many go without. We must look to the realm of distribution. In a world of massive overproduction and widespread poverty, it seems almost embarrassingly obvious that what is needed most is neither more fish nor more fishermen and -women but rather better ways of making sure that the abundant yield of this global industry gets properly spread around to those who are, at present, not getting their share.

But surely, says our productionist common sense, this would be to treat only the *symptoms* of poverty without getting at its underlying *causes*— causes that can only be addressed through providing things like education and training. Yet the fishing example shows what many across the region already know, which is that in these times having training or education is no guarantee of a job, and having a job no guarantee of a decent living. Under such circumstances, one begins to wonder whether the real underlying cause of the deprivation of those with only their labor to sell is not their own failures of preparation (not knowing how to fish) but simply that they have been abruptly cut out of a distributive deal that used to include them. In such a view, getting cut back *in* to the distributive deal is not treating the "symptom" but goes, in fact, to the very root of the matter: the lack of any distributive entitlement is the underlying cause. Indeed, a distributionist (rather than productionist) analysis might revise the "fish" formula as follows: if the proverbial "man" were to receive neither a fish nor a fishing lesson but instead a binding entitlement to some specified share of the total global production, then (and only then) would he really be fed "for a lifetime."

Give a Man a Fish? Productionist Fundamentalism and the Bogey of "Dependency"

This idea—that transforming the situation of the poorest is a fundamentally distributive problem—has a long pedigree in the region, from long-established kinship-based traditions of sharing to the latest forms of nationalist populism.[4] Yet an idea that seems at first blush almost self-evident—that those who have too little should be given more—has long provoked a kind of horror among those who make it their business to "uplift" and "develop" the poor. It has been a kind of truism in such quarters that "you can't just *give* money to the poor!" (Indeed, this refrain is such a familiar one that it was able to furnish the ironic title of a recent text celebrating the rise of cash transfers: *Just Give Money to the Poor* [Hanlon, Barrientos, and Hulme 2010]). But why not? The usual answers have involved arguments that if money or other resources are simply given away, the recipients will misuse them ("They'll just drink it away") or use them unproductively ("wasting" them, and leaving the poor recipient in an untransformed condition, "right back where they started"). Worse, recipients may fall victim to "dependency," losing the incentive to work and coming to expect that they will be provisioned by the state. (The history of ideas of "dependency" in the United States is traced in Fraser and Gordon 1994; for the South African case, see Meth 2004; Davie 2005.) Against this, "teaching a man to fish" seems to promise something more substantial, more lasting, more *fundamental* than simply being fed. Instead of "dependency," a job promises independence and the opportunity to autonomously provide for oneself and one's family. Instead of passively "taking" from productive others, a person in productive labor makes a contribution to society, thus gaining a well-earned sense of pride and dignity. And by contributing to the production system, the person helps to create the wealth that is the true foundation of the economic system, since any distribution presupposes a prior production. Direct distribution of goods may meet a poor person's immediate needs, but it brings about no real change; in altering a person's relation to the system of production, on the other hand, one has produced a transformation far more profound, more "structural."

As we shall see, there are very good grounds for doubting each one of these arguments. Those in wage labor are just as dependent on others for their livelihoods as anyone else, as they often find out when plants abruptly shut down, or mines close, and workers find themselves "right back where they started." Indeed, Fraser and Gordon (1994, 313) have pointed out that being "dependent," in preindustrial Western societies, meant precisely "to gain one's livelihood working for someone else." Nor are those who receive wages noticeably less likely to "drink them away" than those who receive social payments. In fact, wage labor and alcoholism have long enjoyed an extraordinarily intimate embrace across the region, as is well documented (see van Onselen 1976; Crush and Ambler 1992). As for the idea that potential workers are on the brink of losing their will to work, that seems an even less plausible worry in these times. The would-be workers who stampeded the gates of the Mpulungu fish plant did lack many things, but the motivation to work for wages was surely not one of them. And as for making a contribution to society, there is simply no basis at all for the idea that those not in wage labor make no such contribution. As a long history of feminist critique has pointed out, "housewives" and other women who perform non-waged work in domestic setting are not only among society's hardest workers, they have always been charged with "contributing" many of the things that are *most* highly valued by society (not least the society's—and the labor force's—own reproduction).[5] In the same way, elders and others not in the waged workforce are widely acknowledged to perform extraordinarily valuable services of caregiving to the young and the sick across the region—perhaps never more than in recent years, as southern Africa has endured its time of AIDS. And if it is true that all acts of distribution require a prior "structural" process of production (else there would be nothing to distribute), it is equally true that all production requires prior, and equally "structural," processes of distribution, since workers do not, after all, spring into the world fully formed and ready to report to work but instead in a logically and temporally prior state of utter dependence on others.

To appreciate these arguments fully, however, it is necessary to understand that the horror over giving a man a fish has never, in fact, been simply about poor people being given money or goods. In fact, giving to those in need has always had its approved place in state social programs and private charity alike. But for whom has it been considered appropriate to receive such distributions? As discussed in greater length in chapter 2, both the European social democracies and their colonial extensions were built on the putatively universal figure of "the worker," and the domain we have come to know as "the social" was constructed on the foundation of an idealized, able-bodied male "breadwinner." Indeed, the list of those requiring "social" intervention (the elderly, the infirm, the child, the disabled, the dependent reproductive woman) sketches a kind of photographic negative of the figure of the wage-earning man. It is only the other-than-worker, other-than-man, other-than-able-bodied who is fully authorized to be "dependent"—precisely because the able-bodied man must be, above all, "independent," which is to say, employed. For this reason, systems of social assistance have long been designed as if for an imaginary world where "able-bodied men" are all employed "breadwinners," women and children their presumed dependents, and the state the residual provider for those who (through accident, bad luck, or old age) require a different sort of "dependence."

The fact that the "give a man a fish" slogan renders the fisher a man is not, then, just an unfortunate oversight (to be fixed by changing to gender-neutral language). On the contrary, giving metaphorical "fish" to a *woman* (or a child, or a disabled person) has long been understood as legitimate provisioning (with the state taking the traditional role of husband or parent, and the woman cast as mother, dependent, or both). It's giving a *man* a fish that has really been the taboo—precisely because the man was presumed to be properly a worker. The disdain for distribution, then, is not just about giving away fish; it is about the fish being received by someone who is "supposed" to be a worker and not a "dependent." In the disapproval of "giving a man a fish," that is, it is the "man," quite as much as the giving, that is the problem.

Give a *Man* a Fish?! The Denigration of Distribution and the Gendered Politics of Social Assistance

As was noted in the introduction, the new cash transfer programs that are sweeping the globe are, in one respect at least, entirely conventional. Even though they are typically inserted into contexts where few if any of the premises that governed the creation of the prototypical European welfare states apply, they still (nearly all) are structured in ways that counterfactually presume universal male wage labor. Both South Africa's child support grants and the broader array of cash transfer schemes developed in Latin America and elsewhere understand cash support as something appropriate principally for those categories of people who have long been understood as "dependents" (i.e., children, mothers, old people, the disabled). They proceed as if "able-bodied" men can be presumed to be wage-earners, even under circumstances, such as in southern Africa, where it is plain for all to see just how far that ideal is from the reality. Indeed, in privileging the mother-and-child figure as the key recipients of cash transfers, they have arguably fed a global renewal of a kind of paternalism (Molyneux 2007a)—albeit a paternalism for which actual *paters* appear to be dispensable.

In this respect, the new programs are heirs to a long lineage in which the social support provided by welfare states has been linked to normalizing projects aimed at the working class, projects that both envisaged and (sometimes, in some partial measure) helped to create a world where "able-bodied" men of an appropriate age could be assumed to be in waged employment while serving as "breadwinners" charged with providing for an associated set of "dependents" such as wife and children. As Frances Fox Piven and Richard Cloward (1993) long ago argued for the United States, the apparently paradoxical combination of benevolent and putative motifs in the modern welfare state is only comprehensible in the context of an encompassing project to both manage working-class families and discipline workers. Welfare payments, in this context, were always meant to govern and to stabilize precarious working-class communities while not disrupting the "incentive to work" that was understood as necessary to mobilize and motivate the workforce.

For men (styled not only as "workers" but also as "breadwinners" charged with supporting familial dependents), this meant that it was rendered both difficult and shameful to access assistance of any kind except in cases of disability or old age. As noted above, this is why the list of those eligible for social assistance always seems to form a negative image of that familiar figure, the "able-bodied man." Yet women's apparently privileged position as authorized recipients of "social protection," as a distinguished feminist literature has long insisted, has in fact been linked to a diminished form of citizenship. As Carole Pateman has argued, "the position of men as breadwinner-workers has been built into the welfare state" (1989, 187) and the "independence" attributed to the male wage-earner has been the central criterion for full public citizenship rights that have been denied to women and children.[6] While access to social assistance has indeed enabled certain gains for women, the welfare state's persistent tendency to treat men as "workers" and women as their dependents has, in Pateman's words, "confirmed rather than ameliorated our social exile" (1989, 193) (see also Fraser and Gordon 1994; McIntosh 2006; Fraser 2013).

In spite of the fact that wage labor remained far less extensive than in the "developed world," the very same presumptions about "breadwinners" and "dependents" shaped the development of social protection schemes in Africa, as I show in chapter 2. And to a surprising extent, as I noted above, they continue to shape the new cash transfer schemes.

With respect to the question of social assistance for "able-bodied" working-age men, then, the point is not just that they are normally excluded from such benefits. It is that the very idea that they might be in this way rendered "dependent" is threatening to a certain imagination of masculinity within which "independence" and "autonomy" are the very ground and guarantor of male power. In this context, the specter of any sort of distribution that is not an exchange for labor (such as "giving a man a fish") evokes an undesirable passivity and femininity—in a word, "dependency," that phobic object of so much policy discourse in the spheres of development and social assistance. Non-market distribution in this way comes to be an incitement to a kind of gender panic, in which the very possibility of direct distribution threatens to emasculate the adult male and return him to the humiliating dependencies of the intimate domain. Just how directly contemporary common sense links programs of distribution with the domestic domain is revealed in the widely circulated image of the "nanny state," in which the welfare state is styled a grotesquely powerful nurturing woman while recipients of distribution are attributed a kind of humiliatingly inappropriate immaturity, helplessness, and childlike dependence.

It was one of the founding insights of feminist anthropology to observe that the systematic and worldwide devaluation of women cannot be explained by any attributes that women and men possess as individuals. Instead, as Michelle Rosaldo famously argued (1974), the fundamental inequality is rather a structural one, in which one social domain (the public or political) is more highly valued than its complement (the domestic). It is not as biological individuals that women come to be devalued but as social and cultural beings associated with, or imprisoned within, a structurally subordinated social domain. The key implication, for my purposes, is that the devaluation that is at work here applies not only to women but to a whole domain of "domestic" activities and institutions with which they have come to be associated. And these activities and institutions revolve, conspicuously, around practices of non-market distribution in general, and around the primal dependence of the mother-child bond in particular. It is not surprising, in this light, that the disparagement of distribution is so commonly linked to the denigration both of the domestic domain and of the women deemed to properly inhabit it.[7] This helps to explain why it is that discourses hostile to distribution frequently, and characteristically, embed an often unsubtle misogyny, not only in the ubiquitous images of nanny state and welfare queens but also in such casual throwaway lines as U.S. Senator Alan Simpson's recent disparagement of the Social Security system as a "cow with 310 million tits." Indeed, there may be no clearer image of the very particular sort of antipathies generated by "giving a man a fish" than this: an old man's phobic vision of a nation tragically sapped of its virility via the unlikely mechanism of being overwhelmed by hundreds of millions of tits.[8]

The idea that economic dependence poses a threat to the integrity of the adult male citizen is an idea with a long pedigree in Western thought. Lucy Allais (2012) has recently pointed out, for instance, the extreme distaste that Immanuel Kant reserved for begging. "A poor man who begs," he asserted, "is constantly depreciating his own personhood and abasing himself; he makes his existence dependent on other people." It is not only that charity demeans both the giver and the recipient; the beggar, in making himself dependent on others, thereby abandons all self-respect and "displays the highest degree of contempt for himself." "It is a man's obligation to exert himself to the utmost to remain a free and independent being in relation to others, but as a beggar he depends upon the whims of others, and sacrifices his self-sufficiency" (quoted in Allais 2012, 2).

Such disdain for "dependent," non-productive livelihoods that rely on obtaining direct distribution is today most vociferously expressed in conservative, anti-welfare diatribes against "lazy welfare cheats" or undeserving hordes of parasitic "takers" living on the taxes of the hard-working "makers." But a related antipathy toward distributive livelihoods has also long been visible on what we might call the productivist Left. Orthodox Marxism, after all, always reckoned labor as the source of all value, and the proletariat as history's protagonist. Poor people who failed to make the grade of "proletarian" and instead relied on distributive livelihood strategies were characterized by Marx and Engels as part of the "lumpenproletariat" and persistently described in ways that suggested they were of little human or political value.[9] Indeed, the very starting point for Marx and Engels's entire scheme is the material act of production:

> Men must be in a position to live in order to be able to "make history." But life involves before everything else eating and drinking, a habitation, clothing and many other things. The first historical act is thus

the production of the means to satisfy these needs, the production of material life itself. (Marx 1977, 165)

Distribution, for Marx, was explicitly secondary and derivative. The structure of distribution, in his account, was "completely determined by the structure of production," and distribution had to be understood as itself a product of production—"not only in its object, in that only the results of production can be distributed, but also in its form, in that the specific kind of participation in production determines the specific forms of distribution" (Marx [1857] 1973, 95).[10]

Marx can hardly be blamed, of course, for failing to foresee the rise of massive and institutionalized systems of distribution (such as the schemes of non-contributory grants and pensions that are the focus of this book) in which it is precisely not "the specific kind of participation in production" that determines the specific forms of distribution. But even in much more recent writings from the Left, the stubborn idea seems to persist that while production is primary, structural, and material, distribution is somehow secondary, derivative, or ephemeral.[11] Even where the secondary status of distribution is not explicitly affirmed as a matter of theoretical principle, Marxist approaches have generally told production-centered stories about workers and capitalists while giving much less attention to specifically distributive livelihoods and the supposedly marginal people who are caught up in them.

It is time to recognize these peculiar dismissals and devalorizations of distribution for what they are: prejudices grounded in social realities that no longer exist. The succeeding chapters of this book aim to show that distribution is highly structured, that it is an essential part of the political economy of the southern African region, that it is no reflex of production, and that it rests on forms of labor that are just as real, and every bit as material, as productive labor (see chapter 3). Indeed, in place of the Marxist privileging of production that insists on beginning with a primal act of production (before a man can act historically, he must produce), we might just as well reverse the causal fable. Since childhood (and before that infancy) always precedes adulthood, the slogan of a distributive radical politics might be this: before a man can produce, he must be nursed—that is, the receipt of unconditional and unearned distribution and care must always precede any productive labor. Suckling, that is, rather than producing could be seen as the primal human act, and distribution might be quite plausibly posed as the foundation of production (rather than the reverse). This is not, of course, to say that a one-sided overvaluation of distribution is an intellectually satisfying solution (any more than one might profit from seriously arguing one side or the other of the chicken-and-egg conundrum)—only that a strategic reversal might help us to undo some of the inherited common sense through which we have so long thought about issues of distribution.

There is something about the times that we are living in that invites such a rethinking of this old common sense, and this is perhaps especially true in the southern African case to which I will be giving central place here. The distinctive regional political economy of mining and migrant labor created male identities rooted in labor, and masculine working-class personhood has long been linked to wage labor (see chapter 5). Against this historical backdrop, the recent proliferation of social grants for women, children, and old people has been accompanied by a persistent (if delusional) fantasy that able-bodied men would (and should) all be in gainful employment if only they were not "lazy." (See Barchiesi [2011] for an excellent analysis of this "melancholia of labor" and the history of the nexus of labor, dignity, and autonomous male personhood that lies behind it.) But history has pulled the rug out from under such conceptions, as traditional, low-skilled "men's jobs" have disappeared rapidly (for South Africa, see Seekings and Nattrass 2005; Marais 2011), while women have both new employment opportunities and new sources of non-wage income (including social grants). The old networks of wage-earners and dependents that were so central to the regional migrant labor system have been gradually but steadily replaced by new circuits of distribution and dependence, upon which, more and more, depend the livelihood strategies of men and women alike (see chapter 3).

In this context, I have taken a special interest in two sorts of issues that will be themes running through the rest of this book. First are the campaigns (especially in South Africa and Namibia) for fundamentally new kinds of social assistance that point to some intriguing possible new directions for distributive state policy. Most interesting in this respect has been the campaign for what is called a "basic income grant" (BIG), a universal and unconditional small monthly payment that would be paid to each citizen. (This is discussed at greater length in chapter 6.) The second theme involves a focus on relations of material dependence and the political and social relations that they support and sustain. Many of the key political and economic dynamics in the region today, I will suggest, turn on distributional claims, including claims made on the state. Against the long history of official resistance to "giving a man a fish," today direct distributions such as social grants, along with related transfers such as subsidized housing and other services such as water and electricity, are increasingly central both to poor people's livelihoods and to the political life of the state. And while a language of "rights" often dominates the discursive field of contemporary politics (in southern Africa no less than elsewhere in the world), key contemporary demands for "service delivery" in fact often invoke a kind of distributive politics that is both more fundamental, and sometimes more politically potent, than the neoliberal "rights talk" within which it is often subsumed. Indeed, I will argue in the section below that political claims rooted in nakedly distributive demands for "fish" are both increasingly salient in the region and profoundly challenging to the assumptions of both the traditional welfare state and the usual sorts of rights-based politics.

Rights and Shares: From Abstract Equalities to Concrete Goods

The fact that the decline of wage labor as a mechanism of distribution has occurred during what has been, in southern Africa as in much of the world, an era of unprecedented political democratization has given rise to a cruel set of ironies. Just when people find themselves at last included politically, many find themselves increasingly excluded economically, leading to widespread perceptions that the "liberation" of majority rule has been, in some substantial measure, failed, incomplete, or empty (see chapter 6). Having at last acquired formal political equality, many of those once relegated to the ranks of the "non-white" find themselves in material circumstances that make their nominal equality feel like something of a bad joke. In this context, the rich set of democratic rights (sometimes including social and economic rights) granted by progressive new legal instruments such as constitutions have sometimes come to appear empty, as the abstract freedoms they proclaim often seem to translate into narrow legal claims with little relevance to the actual lives of the poorest southern Africans. This is a major theme, for instance, of

Englund's (2006, 2011) penetrating critique of "human rights" in Malawi, which may be usefully compared with Mamdani's (2002) critical analysis of the Report of the South African Truth and Reconciliation Commission. Deborah James (2007) has similarly provided a thoughtful account of the shortcomings of "rights" constructs in the context of South African land reform, while Patrick Bond (2012, 2013) has developed a stimulating critique of "the limits of rights culture" in the South African debate on water provision.

It is not only critical academics who have come to such conclusions. Consider the following story I was told several years ago in Cape Town. A day-long housing rights workshop was staged by an NGO in a neighborhood of shack-dwellers who had long tried, but failed, to get improved housing. Presentations were made and PowerPoints displayed describing in detail the constitutional right to housing. NGO workers stood up one after another, patiently explaining to the assembled crowd what rights are and who has them, what legal guarantees apply to housing, the history of housing rights in South Africa, and so on. At the end of several hours of this, a tired-looking old man in the back of the room stood up, raised his hand, and said quietly: "I'm afraid there has been some mistake here. All I have heard about today is that I have the right to a house. Now that is all very well. But the problem is I don't *want* the right to a house. A heavy silence settled on the room, as the workshop leaders looked at one another in confusion. At last, the man continued: "I want a *house*."

In a polity where millions are unhoused even as everyone has the constitutional right to housing, there is some reason to believe that such a direct claim to material goods is rather more forceful than the affirmation of legal abstractions such as rights, even when those rights explicitly go beyond the traditional "liberal" package of political and civil rights to address socioeconomic conditions such as housing. Certainly, the man in the story is far from being the only one in the region whose most fundamental aspiration is not to recognition of a notional "right" but to the ability to access actual goods.

Such simple and direct demands often seem to be understood as a primitive or immature sort of politics. Like the child who simply says "I want that," the direct distributive demand simply articulates a need or a desire without grounding it in a recognizable framework of justification. Hence the desire to "teach" people "how to have rights" (Englund

2006). Like the "independent man" whom Kant contrasts to the shameful beggar, the rights-holder is not some pathetic figure of dependence and need asking to be cared for but instead an autonomous, property-holding individual—that is, a person who owns certain things ("rights") that must be respected in a context of formal equality.[12]

It is true that the simple distributive claim "I want a house" makes no reference to the equal rights of individuals; indeed, it is not uncommon for such distributive demands to be framed precisely in terms of inequality, with the state understood as having responsibilities of care analogous to the responsibilities that a parent has for a child. But, as I argue at some length in chapter 5, claims made on superiors by their dependents (as anthropologists of southern Africa have long realized) are not some sort of juvenile precursor to "real politics"; on the contrary, they have long served both as fundamental building blocks for the assembling of the region's most important forms of legitimate political authority and as key mechanisms through which resource flows have been distributed.

Jacques Rancière (2010) has spoken of the political demands of the excluded and uncounted as "the share of the shareless."[13] Those who have nothing, who count for nothing, in his account, nonetheless assert themselves through politics, in which domain they are equals; this is the real meaning of democracy. Indeed, the only really substantial democratic politics, for Rancière, is a politics that disrupts the established order through a radical assertion of equality on the part of the uncounted "shareless." In sharp contrast to this conception, what is most striking in the story about the house (as in a host of contemporary social movements focused on "social service delivery") is that the demand is not to be recognized as an equal even though lacking a share. Instead, the demand is precisely *not to be without a share* in the first place. In place of a demand that those deprived of basic material goods should nonetheless be recognized as equals we encounter the perhaps more fundamental claim that such people must be immediately provided such goods. The demand, that is, is not for "equality"; it is for a proper share of things to be distributed to those who ought to have them. It is not a demand for a "right" to such a share; it is a demand for the share itself (a house, not the right to a house).

The idea of "right" is hardly absent from such formulations, since the revised distribution of shares that is proposed in demands for services or social assistance is normally considered "rightful." But it is not that "rights" are first distributed equally to individuals, as a prior distribution that provides the grounds for making certain material claims. It is the share itself that is considered rightful—rightful precisely because certain states of affairs are understood to be proper and right while others are not. The idea of a "right" as a thing that one may "have" may be, as has often been claimed, an invention of the modern West. But, as Richard Dagger (1989) has pointed out, that does not mean that ideas of "right" and "rightfulness" have been absent in other places and times. The shift in the West was not (as it sometimes ideologically proclaims itself to have been) a transition from a situation of generalized rightlessness to one where rights were at last recognized and respected but instead a move (and it was only ever a partial one) from conceptions of "rectitude or rightness" to a contrasting conception of "a" right as "a kind of personal possession, something one can 'have.' " It is the difference, as he puts it, between the belief that "I may do something because it is right" and a belief that "I have a right to do it" (Dagger 1989, 294). And while I have suggested that abstract notions of individual rights can often amount to something of a detour in understanding forms of distributive politics that make direct demands on goods and services, this broader notion of rightfulness—that something should be done "because it is right"—is very much to the point. As discussed in chapter 6, contemporary political discourse across the region links material shares to notions of rightfulness via several different sorts of normative principles, including the idea that the state owes its citizens the kind of care and provisioning that is due to the members of a family; the idea that certain duties of care for, and sharing with, vulnerable others are required by Christian morality; and the idea that the people are properly the owners of all of the country, and therefore should receive a share of its wealth. On such grounds of rightfulness, one might (like the man in the housing workshop) without contradiction take little interest in one's constitutional right to a house while forcefully demanding a house. As I will suggest in the chapters to come, such reasoning is pervasive in the region, and while the surfaces of political discourse are generally coated with at least a veneer of liberal rights talk, it is often this deeper sense of rightfulness that is really at stake.

A more developed notion of a rightful share is elaborated at some length later in this book (see chapter 6). Here, the point is just that some of the most potent and radical political demands in the region today turn less on abstract rights than on very specific claims to a share of material goods. It is this that I call here a politics of distribution.

Revalorizing Distribution

Any new approach to state policies of distribution immediately confronts the question of legitimacy. If someone is to receive a fish—or a house— this question must be answered: What warrants and justifies that allocation? And that question (in a capitalist society) has long been understood as fundamentally a matter of exchange—you get something (a wage) because you give something (labor power). As I have noted, direct distribution is something policymakers have often been willing to accept as legitimate in the case of women and children (for whom the state can stand, in some sense, as provider/husband/father). But, according to the old common sense, a *man* must be taught to fish for himself.

But if wage labor no longer has any real prospect of being universalized, then this is a fantasy, and it remains to be discovered what foundation citizenship, social inclusion, and adult personhood can rest upon. On what grounds will necessary goods be distributed to people if not as an exchange for labor? Is "the gift"—with all its implications of charity, inequality, and subordination—really the only alternative to "the market" in which labor is exchanged for goods and services? As I argue at some length in chapter 6, an important alternative to this widespread binary conception exists, in the form of the share. A share is neither an exchange nor a gift. Shares belong to owners, and when one receives one's rightful share, there is no relation of exchange or debt thereby set up.

It is not true that capitalism does not understand sharing. The share is a capitalist form. What a capitalist owns, in the first instance, is shares of firms—and dividends, appreciation, or other returns on those shares provide the most important source of return on capital. Indeed, for all its rhetoric of competition and individualism, the modern corporation is a *collective* cultural and organizational form, one fundamentally based on cooperation and sharing among an ownership group. Procedures of accounting, auditing, shareholder meetings and elections, and so on all attest to the fact that capitalism takes sharing very seriously and has developed elaborate and effective procedures for ensuring that shares are properly accounted and rewarded. Of course shares, in capitalism, are available only to those who can afford them (shareholders). Other conceptions, however, *are* possible. And here (the foundational question of who owns the production system, and who has a right to a share of its proceeds) may be the place to begin a different kind of radical critique of capitalism.

Who really owns, or ought to own, the vast wealth produced by our advanced industrial society? The Left has traditionally answered with the simple reply "the workers!" Today, however, the idea that wealth properly belongs only to "workers" has little to offer to the growing masses whose predicament is precisely to be excluded from that role and left in the structural position that Marx could only know (and, as I have noted, disparage) as "the lumpenproletariat." Just as new political-economic conditions have undercut what Marxists used to imagine as the transcendental historical destiny of the proletariat, so have they simultaneously rendered increasingly implausible the automatic fusion of "the workers" with "the people" that once allowed a productionist working-class politics to assume a universalistic guise. But we have perhaps been too quick to reduce the question of socialism to the question of Marxism, in the process forgetting a rich legacy of non-Marxian radical thought that has been less preoccupied with productive labor and more willing to contemplate other sorts of bases for radical political challenges to capitalism.

We have, in fact, more intellectual resources than might be immediately apparent for putting questions of distribution and shares at the center of our critical analysis. As advocates of basic income have pointed out (e.g., Van Parijs 2013), the predominantly productivist bent of Western thought has been regularly interrupted by powerful political arguments focused on direct distribution. Thomas Paine argued as early as 1796 that a substantial cash payment, along with an old age pension, should be provided by the state to "every person, rich or poor," a distribution that he argued was warranted both as a kind of "ground-rent" paid to owners (since the entire earth was properly "the common property of the human race" [1830, 402–3]) and as a repayment of a debt, since all those who have accumulated have done so "by living in society" and therefore rightly owe "on every principle of justice, of gratitude, and of civilization, a part of that accumulation back again to society from whence the whole came" (1830, 412). In the early years of the twentieth century, the brilliant

G. K. Chesterton articulated an original and iconoclastic approach to political economy, today largely forgotten, that he termed "Distributism," based on a program of universal direct distribution of property that he conceived as incompatible with either capitalism or socialism (Chesterton 1912). At about the same time, Bertrand Russell proposed to reconcile the conflicting attractions and dangers of socialism and anarchism by supplementing remuneration for labor with the state provision of "a certain minimum" that would provide for "the subsistence of every member of the community, whether capable or not of labour" (Russell [1918] 2008, 73).

Nor are such resources only to be found in the Euro-American canon. Indeed, as noted in chapter 6, a self-consciously "African" socialism explicitly distinguished itself from Marxism by making distribution central to its concerns, taking practices of sharing and mutualism that were understood to be positive legacies of African tradition as a paradigm for a sharing, distributive socialist society. Thus, in Tanzania, Julius Nyerere famously described socialism as based on the "African" principle of *ujamaa* (familyhood); in Zambia, Kenneth Kaunda made similar arguments under the banner of "African humanism."[14] During the struggle against apartheid, Steve Biko, too, expressed an allegiance to socialism that was plainly rooted in distributive aims and suggested that the specific arrangement of "the ownership of the means of production" should be subsidiary to what he seemed to regard as more fundamental questions about "the distribution of wealth." As he put it in his affirmative 1977 response to an interviewer who asked whether he was advocating a socialist society:

> I think that there is no running away from the fact that now in South Africa there is such an ill distribution of wealth that any form of political freedom which does not touch on the proper distribution of wealth will be meaningless. . . . BCP believes in a judicious blending of private enterprise [and state ownership]. Now in that kind of judicious blending we hope to arrive at a more equitable distribution of wealth. (Biko 1979, 149)

In fact, if we can stop reducing socialism (whether European or African) to Marxism, we will see that we are heir to a rich set of alternative Left traditions focused on distribution. Some of these seem highly relevant to our current situation. While Marx always began with production, for instance, the anarchocommunist Peter Kropotkin always insisted on starting with distribution and claims of distributive justice. Why is capitalism unjust? One must begin with a historical account of where wealth comes from.

> For thousands of years millions of men have laboured to clear the forests, to drain the marshes, and to open up highways by land and water. Every rood of soil we cultivate in Europe has been watered by the sweat of several races of men. Every acre has its story of enforced labor, of intolerable toil, of the people's suffering. Every mile of railway, every yard of tunnel, has received its share of human blood. . . . Millions of human beings have laboured to create this civilization on which we pride ourselves today. Other millions, scattered through the globe, labour to maintain it. Without them, nothing would be left in fifty years but ruins. . . . There is not even a thought, or an invention, which is not common property, born of the past and the present. . . . By what right then can anyone whatever appropriate the least morsel of this immense whole and say—This is mine, not yours? (Kropotkin [1892] 1995, 14–16)

And the political conclusion, for Kropotkin, followed directly (in words that sound oddly tuned to our own times, in spite of the fact that they were written in 1892):

> We must recognize, and loudly proclaim, that everyone, whatever his grade in the old society, whether strong or weak, capable or incapable, has, before everything, the right to live, and that society is bound to share amongst all, without exception, the means of existence it has at its disposal. . . . A "right to well-being" means the possibility of living like human beings, and of bringing up children to be members of a society better than ours, whilst the "right to work" only means the right to be always a wage-slave, a drudge, ruled over and exploited by the middle class of the future. The right to well-being is the social revolution, the right to work means nothing but the treadmill of commercialism. (Kropotkin [1892] 1995, 28, 30)

It is not the worker (as worker) whose claims are prioritized here but the member of society, the inheritor of a great common estate (in which each and every one of us has a share). It is not just labor that founds that

inheritance, in this view, but also things like suffering, bloodshed, ingenuity, and shared experience; it is therefore the entire society that is the
source of value. Elements of this argument should be familiar to anthropologists, as Claude Lévi-Strauss long ago suggested that the material
riches of the modern era had to be understood as a kind of inheritance
from millennia of experimentation and innovation. Indeed, in his account, "the greater part of what we call civilization" is still constituted
by the great discoveries of the "savage" past, including the "Neolithic"
innovations of agriculture, animal breeding, pottery, and weaving (Lévi-
Strauss 1976, 347). Lewis Henry Morgan, in whose honor these lectures
have been presented, placed a similar emphasis on the inheritance of invention, innovation, and "germs of thought" in the development of humanity's technological and economic achievements (1877).

Kropotkin expressed the claims of inherited suffering, in particular, in
terms that resonate extremely well with the southern African situation,
nowhere more so than when he touched on the legacies of mining:

The shafts of the mine still bear on their rocky walls the marks made
by the pick of the workman who toiled to excavate them. The space
between each prop in the underground galleries might be marked as a
miner's grave; and who can tell what each of these graves has cost, in
tears, in privations, in unspeakable wretchedness, to the family who
depended on the scanty wage of the worker cut off in his prime by fire-
damp, rockfall, or flood. ([1892] 1995, 14)

Nor is this only a matter of the structural violence of the mining industry. Across a host of domains, contemporary claims are grounded in past
suffering and past contributions that require redress or compensation to
the current generation. Indeed, claims to social payments and social services today are commonly grounded not only in production ("I am worthy
because I have worked hard all my life") and reproduction ("I deserve it
because I am raising five kids") but also in past injuries ("We struggled
against apartheid," "We are descended from those who lost their land,"
etc.), injuries which are often understood as both collective and inherited
across generations.[15]

This fundamental idea, that wealth, being the product of social labor,
social suffering, and social innovation, should be in some way shared by
society as a whole, has been developed in different ways by more recent

theorists, ranging from autonomists (who have developed the idea of the "common" and the theme of society as the ultimate source of both creativity and production)[16] to philosophers working at the radical end of the distributive justice tradition.[17] These formulations are not without their problems, about which I will have more to say in later chapters (see chapter 6 and conclusion). But it is significant that powerful political arguments grounded in the concept of rightful shares are very much in contemporary circulation. In some ways, though, it is Kropotkin's much older formulation that puts things most clearly. For his insistence (following Paine) on a kind of common inheritance goes to the heart of things by grounding rights to distribution not in productive labor at all but in an unconditional claim of ownership. In his account, I don't deserve to receive goods because I produce them; I deserve a share of production because I own (as an inheritance) a share of the entire production apparatus and its output.

As demonstrated in chapter 6, remarkably similar arguments are put forward by advocates for Namibia's Basic Income Grant (BIG) Coalition, who propose that each and every Namibian should be entitled to a monthly cash payment precisely because they, as the nation's citizens, are the real owners of the country and its mineral wealth, and therefore ought "to share in the country's wealth." Receipt of an income, in these arguments, is rendered simply as the receipt of a share that is properly due to an owner. The most basic citizenship right is thus understood not as the right to vote but as the right "to partake in the wealth of the nation." The moralizing "give a man a fish" logic simply does not apply, in this conception, because the "fish" is not a gift in the first place; in "partaking in the wealth of the nation," the nation's owners are simply receiving what is already their own, a distributive process that requires neither reciprocity nor evidence of special disability or hardship.

Such claims—based as they are on the idea of a right to distribution, a rightful share of a distributed common product—are, of course, often not readily accepted. Why should one "rightfully" have a share of a product that one has not helped to produce? Most of the examples where such a claim has been accepted as legitimate seem to involve mineral wealth, where the idea of a birthright or inheritance seems to find traction fairly easily. The Alaska Permanent Fund, for instance, makes all legal residents of Alaska shareholders in a portion of the wealth produced by oil production there, and residents receive an annual dividend check based not on their participation in production but on their legal status as state residents (see Widerquist and Howard 2012). Likewise, a scheme of direct, universal, and non-means-tested cash transfers of oil revenue to citizens was recently implemented in Iran as part of a comprehensive reform of subsidies (Guillaume, Zytek, and Farzin 2011; Tabatabai 2011), while similar measures have been proposed for other mineral-rich states, in what has been heralded as a possible solution to the "resource curse."[18] No such programs of direct cash transfer of mineral incomes have yet been put in place in Africa, but it is significant that Botswana has created a sovereign wealth fund ("The Pula Fund") that is meant to preserve the proceeds of mineral riches for the future generations of the nation, along the lines of the better-known Norwegian Government Pension Fund. And it is clear that in South Africa, as in Namibia, one forceful argument for programs like the basic income grant has been that ordinary citizens should see some minimal share of the vast wealth that is produced by the country's mining industry. In this interpretation, the basic income grant would be what is sometimes termed a "citizen's income," a rightful share of a common stock of wealth.

It seems, then, that there is something especially compelling about the idea of a rightful share when the wealth in question derives from precious substances that almost magically emerge from within the earth. But (as argued at greater length in chapter 6) there is no obvious reason why this sort of reasoning need be restricted to resource extraction. Consider the most advanced forms of manufacturing today, in which small numbers of highly trained workers run highly automated, capital-intensive production processes from which emerge (almost magically) vast quantities of goods. The most radical demand, in previous times, was for the workers to own and operate the factory; more reformist forms of socialism suggested more modestly that the workers should, in various ways, share the profits it produced. But when a tiny number of workers run a highly automated factory, neither of those formulations looks very distributive, and both would leave out the vast majority of the population. Instead, the more radical demand today does not depart from the claims of productive labor at all but from the claims of distribution—a claim for a universal share in socially produced wealth.

If the sorts of distributive claims I have discussed here are to gain any political traction, the idea of rightful non-labor-based distribution has to be legitimated. The old productionist contempt for "handouts" will have to be overcome, and a new regard for the legitimacy of receiving a rightful share will have to be nurtured. This must involve revaluing distribution as a worthy end (and not just a distraction from the "real" work of production). One way of doing that (as I suggest in chapter 3) is to focus on distribution as a social activity and particularly on what I term "distributive labor." But merely establishing distribution as an important and valuable social activity will not be sufficient. In order for a politics of rightful shares to really gain traction, two challenges must be met. First, institutional mechanisms of distribution must be identified or created. Second, there must be frames of political and ethical reference that would allow for shares to be considered rightful in the first place.

To date, whatever progress has been made in establishing viable systems of direct distribution has been largely confined not only (as I have suggested) to certain sorts of distribution (i.e., to legitimate "dependents" such as women caring for children, the elderly, and the disabled) but also to certain sorts of nation-states—those that have what might seem to be a minimum set of political and institutional conditions for the sort of distributive politics I have highlighted here. Certainly, the most impressive distributive systems that have emerged in this new era of "cash transfers" have been in countries (whether South Africa and Namibia or Brazil and Iran) that have not only strong economies generating significant sources of wealth but also relatively high levels of state capacity. This fact rightly raises questions about how widely applicable any political gains secured through distributive politics might be. Indeed, it is difficult to imagine how the distributive state policies that have flourished in South Africa, for instance, could be relevant for, say, the Democratic Republic of the Congo (DRE), which possesses neither its well-institutionalized democratic institutions nor its more or less well-functioning state bureaucratic apparatus. Similarly, one might well wonder how powerful distributive claims can be in a country like Malawi, where (unlike South Africa or Brazil) there are relatively few "rich" who might be taxed to support transfers to the poor. And, of course, the new welfare states, like all those that have gone before them, inevitably encounter the limits of any solidarity conceived at the level of the nation-state when they grapple, as they must, with the challenge of immigration and popular xenophobia that so often accompanies it.[19]

Yet as I discuss in this book's conclusion, new thinking is addressing all of these limits. Institutionally, programs of direct distribution have proved their value in the most institutionally challenged environments (e.g., in situations of famine and emergency), often by dispensing with the usual apparatus of paperwork and identity documents and using biometrics (cf. discussion in chapter 2). Indeed, a recent review concluded that such technology has already proved robust in creating working systems of cash payment in a range of difficult environments (including in the context of the demobilization of soldiers in the DRC) and that the barriers to making cash payments, even in "developing countries" with established records of corruption and "leakage" of public finance, "are no longer technical, but political" (Gelb and Decker 2011, 1). As for the political and ethical horizons of distribution that today seem so firmly bound to the nation-state, here, too we find a world in motion. As detailed in the conclusion, political thinkers are increasingly making arguments for "distributive justice" that insist on conceiving ethical obligations within a global frame and that understand those obligations in terms not far removed from the "rightful share" thinking I have touched on here. Advocates of basic income (see chapter 6 and conclusion) also explicitly see the issue in planetary rather than national terms (the main worldwide organization promoting the issue calls itself the Basic Income Earth Network) and imagine the implementation of basic income not simply as a series of national campaigns but as part of an emerging norm of global citizenship. The International Labor Office (ILO), meanwhile, has begun campaigning for what they term a worldwide "social protection floor," arguing that a state-guaranteed minimum income covering *all* those left out of the labor market (even the "able-bodied" of working age) should be among the basic responsibilities to citizens expected of all nation-states (just as we now expect all "normal" functioning states to provide some form of universal primary education).[20]

These ideas are not yet well developed, and they undoubtedly still occupy the margins of the global political space that we all inhabit today. Indeed, it would not be too much to say that we can hardly even imagine what a practical politics of distribution might look like on a global scale. But this is perhaps a propitious time to start trying. If I am right that the issue of distribution belongs at the center of our politics then we will not only need to have a better understanding of how the crucial work of distribution is in fact being done. We will also need creative ideas about how it might, in the future, be done better. As I have suggested here, recent thought and practice in the new welfare states of southern Africa might be one potent source for such ideas.

Let me conclude by making the following suggestion: a revitalized distributionist tradition (flowing from heterodox socialist thinkers like Kropotkin, through latter-day currents such as autonomism and distributive justice) may be able to intersect the new fissures and possibilities appearing in the new welfare states of the South to create the conditions for a new kind of progressive politics. Existing programs of distribution (in southern Africa and elsewhere) are both extremely limited and hemmed in with unhelpful forms of conditionality. They can hardly be considered anything more than a starting place. But it is worth exploring whether openings are being created for addressing the issue of distribution in new ways that sever the automatic connection between labor and the receipt of a rightful share and that create chances for both new kinds of policy and new kinds of political mobilization.

We do not yet know what kinds of politics may be provoked or enabled by programs of direct distribution in the new welfare states of the South, and there are ample reasons for caution. Populist and chauvinistic versions of distributive politics like those I analyze later in this book (chapter 6), may, in the end, carry the day. And a nostalgic "melancholia of labor" (Barchiesi 2011) still exerts a powerful pull toward "job creation" as the solution to all problems, often making programs of direct distribution more difficult to sell politically than programs of public employment that—whatever their (debatable) virtues as public policy[21]—leave intact the paradigm according to which a "man" legitimately receives a "fish" only in exchange for labor.

Cash transfers, meanwhile—at least in their current form—hardly seem to pose a radical challenge to the status quo. Indeed, critics on the Left are often quick to impute a conservative function to such programs. It is a reasonable worry. President Lula da Silva of Brazil used to say (in defense of the Bolsa Familia program of cash transfers), "It's cheap and easy to look after the poor." As Perry Anderson points out, in quoting this line, there is a moral and political ambiguity in such a statement that leaves us wondering (as he puts it), "Uplifting, or disturbing?" (2011, 12). Are cash transfers a route to the elimination of poverty or just a cheap and easy way to manage it? Are they a progressive response to the legitimate distributive demands of the poor, or do they rather undermine and domesticate what might otherwise become more radical political pressures from below?

These are serious questions. Yet the claim that cash transfers are demobilizing is unproven at best, and there is reason to think that, quite to the contrary, direct state payments to society's poorest may create new engagements and mobilizations among precisely those ragged classes of people that the traditional Left has never known quite what to do with (and that have resisted most traditional attempts at political mobilization). As John Gledhill and Maria Gabriella Hita (2009) concluded in their recent ethnographic study of Brazil's cash transfer programs, actual political responses did not support the idea that social assistance was "promot[ing] 'depoliticisation' of poverty and inequality." Instead, they claim, "applied on the scale of Bolsa Familia, conditional income transfers seem more likely to *encourage* than restrain popular aspirations to go further." Left critics of such programs, they observe, have underestimated what they call "the capacity of some poor communities to seize the opportunities that have emerged to oblige politicians to reengage with both poverty and the roots of social injustice" (2009, 2).

We are dealing, then, with an emergent politics—one full of dangers, it is true, but also of possibilities. Marxists and others on the Left often fear that giving central place to issues of distribution means giving up on radical challenges to capitalism. But what I have tried to suggest here is that, on the contrary, pursuing a truly radical politics today means seeking to find social and moral bases for such challenges *other than* the labor-based claims of an ascendant proletariat. We are, in fact, forced to take on such challenges (as Tania Li 2010 has noted) because the universalization of wage employment seems, in many of the settings where we work, a vanishing dream. But we might also see the disappearance of full employment as a kind of horizon of Left politics as an *opportunity* rather than simply a tragedy.[22] Universal wage slavery, after all, was never what Marx had in mind, and he saw proletarianization as progressive only because he was convinced it was a necessary stage on the road to a socialism that would redeem its manifold sufferings. But thinking (as we must today) without that transcendental storyline, there is no reason to valorize receiving a wage over other kinds of distribution, and every reason to consider the emergence of new distributional claims as a central arena of a new progressive politics.

Where the emergent distributive formations I have discussed here may lead, and to what effect, remains profoundly unclear. But it might be wiser to approach such questions with a spirit of curiosity and discovery rather than one of summary judgment. We academics know perhaps a little too well how to "critique" the emergent and often ambiguous new forms of the post-neoliberal global order. But along with this, I hope we can also learn from, and take inspiration from, the rich world of actual social and political practice that is unfolding in the new welfare states of the South. That is a world still full of invention and surprise, where the landscape of political possibility and constraint that we have come to take for granted is being redrawn even as we speak.

2. What Comes after the Social?

Historicizing the Future of Social Protection in Africa

As I have observed in the previous chapters, one finds today, across a host of southern African states (especially in South Africa, but also in Namibia, Botswana, and several other countries), remarkably extensive programs of social payments, which include old age pensions, child support grants, and disability grants that provide support to very substantial proportions of the population. Such extensive programs of "social protection" (as they are today termed) are often understood as part of a new worldwide embrace of cash transfers that has seen the proliferation of programs across the global South that transfer small amounts of cash directly to targeted "poor" recipients, in what has come to be regarded as the new "big idea" in international anti-poverty policy. (See the review of these programs in this book's introduction.) But while the southern African region's social schemes have been rightly hailed (along with Latin American exemplars like Brazil and Mexico) as pioneers in this global development, they also have deep roots in a quite particular social and political history, a history that sheds much light both on how and why contemporary programs have taken the form that they have, and on what sorts of future developments may be possible for systems of "social" transfers in the future. Indeed, I will argue here that only a properly historical understanding of contemporary regimes of state distribution programs can enable us to think in a suitably open-ended way about possible futures for state systems of direct distribution.

The historical specificity of southern Africa's systems of direct distribution also raises questions about what the prospects may be for the expansion of programs of cash transfer in other places (notably, what South Africans like to call "the rest of Africa"), settings in which extreme poverty coexists with state apparatuses that have neither the institutional and financial capacity of states like South Africa and Namibia nor the specific history of "social" provisioning that I will trace here. This raises a larger question (which I treat in the final section of the chapter) about the extent to which programs of social protection necessarily imply the sort of extensive institutional and informational apparatus associated with the European "social" and to what extent new "techniques of the social" (including biometrics) may instead be making it possible to envision new kinds of distribution based on new sorts of political and technical recognition.

The Invention of the Social

In approaching the question of social assistance today, I take as a starting point the important literature on what Jacques Donzelot has termed "the invention of the social" (see also Foucault 2003). As Nikolas Rose has observed, many of the issues and problems that would be identified in twentieth-century Europe as "social" were previously understood as moral problems that might best be addressed through some combination of religious institutions and what were known as "the moral sciences." Problems such as vagrancy, idleness, thieving, and prostitution, in this optic, were the result of the faulty "character" and "morals" of the poor. This was partly a matter of good old-fashioned sin, of course, the responsibility of the Christian religious institutions that had dealt with such matters for centuries before. But by the early nineteenth century, the response to such "problems" had also come to include a host of scientifically informed disciplinary "moral technologies" whose purpose was to improve the moral hygiene and character of the poor. Pauper schools, reformatory prisons, lunatic asylums, public baths and wash-houses—these "great machines of morality," Rose has argued, "took the characteristic form of enclosed sites for the manufacture of character" (1999, 103). Such things as thievery, vagrancy, and prostitution were forms of immorality, and remedies were aimed at this fundamental cause.

Over the course of the nineteenth century, however, it became possible to pose the problem in a fundamentally different way. Thanks to the emergence of an idea of "society" as a natural system with regular and even calculable properties, it became possible to reinterpret what had been understood as moral failings as instead (in Durkheim's famous phrase) "social facts." Early socialist thinkers were already stretching the notion of "character" in ways that foreshadowed the late-nineteenth-century notion of social causation. Already in 1813 Robert Owen wrote:

> In those characters which now exhibit crime, the fault is obviously not in the individual, but the defects proceed from the system in which the individual was trained. Withdraw those circumstances which tend to create crime in the human character, and crime will not be created. Replace them with such as are calculated to form habits of order, regularity, temperance, industry; and these qualities will be formed. ([1813] 2004, 30)

But this vision was given real substance only following the nineteenth-century "avalanche of numbers" (Hacking 1990) that revealed astonishing regularity in a broad range of observable and enumerable phenomena once sufficiently large samples were acquired. For "vices" such as crime and vagrancy (once properly documented and compared across time and space) could be shown to follow, like suicide rates, their own predictable and determinate laws. No longer would it be necessary to see the cause of the crime in the moral failing or innate traits of the criminal, for crime rates were demonstrably caused by (again Durkheim) "other social facts" and not by underlying factors of character or psychology. Crime, then, was not a matter of immorality or the "criminal types" of criminological anthropology but rather a measurable social phenomenon whose rate varied in a more or less determinate correlation with other measurable social facts (such as unemployment, family structure, or urban geography). In this sense, crime is no longer principally a moral or biological problem; it is precisely a *social* problem. And if social problems have social causes, they must also have social solutions. A host of new institutions and occupations arose during this period to observe, measure, manage, and correct this new object—social work, social statistics, social reform, the social policy expert, and, of course, the social scientist.

A key focus for "social" intervention, from the very start, was the family. Social reasoning, of course, required a whole new level of interest in childhood, upbringing, and "social background" as causal "factors," and anxieties over the pathologies of "society" quickly settled on the family as both blameworthy cause and supremely valuable solution (Donzelot 1979). It would not be enough to morally correct the prostitute, or even to reeducate her; it is the social milieu that produced her that is the problem: the deficient family structure, the alcoholic mother, the absent father— all this would have to be corrected. Thus was born an extraordinarily ambitious project (uniting the "social" and the "psy") of surveillance and correction of intimate life, what Donzelot (1979) famously described as "the policing of families."

A crucial additional development, according to most accounts, made it possible for the regularities of social phenomena to be turned into institutionalized solutions to social problems. This was the development of techniques of social insurance. As François Ewald (1986) argued in a groundbreaking account, the regularities that had been discovered in such things as accidents, illnesses, and life span created the possibility of what he termed a new "political technology," the technology of risk. Starting with wage laborers in large firms, measures began to be taken to calculate risks (especially the risks of workplace accidents) and to socially distribute them via pooling. An early emphasis on "prudence," which encouraged workers to voluntarily join associations provided by trade associations or friendly societies, started to give way (around the turn of the century, in most European countries) to national schemes of compulsory social insurance (Ewald 1986; see also Defert 1991; Dean 1992; Horn 1994; O'Malley 1996). These schemes applied only to formal-sector workers (who made contributions to the system via their paychecks); others were included (if at all) via their status as "dependents" of recognized workers (i.e., wives and children). The family thus became a key relay or point of conjunction, linking institutions focused on wage laborers with the larger urban population via the construction of the recognized dependent.

The workplace accident (like the crime) was now not principally a moral or legal problem (Who is at fault? What is the wrong, and who is responsible for it?) but a social one (What is the risk, and how is it insured?), requiring a social solution (compensation, not justice). Like life expectancy or the chance of going blind, the accident is probabilistic and calculable—and therefore manageable via institutions for pooling risk. The social thus becomes available for a new kind of intervention that would be principally technical rather than moral. The poor child needs educating not because we feel sorry for him but because it is good for society, just as the Keynesian economist argues that laid-off workers need unemployment insurance not because they deserve it but because the economy needs their economic demand to offset a dip in the business cycle. At the same time, such technical interventions relied on, and helped to buttress, a new moral sentiment, which takes many names, but is probably most recognizable under the label "solidarity." If honesty, thrift, and so on are "bourgeois virtues" (McCloskey 2006), then it is solidarity that is surely the first among what we might call "the social democratic virtues."

The welfare state was therefore founded on a set of techniques for managing "the social" that depended for their efficacy on a refusal to reduce social problems to either morality or the market. In this way, new circuits of distribution became possible. At the same time, it became possible for such circuits of distribution to be justified and legitimated in radically new ways. In the new dispensation, a disability pension or a free education was neither the price of a commodity (like a wage) nor a religiously inspired gift or donation (like charity). It was a social intervention (understood technically) and an expression of social solidarity (understood normatively).

In recent years, a number of authors have suggested that this conception of the social, along with the institutions based upon it, has weakened or broken down. Peter Miller and Nikolas Rose, for instance, have suggested that recent years have seen something resembling "the death of the social" (2008). In this account, neoliberal restructuring has not only (or even principally) been about "rolling back the state" or opening a path for "free markets." Rather, what has occurred has been the development of new rationalities of government that make it possible for "the conduct of conduct" to be guided in ways that rely on market mechanisms to achieve governmental ends. Individuals are increasingly induced to take responsibility for managing their own risks (what Rose has termed "responsibilization"), while an "enterprise model" is increasingly applied not only to capitalist firms but to government agencies, nonprofit entities such as universities, and even individuals (now conceived as the proprietors of their own "firm" and promoters of their own "brand").

Along with this, Miller and Rose argue, comes an increasing value placed on "community." In place of a "society" governed by social forces, an alternative conception gains traction, within which communities are composed of individuals who share certain attributes ("identity," "culture," sexuality, a disease status, etc.) and associated interests (against the solidarity of "society," we have the fragmentation into "interest groups"). "Communities" are charged with attending to those responsibilities that the state cannot or will not continue to accept (thus voluntary "community safety programs," etc.), while marginalized populations (who cannot or will not be "responsibilized" and who evade being governed via "affiliation" with a "community") are increasingly relegated to a zone of abjection: dispersed, invisible, and cared for only by privatized and re-moralized "programs" fragmented by niche (drug treatment, homeless shelters, etc.)—if not actually incarcerated in the rapidly expanding prison system that Loïc Wacquant (2001, 404) has argued is an integral part of contemporary neoliberal governance.

An anthropology of contemporary social distribution must address two questions about all this. First: isn't this whole discussion hopelessly Eurocentric? Much of the conceptual and institutional apparatus of "the social" that this literature describes was never well established in the global South, where neoliberal restructuring represents not a "rolling back" of a Keynesian welfare state but the very context within which new forms of social protection have been pioneered. Given the importance of institutions of social welfare in the global South—and the inapplicability there of much of the account provided by Rose, Donzelot, and Ewald—do we not need new sorts of historical narratives to understand contemporary struggles around distribution? And second: if the sort of "social" that this literature describes is in fact going through fundamental changes (if not, as Rose et al. hyperbolically put it, facing "death"), then what comes after it? That is a question that has been addressed, at least to some extent, for the so-called advanced liberal countries of the global North but one that few have yet begun to think about in the postcolonial South. And the word *neoliberalism* is hardly an answer—particularly when (as I have elsewhere argued—see Ferguson 2010) neither neoliberal economic policies nor neoliberal techniques of government are by any means incompatible with certain forms of social protection.

The African Social

We might begin by asking whether "the social" (in the sense intended by authors such as Rose and Donzelot) ever really existed in the colonies. I treat here only the case of Africa, with a special focus on the anglophone countries of southern Africa. In this context, it is clear that as "social" techniques swept across Europe—starting in the early twentieth century, and with much greater intensity after the Second World War—there were attempts to introduce them in the African colonies. Such projects were sharply limited, though, by a number of factors.

First, the populations of the African colonies were overwhelmingly rural, with land generally abundant and small-scale agriculture the main source of subsistence. Under these circumstances, it was easy for colonial officials to imagine that social security was "naturally" provided by what they conceived of (usually in highly idealized terms) as "the extended family." Rural kin did, of course, do most of the heavy lifting when it came to assisting the sick, the injured, the disabled, and the destitute. But there was also evidence all around of the inadequacy of such provision. Rural famines revealed stark limits to kinship-based sharing even in the countryside, while colonial towns quickly became peopled with ragged beggars, vagrants, "delinquents," and so on. Yet such manifestations of need were determinedly interpreted as signs of the "breakdown" of "traditional" institutions. (On the idea of "breakdown," see Iliffe 1987; Moore and Vaughan 1994; Hunt 1999.) This is empirically dubious—as John Iliffe has noted, "There was nothing new either in the fact that families did not always care for everyone or in the fact that most families did care for most of their unfortunate members most of the time" (1987, 213). But the caring "traditional African extended family" was a powerful imagined reality that shaped the whole discussion of social security in the post–World War II era.

If people were left in acute need only through the "breakdown" of old institutions, then what might have been identified as urban "social problems" could be seen instead as pathologies of "urbanization" requiring not new institutions of the social but rather projects of restoring rural "tradition." Again and again, as one reads the discussions and debates from the period, one finds that attempts to extend the sorts of projects of "social" reform that were flourishing elsewhere in the empire were countered by strategies that sought to reduce the problem of security to the need to restore and revitalize what was imagined as a degenerated rural society. And the persistent linkage of the urban with the rural via the institution of migrant labor (found throughout colonial Africa, but especially visible in southern Africa) meant that even the poverty of the most thoroughly urban people was read through the lenses of an imagined rural "home."

The result is that what looked like it might become a project for encompassing African poverty within the terms of "the social" became something rather different, namely "rural development." Strategies of supporting and developing peasant agriculture were here tightly bound up with fantasies of a communal and caring rural sociality that had to be restored. And the solution this implied for problematic "lumpen" urbanites such as beggars, the handicapped, thieves, and prostitutes was that they should be restored to the countryside, under the care of "their people." In this way, urban poverty came to be a problem not of social assistance and welfare but of "development." Rhodesia, following the international trends, had created a team of African "welfare officers" after the war, but by 1950, they had their titles changed, tellingly, to "district officers—rural development" (Seekings 2005, 54), just as the Tanganyika Social Welfare Department became the Social Development Department, charged principally with rural "community development" (Iliffe 1987, 204).

But the project of creating an African "social" encountered another problem that was perhaps equally fundamental, because the sorts of moralizing understandings of poverty and crime that Miller and Rose argue were displaced by "the social" in Europe continued to hold a much more central place in the southern African colonies. The power of the Christian missions (together with the relative weakness of the state) meant that institutions like education and health care were never really secularized, and explicitly moral and religious ideas remained considerably more prominent than they did in Europe (Iliffe 1987). (To be sure, this is only a matter of degree, since "social" problems have never ceased to be understood at least in part in terms of moral faults and defects of character— not least in the United States.)

The result is that the prostitute and the beggar did not (with a few exceptions) become the charges of the social worker but remained (to the extent that they were attended to at all) a problem for the church (as a matter of sinfulness and bad character) and a problem of urbanization (insofar as urban "hangers-on" could be dealt with by sending them "back to their people" in the countryside) Thus, the dominant formation for dealing with the problematic urban classes was not "the social" at all but what we might call the "moral-developmental."

But if "lumpen" urban hangers-on required removal or moralization, proper workers required something more, and this is where something like "the social" did manage to obtain a small foothold. Workers, according to dominant colonial conceptions, ought to become civilized, live in proper families, learn the dignity of labor, and so on. But how could they live proper urban lives without the incomes, housing, and social security that would support this? The circular migrant laborer might be cheap, but he could never become modern (and disciplined, stabilized, skilled, etc.), and this was seen to be problematic by industry leaders and colonial planners alike (Cooper 1996). But in the absence of the social security that would enable continuous urban residence, even in retirement, how could migration cease to be circular? In this context, a range of "social" institutions were created for relatively small groups of formal-sector workers in many African colonies. Probably the most ambitious of these was the system of family benefits in the French colonies during the 1950s, which provided cash allowances to workers' families for the support of children (Cooper 1996, 318–21; see also Iliffe 1987). Southern African examples were less ambitious but still important. The major mining companies on the Zambian Copperbelt, for instance, provided modest pensions to mineworkers (Ferguson 1999), while Union Minière in Katanga went further by providing a broad package of social support meant to encourage the "stabilization" of the workforce (Perrings 1979; Higginson 1989).

Such provisions were linked to a colonial vision that African workers (or at least some "advanced" subset of them) might become what were sometimes termed "proper workers"—and part of being a "proper worker" was living in "proper," "European-style" nuclear families (cf. Ferguson 1999). An ideology of familism was thus central to all of these schemes, which were meant to support not just a worker but also the recognized dependents of that worker (the latter Eurocentrically understood as "wife" and "children"). The wider population (i.e., beyond the formally employed, recognized workers) was therefore provided for only

via the relay of an idealized nuclear family. Thus the French family allocation system involved payments to parents to help support the raising of
children—but the funds were dispersed not to mothers or children but as
a supplement to the father's paycheck (Cooper 1996, 319).

The functioning of such systems (let alone their extension to a broader
population) was sharply constrained by a paucity of social and demo-
graphic documentation. Family-based schemes, for instance, required
documentation of births as well as reliable ways of assigning particular
children to particular families and a single, bona fide wife to each wage-
earner. Even among the "advanced" formal-sector workers that these
schemes targeted, such information was rarely complete or accurate
enough to inspire confidence (Cooper 1996, 334). The near-absence of
such documentation for much of the wider population posed an informational barrier that made it difficult even to imagine how "social" schemes
could be generalized to an entire society, leaving the question of "the social" very much a question of the formal wage laborer.

In this context, "social" institutions were not so much about taking
care of the needy as they were about trying to solve what Frederick Cooper
has described as "the labor question" (Cooper 1996). Thus "social welfare" work (sometimes styled urban community development) tended to
be focused on such things as setting up recreational activities and adult
education classes for workers in privileged industries and occupations—
among the most (rather than the least) secure sections of the urban population. A Nyasaland provincial commissioner tellingly complained in 1952
that local Social Welfare Committees were not looking after the needy at
all but instead "organizing 'snob classes' among the 'intelligentsia' and
their wives, such as knitting classes, basket-ball classes, football teams,
and such like" (Iliffe 1987, 205). Yet such a focus on recreational and social
activities for the better-off was found across the region (cf. Ferguson 1999),
reflecting the fact that "social welfare" had become a way not of helping
the poor or insuring against risk but of providing "modern" facilities to a
small and privileged minority of recognized, formal-sector workers.

The ironic fact that the apparatus of the social was most available not
to the destitute but to a kind of elite recalls T. H. Marshall's famous definition of "social" citizenship as entailing "the right to live the life of a
civilized being" ([1949] 1987, 8). While Marshall intended this as an argument for universal social rights (since all British citizens were entitled to

live the life of civilized beings), under colonial conditions the association of the social with the civilized had the opposite implication. "Civilization" was not a universal entitlement but the property of a privileged minority, and the association of "social" rights with this attribute was precisely a principle of restriction, so that social assistance was available *only* for the "civilized," the "stabilized," the "*évolués*" (with "the African extended family" the imagined remedy for the less civilized rest).

"Social" provisions were obviously important for those few who held the most securely institutionalized formal-sector waged employment, but the effect on the wider society was far more limited. Formal-sector workers were everywhere a small minority of the population, so "social" institutions that were restricted in this way never had any chance of approaching full "coverage" of the society. On the contrary, as Cooper has noted (1996, 283), what colonial attempts to "stabilize" the working class reveal most starkly is "a desire to treat it as a wholly different world from rural Africa." Fundamental obstacles, prominent among which were the paucity of funds and the lack of an adequate informational basis, meant that the generalization or universalization of "the social" under colonial conditions could be neither achieved nor even convincingly advocated. As a British Colonial Office specialist on social security put it bluntly in 1961, "Obviously a genuine insurance scheme is out of the question" (Cooper 1996, 333).

In the settler colonies, however, a much more fully realized "social" was established, the history of which sheds much light on the nature of the systems of social assistance that now play such a prominent role in the region's political economy. South Africa, with by far the largest population of white settlers on the continent, led the way. Starting in 1928, a non-contributory social pension was introduced for white "Europeans" and mixed-race "Coloureds," conditioned on age (men over sixty-five, women over sixty) and means testing (Devereux 2001; Seekings 2007). "Natives" (also known as "Africans") were excluded since they were supposed to be able to rely on their "Native custom which makes provision for maintaining dependent persons" (Pienaar Commission, cited in Devereux 2001, 2). In addition, white settlers in the 1930s came to enjoy a range of other social protections, including unemployment benefits, job programs, farm assistance, child welfare, invalid and blindness pensions, and public health provision (Seekings 2008b). By the late 1930s (even before the substantial expansions associated with the 1940s and the worldwide postwar boom in welfare states), the foundations had been laid for what Seekings has described as "a remarkable welfare state," one which, already in 1938, was budgeting some 20 percent of total public expenditure on "services of an essentially social welfare nature" (Dept. of Social Welfare, cited in Seekings 2008b, 515). Indeed, the University of the Witwatersrand professor of sociology J. L. Gray could boast (with only a little exaggeration) that "today the provision for [the] European population . . . is scarcely less complete than that of Great Britain" (cited in Seekings 2008b, 516).

What motivated this extraordinary development? The coalition ("Pact") government that came to power in 1924 was based on an alliance between the National Party (NP), representing largely poor rural Afrikaners, and a smaller socialist Labour Party, with its base among white workers in the gold-mining towns on the Rand. And its principal purpose in pursuing social protection was to protect the "civilized standard of living" of whites, especially the "poor whites" whose racial privilege was endangered by the economic conditions they increasingly shared with blacks. As Seekings (2007, 378) has put it:

> The most important factor was the imperative—for the NP—of raising its "poor white" supporters out of poverty and the attendant risks of becoming subordinate to or intermingling with African people. Old age pensions constituted one cornerstone of the "civilized labour" policies by which the Pact Government sought to raise all white people to "civilized" standards of living, above rather than below or alongside the "native" (African) population. South Africa's welfare state thus has its origins above all in the Pact Government's general strategy of racial segregation (and discrimination) in response to the *swartgevaar* (black peril).[1]

While these early forms of social assistance and social protection explicitly excluded "Africans," this began to change starting in the 1940s, as South Africa joined much of the rest of the world in seeking to expand and rationalize its various programs of social assistance. In this "radical moment" (as Seekings [2005] has called it), key features of the South African welfare state were extended to include all South African citizens. The 1944 Pension Laws Amendment Act, crucially, extended disability grants to "Coloured," African, and "Indian" people, and extended the non-contributory old age pensions (already enjoyed by whites, "Coloureds," and "Indians") to include Africans as well (Seekings 2005, 47–48; see also Posel 2005; Iliffe 1987; Devereux 2001; Devereux and Lund 2010). But while this involved a kind of universalization of the social, it operated explicitly according to what the government called "a principle of discrimination" (Devereux 2001, 4). From the beginning, benefits were pegged to a starkly unequal racial scale, and benefits for Africans were never more than a small fraction of what they were for whites—indeed, in 1965, the ratio of white pensions to "Coloured"/"Indian" and African pensions was 11:4:1 (Devereux 2001, 4). While welfare states in the North are generally thought to be committed to a kind of economic and ideological egalitarianism (such as we might associate with a country like Sweden), South Africa shows us a very different formation of the social, universal in its reach but specifically designed to support and maintain an explicit racial hierarchy.

Similar trajectories unfolded in the other settler colonies in the region. In the South African trust territory of Southwest Africa (which would become the independent state of Namibia), pensions and other benefits for whites were introduced in 1949, on the South African model. They were later extended to "Coloureds" in 1965. Finally, an African pension was introduced in 1973—presumably motivated in part, as Devereux has suggested, by the need to win "hearts and minds" during the national liberation struggle (Devereux 2001). As in South Africa, the system had grown to address the entire population in some minimal sense, but again social expenditures were overwhelmingly focused on maintaining white standards, and the allocation of benefits was highly unequal and explicitly racialized. Even by the time of independence, the ratio of white pension benefits to African benefits was still as high as 7:1 (Devereux 2001).

In Southern Rhodesia (later to become the independent Zimbabwe), too, a quite ambitious welfare state was constructed for "non-Africans" starting in the 1930s. The provision of old age pensions (along with widows', orphans', and war pensions), public assistance for the destitute, free public education, and subsidized meat (Kaseke 2002; Iliffe 1987; Henderson 1972) meant that by the end of the Second World War, Rhodesia's European settlers "had little to complain of," as Henderson (1972) has put it, enjoying "a welfare state with comprehensive social services at little cost" (1972, 398). Africans, however, were entirely excluded from these schemes, on the grounds of their allegedly "simple needs" and the idea that the rural reserves "provided a form of indigenous pension which enabled them to support the aged and destitute Africans" (Kaseke 2002, 222–23; see also Iliffe 1987, 206). For Africans living in town, therefore, destitution, far from triggering access to benefits, "became a justification for the colonial regime to remove them from urban areas" (Kaseke 2002, 222). Attempts in the 1940s to expand welfare services to urban Africans did not get far. African urban welfare was generally left to municipalities or voluntary organizations, "both of which concentrated on recreation," according to Iliffe (1987, 206). The isolated progressive experiment of the city of Bulawayo in providing more comprehensive urban services to Africans (Brokensha 2007) did not survive the 1965 unilateral declaration of independence (UDI), which, as Iliffe (1987, 206) put it, "subordinated everything to white survival."

In the southern African settler colonies, then, in matters of social policy as in so many other domains, there were two governmental systems, not one. For the whites, a genuine (and in some ways quite robust) version of the Beveridgian "social" was established. Blacks were able to participate only marginally in this, and on decidedly unequal terms. They were, however, included (however unequally) in a few significant programs of social support. In particular, the extension of key social benefits to black South Africans in 1944 must be regarded as of enduring significance. While some such gains (e.g., unemployment insurance) were reversed by the reactionary triumph of the Nationalist Party (NP) in 1948 that inaugurated an explicit policy of apartheid, the NP never abolished the non-contributory old age pensions and disability grants, a fact that would come to be highly significant for post-independence developments.

Given all of this, it seems necessary to shift our question: it is no longer a matter of what comes after *the* social but of what comes after *this* "social"—that is, the historically particular and decidedly non-egalitarian "social" of white settlers and black labor aristocracies in southern Africa.

What Comes after the Southern African "Social"?

The most interesting place to explore this question is surely South Africa, where a racially highly unequal system of pensions and grants dating from the 1940s was deracialized, and benefits equalized, in the years leading up to the transition to majority rule in 1994. That was, for the black majority, already a huge expansion of social assistance, since the new, racially equal rates were far higher than the old, racially discriminatory "African" rates had been. The years since 1994 have seen continued expansion, both in terms of amounts of money distributed and numbers of recipients. According to South African government figures, social assistance programs today pay grants to nearly fifteen million South Africans, some 30 percent of the entire population. Of these, nine million are caregivers of children (who receive a child support grant), while most of the rest are recipients of old age pensions and disability grants. In 2010–11, the government spent R89 billion on social grants, raising expenditure on social grants to 3.5 percent of the gross national product (South Africa 2011). In South Africa's poorer provinces, such as Limpopo and the Eastern Cape, nearly 60 percent of all households now receive some sort of grant (Statistics South Africa 2013, 19–20).

Given this extraordinary extension of pensions and grants to the entire population, one is tempted to say that the black South African majority got "the social" at just the moment when it was being declared dead in the West. But that is not quite right. As argued earlier in this chapter, the old European "social" was based most fundamentally on wage labor and insurance rationality. But in contemporary South Africa, grants are mostly not based on insurance mechanisms, and they are most significant as means of support for individuals and communities that lack wage labor altogether.

This combination of society-wide social assistance with staggering levels of mass unemployment is something that the engineers of Europe's systems of social assistance could never have imagined. Indeed William Beveridge, in his world-conquering 1942 report on social insurance, regarded it as obvious that "a satisfactory scheme of social insurance assumes the maintenance of employment and the prevention of mass unemployment" (1942, 163). This was so for technical and fiscal reasons (having to do with the insurance mechanism that was central to his scheme), but also on grounds of first principles (since, for him, the battle against what he called "Want" had to be complemented by coordinated attacks on the other "giant evils," among which "Idleness" stood coequal with "Disease" and "Squalor" [Beveridge 1942, 170]).

Colonial officials in southern Africa were likewise unable to imagine any applicability for widespread social assistance in circumstances where earning a decent wage was an exceptional circumstance rather than the general rule. Southern Rhodesia's social security officer, F. T. Russell, explained clearly why Beveridge's ideas of social security could not be applied in southern Africa:

> The Beveridge Committee dealt with a radically homogeneous community in which three-quarters of the existing poverty was due to the interruption of normal earning power by sickness, accident and unemployment, and its termination by old age or premature death. Most of the remaining poverty in Great Britain was found in families too large for the breadwinner to support adequately on normal earnings; low earnings as a cause of poverty were relatively of minor importance. In Southern Africa, on the other hand, it is not so much the interruption of earning power as the inefficiency of earning power which causes poverty. The great majority of the population is in poverty, in work and out of it. (cited in Seekings 2005, 55)

What has changed? How is it that a massive apparatus of social assistance that was never regarded as a serious possibility in the days when welfare states ruled the roost came to be considered (under "neoliberal" conditions supposedly antithetical to welfare) not only thinkable but practical, and even necessary?

A difficult question, to be sure. But we can at least start to answer it by pointing out that the South African state's willingness to expand the system of social support so substantially is surely linked to two quite fundamental predicaments. First, post-apartheid planners have had to come to terms with the radical deterioration of agrarian livelihoods in the old "native reserve" areas of South Africa. In earlier decades, dreams persisted (however unrealistically) that black poverty could be contained (if not actually overcome) through strategies of "re-agrarianization." By 1994, the decisive political defeat of apartheid's "Bantustan" project (and the forced removals it had entailed), together with the grim economic state of the reserves, made it only too clear how limited were the possibilities for a rural "fix" to the problems of poverty and unemployment. At the same time, though, another fundamental predicament appeared, which was the failure of the new ANC regime's economic policies to produce robust employment growth. Neoliberal restructuring did bring some economic growth, but (as discussed in this book's introduction) it was largely "jobless growth," and unemployment rates (especially among poor and low-skilled blacks) rose to alarming levels (sometimes reckoned at some 40 percent, though official figures are lower).

The conjuncture of these two crises has yielded a fairly abrupt, and more or less simultaneous, end to both of the great fantasies of familism that long sustained social policy in Africa—the rural "extended family" (based on an agricultural rural homestead) and the urban "nuclear family" (based on the "breadwinning" male wage laborer).

Importantly, in current policies on social assistance, we see not only expanded levels of assistance and increased "coverage" but at the same time a questioning of traditional ideas of the family as a basis for calculating eligibility for grants. Since 1998, the huge program of child support grants has had no requirement that the recipients of the grants be in any prescribed familial relation, either conjugal or filial. The recipient need not be married, may reside with or without a partner (of either gender), and is not required to be a parent, or even a relative, of the supported child. All that is necessary is that the person receiving the grant be recognized as the "primary caregiver." In contrast with older forms of social assistance (such as the old State Maintenance Grants), there is no longer any attempt to identify the "real parents," to impose responsibilities on fathers, or to impose "proper" family forms.[2] Poor women, for their part, have become increasingly reliant on child support grants and are increasingly unlikely to see any benefit in marriage (Hunter 2010).

An even more radical break with welfare familism is represented by the recent campaign for a basic income grant. This proposal would ignore all distinctions of family status (and indeed, of every other sort as well) and simply provide a minimum monthly cash payment (the amount initially proposed was R100, or about US$16) to each and every individual. There would be no means testing of any kind, so all South Africans would receive the grant (though the better-off would have their $16 and more recouped through the tax system). The BIG campaign illustrates with special clarity something that is also evident in many other areas of social policy, which is a new willingness to contemplate decoupling assistance for the poor from calculations about wage labor and family structure alike. In such conceptions, what we used to call social assistance starts to look like simply assistance (just as cash payments themselves, in technocratic discourses, are increasingly described not as "welfare" but simply as "transfers" [see chapter 6]).

Nor is this only a matter of South Africa. Old age pensions on the South African model have recently been introduced into several other African countries, and a pilot basic income scheme has been established (with international funding) in Namibia, where discussion of the BIG remains lively and serious (see chapter 6). What is more, what are known as conditional cash transfer schemes have flourished all across the world (especially, but not only, in Latin America). The "conditions" usually involve an income cut-off and a requirement that recipients' children attend school and make regular visits to the clinic. Unlike with the basic income grant, there is here an explicit aim to govern behavior in some minimal sense, usually justified by the need to "enhance human capital." But it is noteworthy that the ambition to mold or discipline recipients remains much scaled back from "the social" of old. And as in the South African examples, these policies of cash assistance make no reference to particular configurations of employment (the wage laborer, the breadwinner) or family structure (the "proper family," marriage, the father). A recent major World Bank report (2009) assesses such schemes in twenty-seven countries and makes a vigorous argument for their expansion as a central part of any strategy for fighting poverty.

This raises a number of questions, all of some importance for thinking about the future of "the social" and about where what I have termed the new politics of distribution may be headed.

First: why is it that the fear of "handouts" seems to be abating? Twenty years ago (or forty years ago), mainstream development institutions would have reacted in horror to any proposal to "just give money to the poor," citing a familiar litany of dangers that would have included "dependency," misuse of resources ("they'll just drink it away"), and (above all) a potential reduction of the incentive to work. Today, however, the World Bank is a leading advocate of expanded cash transfers to the poor (World Bank 2009), while a new book by an eminent group of development studies academics is titled precisely *Just Give Money to the Poor* (Hanlon, Barrientos, and Hulme 2010). What has changed? Part of the answer must be the massive contemporary oversupply of manual labor, which means the age-old bourgeois task of getting the poor to make their labor available on the market no longer appears especially pressing. The problem is rather what to do with the surplus millions who would be only too happy to work for wages but for whom no jobs can be found. Here we find a new governmental interest in vernacular ways of surviving that do not involve wage labor ("livelihoods," the "informal economy") and a new appreciation of the virtues of cash as a "flexible" resource that can "catalyze" other economic activities. Emergent in all this, perhaps, a new rationality of poverty is becoming visible.

Second: why the new openness to questions of family and household composition? If the welfare state of old was based on the figure of the family, quite as much as that of the nation-state and the wage laborer, the disappearance of that figure in the new welfare states of the South is striking. Again, the declining role of wage labor seems crucial. With the figure of the male wage-earner or "breadwinner" displaced, the very idea of "dependents" becomes artificial. Increasingly, "society" comes to be imagined not as an assembly of families, each with a "head," but as a network of flexible individuals, where only some have "real jobs" and all are opportunistically adapting to changing conditions. There remain crucial domestic alliances and commitments, to be sure, but planners increasingly ask themselves whether it is wise to prejudge their nature. In the most ambitious rethinkings, the flexibility of cash is matched by the flexibility of unqualified eligibility (thus, any caretaker gets the South African child support grant, and every individual would be eligible for the BIG), and recipients are then free to use their "transfers" to make whatever domestic and intimate arrangements they wish.

Third: what possibilities and challenges does this raise for progressive politics? It would be easy enough to label these new developments "neoliberal" and then (with a great "Aha!") denounce them. But as I have argued elsewhere (Ferguson 2010), such easy denunciations do not really get us any further in thinking about progressive possibilities and may even blind us to recognizing some of the more hopeful forms of new thought and practice that are emerging in new welfare states like South Africa. Instead, we need more engaged and pragmatic analysis of what strategies might be effective on this new terrain. What are we to make of things like the basic income grant campaign? Does the increasing reliance on cash transfers (with its implicit acceptance of decommodified livelihoods that do not depend on an exchange of labor for wages) simply acquiesce in the failure of the state to pursue job creation more effectively? Or might it create openings for new sorts of political strategies, strategies that might go beyond the twentieth-century horizon of "full employment" to pursue goals that would be both more realistic and, in some sense, more radical?

Historicizing the Future

I have emphasized the importance of understanding the way that any project for remaking "the social" today must encounter distinct layers of sedimented history that shape and constrain the field of possibilities. As John Clarke has pointed out, attempts to govern "through" the social must always confront such historical layers, and new "mappings" (in his terms) must always negotiate other preexisting and emerging mappings (2007, 7). But this is not only a matter of the past acting as a drag or constraint on the present. Indeed, the historicization of "the social" that I am pursuing here is perhaps most fundamentally not about the past or the present at all but about the future. After all, to say that something has not always existed implies the possibility that what once appeared may also one day disappear. If there was a time before "the social," that is, it may also be possible to imagine a time when that same figure fades into obscurity or mutates into something different altogether.

If "the social" was constructed on such pillars as the male wage laborer, the nuclear family, and the interventionist, social-engineering state, the contemporary southern African scene gives us reason to take such a possibility seriously. In South Africa, long the African site where conditions came closest to approaching the Western ideal of social inclusion via formal-sector employment, mass unemployment remains stubbornly entrenched, and young black men in much of the country see slim and declining prospects for the sorts of formal-sector jobs their fathers and grandfathers held. Marriage is also a radically diminished institution, as poor and working-class women (often receiving child support or other grants from the state) may see little to gain from bringing an unemployed man into the household. Elsewhere in the region, formal employment plays a far smaller role, while the rural livelihoods that once supported the largest part of the population are in sharp decline. The result is the emergence of massive urban populations that lack formal (and often even much informal) employment and increasingly lack meaningful rural connections as well. Such people were once designated as "the lumpen" and understood (by colonial officials and Marxist theoreticians alike) as a small and dangerous residuum. Today, they may well consti-tute the majority of the population in most African cities.

Historizing helps us to see this circumstance as something other than simply decay and degeneration (à la Mike Davis [2006]). The idea that Africans leaving agricultural village life for the city would be incorporated into a stable, Fordist industrial working class where unemployment and destitution would be atypical conditions, stabilized through insurance mechanisms, is increasingly implausible. But if we make ourselves aware that what is being lost is not any possibility of a decent future but instead just one very particular formulation of what such a decent future might look like, then we can perhaps learn to free ourselves from a politics of nostalgia and see new sorts of futures, and new sorts of politics, that only a properly historicized sense of the future might be able to detect.

In a world of urban dwellers increasingly unanchored from both sub-sistence farming and the certainties of formal-sector wage labor, what sorts of demands for economic inclusion and assistance are likely to emerge? What sorts of strategies for governing such populations will prove viable? As my brief discussion of cash transfers above was meant to imply, social transfers, in some form or other, seem to be emerging as part of the answer to both questions.[3] But it will be a very different sort of "social" that will be in play, one whose dangers and possibilities, for the most part, remain to be mapped.

New Techniques of the Social? Recognition beyond Documents

Finally, let us turn to the question of how the new programs of direct dis-tribution may be changing the rules of the "social" game by developing new technical methods of identifying, recognizing, and paying recipi-ents of cash transfers. Like "the social" itself, these technical methods must be understood as having both a past and a future. The particular formation of the social that enabled the classical Northern welfare states depended upon a whole range of other institutions, which constituted its conditions of possibility, and on which all "social" technologies de-pended (the short list would include widespread regularized wage labor, the male-headed family, insurance mechanisms, and the nation-state as bounded membership group). All of these had technical documentary and informational entailments (attesting to where one was born, when, to whom, to whom one was married, when one died, whose children belonged to whom, and especially, of course, membership of the bounded entity—parish, town, or state—providing the vital entitlements). Pushing this observation into the future, then, we might ask, what would be the informational and documentary entailments of possible future forms of social distribution?

Is it the case that social protection in Africa must wait on the development of the economic, political, and documentary institutions that enabled it in the West? Does the effective distribution of social payments in fact require the kind of state that knows things like how old every citizen is, who lives in which house, what each household's income is, and which children belong to which parents? It is not possible to say for sure, but the present holds some clues. Promoters of the idea of a basic income grant, for instance, make interesting arguments about the reduced need for documentation entailed by unconditional social transfers and the role that new technologies might play in providing new kinds of bureaucratic recognition. In an ideal system, in some of these accounts, a monthly BIG payment could be obtained by any recipient simply by being biometrically recognized (e.g., through fingerprints and an iris scan) as a unique individual at any ATM. Instead of all the paperwork, files, and social workers that conditional schemes require to sort out who qualifies and who does not (what's your name, where were you born, how many children do you have, are they really yours, what is your income level, etc.), the BIG and its biometric recognition scheme would have to answer only one question: have you already been paid yet this month or not? (Restriction of the benefit to citizens, of course, would require a second—and extremely difficult—question: are you [really] a citizen?) Thus is a radically stripped-down form of recognition envisioned, one that requires far less from the state (in informational and registration terms) than the social of old.

There are ample reasons to be skeptical of such proposals, given both the general tendency of our time to seek reductive technological solutions to complex political problems and a more specific South African history of hyped claims for the efficacy of biometrics (Breckenridge 2005). But the idea that biometrics can facilitate the delivery of services to marginal and geographically remote people is not just a fantasy, either. Pensions and other social grants are paid quite effectively in Namibia, for instance, through the use of biometric "smartcards" that, together with fingerprint readers, allow people in even the most remote parts of this vast and lightly populated country to receive payments each month, either at the nearest NamPost (post office) or via mobile pay-points mounted on trucks (accompanied by armed guard where necessary). India, another state with many rural poor and a checkered history of identity registration systems, has pioneered the use of biometrics (using a combination of iris, face, and fingers) for establishing unique IDs for purposes such as distributing ration cards and is now rolling out a comprehensive scheme for a nationwide biometric identification scheme that proponents claim will both improve service delivery to the poorest while reducing opportunities for corruption (Lakshmi 2010; cf. Cohen forthcoming). A recent review of these technologies of recognition concluded that they have already proven their value in creating working systems of cash payment in a range of difficult environments and in making effective distribution of cash payments technically viable even in countries with established records of corruption and "leakage" of public finance (Gelb and Decker 2011, 1). Keith Breckenridge's (2010) review of Ghana's current effort to introduce what has been called "the world's first biometric money supply" has highlighted the dangers of such schemes and the likelihood of their being deployed in ways that respond principally to the needs of banks and wealthy depositors. But at the same time, Breckenridge acknowledges "that these systems of biometric registration can, as has been the case in South Africa, serve as technologies of inclusion, working, very efficiently, to provide the old, infirm and the young with a measure of social security" (2010, 656).

Biometrics are often imagined as scary instruments of control at the disposal of a potentially totalitarian state. Indeed, in a traditional Left perspective, discipline and surveillance are fundamentally capitalist tools used for extracting and controlling labor. Resisting such forms of discipline as enumeration and registration, in such a perspective, can thus easily appear as a way of protecting and defending one's own life and labor, which someone is trying to take from you. But today, under conditions in which labor is in surplus, the poor and cast off may actually aspire to certain forms of surveillance and enumeration (Robins 2008, 77–99), just as they aspire to certain forms of biopolitical care (McKay 2012), seeing in them forms of incorporation, recognition, and support that are otherwise unavailable. Here, inclusion in systems of registration and accounting may appear less as an oppressive system of control than as a valued token of recognized membership.

In this context, I suggest that the development of more effective and inclusive techniques for identifying biological individuality should not be thought of as *automatically* regressive or politically objectionable. Indeed, under the conditions I have described, new technical forms of identity documentation and recognition have some attractive political features, features that could in fact facilitate more effective and inclusive forms of state support and recognition even while requiring less, rather than more, intrusive surveillance. To appreciate the case for the biometric, it is useful to remember that current regimes of (paper) documentation in Africa have some quite obvious and severe problems. First of all, it is well established that the burdens of obtaining and retaining documents fall hardest on the poorest and most marginal members of society (just those who are most in need of social protection), who often fail for this reason to qualify for schemes ostensibly meant to benefit them. In addition, widespread fraud (through forged documents, etc.) both wastes resources and (even more important) undermines political support for social transfer programs. Reliance on local officials to issue or certify documents creates vast opportunities for corruption, while linking benefits to the holding of specific cards or identifying documents allows social stigma to be attached to the receipt of payments. In contrast, the mechanics of bio-recognition appear to fit well with the universality of unconditional cash transfers, where everyone with a unique iris scan is entitled to get a transfer once a month. In this scenario, many of the identity-related documents the "social" state has always needed can be dispensed with, and resources that would otherwise be spent tracking down who really qualifies for the income cut-off or who really lives at what address could be used instead to provide benefits. Critical skepticism toward such ideas is of course important, but I am increasingly convinced that it is equally important to allow ourselves to be open to the political possibilities that such new "techniques of the social" might enable.

It would be easy to say that what the "lumpen" masses of Africa's cities really need is "proper jobs" and the whole range of "social" rights, state protections, and documentary entailments that (at least in European welfare states) have long been understood to come with them. But such a demand seems increasingly irrelevant in places where state capacities are

extremely limited, where a formal-sector job is a distant rumor, and informal hustling the dominant livelihood. To find forms of social assistance
and state services—and perhaps also forms of political mobilization—
that can be effective in such circumstances, we may require both a historically informed sense of the future and its possibilities and a willingness
to envision new forms of legibility that might correspond to new forms of
social and political recognition.

3. Distributed Livelihoods

Dependence and the Labor of Distribution
in the Lives of the Southern African Poor
(and Not-So-Poor)

It is common to suppose that people make their livelihoods by being "productive"—that is, by producing, via their labor, goods and services that either meet their own needs directly (as in subsistence farming) or meet the needs of others in such a way that either their goods can be marketed (e.g., peasant production) or their labor can be sold (via wage labor). In fact, that has never been an adequate account. In no modern industrial society does the number of people directly engaged in productive labor come anywhere close to accounting for the entire population. But the idea that the normal condition is one where most people earn their daily bread by either directly producing things or being paid for their labor remains a kind of common sense. Recent developments in the spatial and social organization of production, however, put that common-sense linkage of livelihood with production under considerable strain. As any observer of the contemporary world cannot fail to have noticed, more and more of the things in the world are produced by smaller numbers of people who specialize in it. Plastic toys for children are overwhelmingly made in China. Wheat is grown in Canada on a scale and at a price that few can compete with. And so on.

This is not simply a matter of the sort of functional global division of labor that is evoked by the phrase "comparative advantage." For the fact is that whole regions and populations find that they have no "advantage" of any kind and are (in some significant measure) simply left out of the global production regime. Even where valued products are exported, it is often in ways that do not generate much employment (as in the case of oil exporters and mineral export economies generally), even as the labor-intensive small agriculture that once supported most of the world's populations is in decline, being displaced by agribusiness, or both. In such situations, we have massive new populations that are, from the point of view of the production system, "redundant." Tania Li (2010) has recently posed the question as a matter of "surplus populations" (echoing from an Asian vantage an earlier critical discussion of apartheid South Africa's approach to "surplus people" [Platzky and Walker 1985]) that have been expelled from rural agricultural production systems but not incorporated into urban industrial working classes in the way that dominant developmental paradigms expected. Such people, now largely excluded from *any* significant role in the system of production, may often be found engaged in tasks whose fundamental purpose is not to produce goods at all but to engineer distributions of goods produced elsewhere by accessing or making claims on the resources of others. Such distributive processes have always been there, of course, but they take on a new centrality when more and more people are seeking to make livings without being able to rely upon either land-based livelihoods such as peasant production or those based on wage labor. Processes of distribution have thus come to acquire an extraordinary salience in the lives of those who inhabit the margins of the global economy, even as they have remained underdeveloped in our theoretical and analytical protocols.

It is time, then, to revisit the issue of distribution. This is, of course, a topic that was central to the "economic anthropology" of another anthropological generation (whether Malinowski's foundational account of the Trobriand *kula* ring, Mauss's brilliant treatment of gift exchange, or Karl Polanyi's influential analysis of systems of redistribution). Today, clearly, we are less concerned than we once were with hereditary chiefs and piles of yams and more concerned with such things as state bureaucracies, taxation, and programs of social protection. But it is worth insisting on at least one key anthropological insight that remains of great relevance: distribution is a crucial social activity that is constitutive of the social (and not only the economic) order. Accordingly, we need to pay attention to the idea of distribution as a necessary and valuable social activity within what Keith Hart and his colleagues have called "the human economy" (Hart, Laville, and Cattani 2010).

From Lumpenproletariat to Informal Economy to Distributed Livelihoods

Processes of distribution are ubiquitous, and of greater economic importance than is sometimes imagined. As noted in the introduction, even in the highly industrialized and relatively welfare-unfriendly United States, wage labor directly supports far less of the population than is commonly supposed. The idea that distribution is accomplished principally via direct remuneration for productive labor is even less satisfactory when we take a broader geographical view. Certainly, when we consider southern Africa, an account of distribution proceeding via wages and markets immediately and massively fails to account for how most people in fact obtain goods. For a huge majority of the African poor are not wage laborers and do not in fact access most of the goods and services they need by selling labor in a market of wage labor. Even in highly proletarianized South Africa, as we will see in the following sections, broad sectors of the population are largely or wholly excluded from the world of wage labor and instead piece together livelihoods through a complex mix of other activities. All across Africa, indeed, wage laborers (in the normal sense of the term) make up only a small percentage of the population. Nor are those who fall outside of the realm of regularized wage labor necessarily peasants or subsistence farmers, either. Instead, as was discussed in the introduction, Africa's fast-growing cities are increasingly inhabited by people who lack both land and formal-sector jobs and who improvise complex and contingent livelihoods through a combination of petty trade, hustling, casual labor, smuggling, prostitution, begging, theft, seeking help from relatives or lovers, and so on.

Marx long ago identified the presence of a stratum of urbanites that fell outside of the production-based class categories of proletarian, bourgeoisie, petty-bourgeoisie, peasant, and so on. These he identified as the *lumpenproletariat*, whose members he famously characterized in the following colorful terms in *The Eighteenth Brumaire*:

Decayed roués with dubious means of subsistence and of dubious origin, ruined and adventurous offshoots of the bourgeoisie, rubbed shoulders with vagabonds, discharged soldiers, discharged jailbirds, escaped galley slaves, swindlers, montebanks, *lazzaroni*, pickpockets, tricksters, gamblers, *maquereaus*, brothel keepers, porters, literati, organ-grinders, ragpickers, knife-grinders, tinkers, beggars—in short, the whole of the nebulous, disintegrated mass, scattered hither and thither, which the French term *la bohème*. (Marx [1852] 1978, 73)

While this vivid list is, as has often been noted, something of a grab-bag in sociological terms, it correctly identifies something that more recent social scientific treatments often sidestep or seek to minimize, which is the prominent role of specifically *distributive* processes in sustaining the livings of those on the urban margins. While a contemporary neoliberal policy literature seems to be sure that every poor person scrambling for a livelihood can be treated as one or another sort of productive entrepreneur or firm, Marx's account of the lumpenproletariat emphasizes livelihood practices that rely on direct distribution, including thieves and pickpockets, vagabonds and beggars, tricksters and gamblers—all those "living on the crumbs of society" (Marx [1850] 1964, 50). But the insight into the distributive basis of many marginal urban livelihoods is blunted by the unmistakable moralizing contempt with which such "parasitic" ways of life are understood. As noted in chapter 1, the Marxian overvaluation of production has made it difficult for those working within this tradition to see those outside of productive labor as anything other than a proletariat-in-waiting (as in Marx's concept of the "industrial reserve army") or else a kind of social refuse, of neither economic nor political value—the "scum, offal and refuse of all classes," as Marx himself put it, seeking "to benefit themselves at the expense of the laboring nation" (Marx [1852] 1978, 73).[1] And while Marx clearly recognized the role of direct distribution in politics (it is central to his analysis of the political triumph of Louis Bonaparte), he could understand such a politics only in entirely negative terms, as the means by which a reactionary populism could buy itself a lumpen following by plying them with sausages (Marx [1852] 1978, 124). Missing is any sense that achieving distributive results (i.e., "living on the crumbs of society") might in itself be a valuable social activity, along with any recognition that the distributive claims emerging from such forms of life might be either legitimate, or part of a progressive political mobilization.[2]

In more contemporary writing, the ragged and miscellaneous livelihoods that Marx analyzed as "lumpen" are more often described in terms of a so-called informal sector or informal economy. But this discussion, too, is not adequate to the problem for at least two reasons. First as Kate Meagher has pointed out, the sorts of economic activities the term was originally intended to capture have become so pervasive as to call into question the very concept of an "informal economy"; in her view this has led to "the collapse of the informality paradigm" (2010, 11). Indeed, the originator of the very term *informal sector*, Keith Hart, has suggested that in many countries informalization has now become so pervasive that it no longer makes any sense to seek to identify a distinct sector or type of activity. As he has put it, "When most of the economy is 'informal', the usefulness of the category becomes questionable" (2007b, 28). In this perspective, calling a domain of economic activity "informal" may be no more helpful than categorizing a language as "non-Chinese."[3] South African scholars, for their part, have long chafed at the very idea of a distinct "sector" or "second economy" defined by "informality," pointing to the many points of connection and integration between the livelihoods the terms seek to capture and the dominant, supposedly "formal," economic system (see van der Waal and Sharp 1988; Du Toit and Neves 2007; Valodia and Devey 2012).

Second, it is not at all clear what the word *informal* means here. A critical literature seems agreed on the term's inadequacy but has failed to produce an alternative terminology.[4] It is far from clear that formalization in any of the usual senses (documentation, bureaucratic regulation, paying taxes, adherence to law, etc.) is really the key dynamic at work. A small street hawker's fundamental situation is after all not much changed by having or not having a license, while even very large and well-organized corporations often evade regulations, laws, and taxes. Instead, I will suggest that the picture that emerges from ethnographic research in southern Africa suggests that the more fundamental characteristic of the ragtag livelihoods that support more and more of the region's population is that they are almost unbelievably precarious and insecure and that those who navigate them manage to avoid the worst only through a continual process of flexible improvisation.

This combination of precariousness and flexibility is not well captured by either the languages of "informality" or that of the "lumpen." I here therefore prefer to avoid both terminologies and to speak instead of a kind of *improvisation under conditions of adversity*.[5] At the bottom of the economic scale, such improvisation may in fact be a matter of real or perceived survival, a fact that once led Rogerson (1996) to speak of such informal enterprises not as the "micro-enterprises" that are often celebrated as sites of accumulation or advancement but rather as "survivalist enterprises," driven by a spare logic of simply making it from one day to the next. With such distinctions in mind, I characterize the precarious livelihoods of the southern African poor not in terms of "informality" but of *survivalist improvisation*—a term that finds support in the vernacular usage (which I have encountered especially often in Zambia) that provides a common response to questions about how someone is faring: "I am just surviving . . . " But the larger point I wish to make (and will argue at some length in the sections to follow) is that this work of "surviving" is in fact less about producing goods and services (though that is of course a part of the story) than it is about securing distributive outcomes. It is in large measure, that is, about accessing or making claims on the resources of others.[6]

If this is true, then the precarious survival strategies of the southern African poor might best be understood as neither the vicious predations of a lazy lumpenproletariat nor the bustling entrepreneurialism of an "informal economy" but rather as what might be described as a system of distributed livelihoods.

Distributive Labor and the Hard Work of Dependence

"Money does not stay with a person." So it was explained to me during my first research in Lesotho, as I sought to understand why villagers avoided converting assets such as cattle into cash (Ferguson 1990). It was not just that resources in the form of cash might be spent impulsively or unwisely; the greater danger was that they would become the object of perfectly legitimate (indeed, morally binding) demands for the care of others to whom one was bound: blankets to warm an older relative, school fees for a sister's children, taxi fare for a sick neighbor's trip to the clinic. The force of such demands always lies in the background when poor households across the region manage their economic affairs, and it explains a great deal about how both income and assets are handled. This is a theme that has been explicated at some length in an impressive regional literature on migrant labor and the ways that it historically supported workers' families and communities of origin (see, e.g., Murray 1981; Moodie 1994). But the larger point I wish to explore here is that such distributive pressures are not only brought to bear around migrant labor. Instead, they provide a crucial context for the social reception of *all* sorts of income streams.

In fact, any poor person who receives an income (from employment, to be sure—but also from disability payments, old age pensions, inheritance, or any other source) is likely to encounter strong claims on that income. The strength of these claims can be gauged by the extreme measures needed to resist them. As I found in Lesotho, money needs to be guarded—not just against illegitimate attempts to seize it (via crime) but equally against more or less *legitimate* takings in the form of social and moral claims by those to whom one has recognized obligations. In an influential recent study, a group of development economists reported the "perplexing" finding that the world's poor often save not by making deposits that earn interest but by drawing on informal mechanisms such as "money guarding" (i.e., paying someone to keep a sum of money and return it at a later date) to keep their small surplus funds secure for a certain period of time (Collins et al. 2009). Indeed, in some cases, they note that quite high rates of "negative interest" are paid for such services (they cite West African examples in which effective rates paid to a money guard are negative 3.3 percent per month, or a negative 40 percent at an annualized rate [2009, 21]). The widespread existence of such practices (in southern Africa and beyond) provides strong confirmation that "saving" (that is, keeping to oneself more money than one at present needs) is, in the midst of generalized deprivation, a very difficult thing to do. What is more, the ethnographic record suggests that the reason for this is not just lack of discipline or the "temptation" of immediate consumption (as the report seems to suggest [2009, 22]) but also the pressing and (often) socially legitimate demands of others.

Such, at least, has long been observed in the ethnography of southern Africa. Saving for retirement, for instance, has been noted to be associated less with bank accounts and stores of money than with the accumulation of assets such as cattle, even under circumstances (including limited and degraded grazing and high rates of theft and herd mortality) that would seem to make for a losing "investment." In Lesotho, a cultural disapproval of the conversion of cattle to cash (which I termed "the bovine mystique") enabled assets to be protected from the immediate needs and demands of a wage-earner's dependents, thereby slowing the inevitable dissipation of a fund of resources accumulated while working (Ferguson 1990). Similar dynamics have been observed around other sites where savings of some sort are required, such as funerals. Southern Africans have a long history of dealing with such problems collectively, via rotating credit and other saving schemes such as the South African *stokvel*, which enable funds to be detached from an individual and sheltered within a collective group that is less vulnerable to the daily needs and demands that make saving so difficult at the individual and household level. (The history of these schemes, and their latter-day revisions and updatings, have been described in Bähre 2007b and James 2012.) As in the case of cattle-keeping, we see here elaborate mechanisms for building assets in the face of strong distributive pressures.

As such details suggest, funds *not* carefully secured in such ways are likely to be subject to claims that may be very difficult to resist, and a great deal of the day-to-day activity in the region's low-income communities is related to making, negotiating, contesting, and sometimes evading the social and affective claims that can be made on the meager streams of income and sources of wealth that such communities contain. As discussed at some length below, such claims have long been brought to bear on the earning power of wage-laborers in the southern African region, but today even the very small income streams that come from social grants and pensions may be subject to similar claims. The amounts thus transacted are often pathetically small, but this does not mean that the impact is insignificant; on the contrary, the small dribbles that come to the poorest clearly provide at least part of the answer to the question (one that has vexed many an observer of urban Africa) of how people with no visible means of earning an income in fact manage to survive from day to day—a fact that has led some researchers to speak of a system of "informal social protection" (Du Toit and Neves 2009a).

Africanist scholarship has long noted the reliance of African political-economic systems on processes of diversion, division, and tapping into flows. Jean-François Bayart (2000) has seen in such processes the roots of a distinctive modality of political power keyed on controlling externally oriented resource flows ("extraversion"), and has pointed to the widespread use of such control to establish networks of clientage and patronage, in ways that remain crucial to understanding contemporary politics across the region. And a massive body of ethnographic evidence from anthropologists of Africa, assembled across the last century, documents a remarkable elaboration of mechanisms of distribution, thanks to which sources of wealth and streams of income are divided into smaller and smaller slivers as they work their way across social relations of kinship, clientage, allegiance, and solidarity. These practices of distribution have changed in form over time, and we know them by a wide variety of names (remittances, kin-based sharing, political clientage, "corruption," etc.). But they are visible, and even prominent, in any detailed social study that attends to the micro-social level, where we find that those with access to incomes inevitably encounter a wide range of social claims on that income—claims that may be honored or scorned, to be sure, but in any case cannot be easily ignored.

But while the existence of such practices is well documented, we have perhaps not fully appreciated the extent to which the livelihoods of today's urban poor in fact depend on these ongoing processes of seeking and securing distributive outcomes. The ability to make successful distributive claims does not come easily, and long and careful work goes into building the sorts of social relationships that make such distributive flows possible. That is to say that material dependence on others is not a passive condition—it is a valued outcome of long, hard social labor. "Dependence"—that bogey of moralizing social policy—can in this respect be understood (in Bayart's felicitous phrase) "as a mode of action," and even as an achievement (Bayart 2000, 218; cf. chapter 5). For while "dependency" is obsessively decried as a problem or a trap in social policy discourse, an ethnographic view suggests that it is really only via relations of "dependence" that most of the population survives at all. Dependence is, in this respect, not the name of the problem; it is the name of the solution.

In this spirit, I propose an analytical focus on what I call "distributive labor." To appreciate the way that distribution can be the object of labor, I will suggest, we must be prepared to sever what has become an unthinking and dogmatic coupling of the concept of labor with the process of production. If we can do this, we will be able to arrive at new understandings, both of labor and also perhaps of the problem of distribution.

In reading the social scientific and policy literature, I have been struck by what seems to me a persistent misrecognition of the livelihood strategies of the poor, a misrecognition that I term "productionist." This misrecognition takes several different forms. On the political Right, the attempt is to see urban improvisatory survivalists as "microentrepreneurs"—if not actually capitalists in miniature, then at least "self-employed businessmen/women" or proprietors of (as the phrase has it) "small, medium, and micro enterprises." On the Left, the urge is to see the same people as "workers," implicitly sharing a class position (and potentially a politics) with the wage-earning proletariat. The policies and politics that such visions inspire are varied and ideologically opposed (ranging from Hernando DeSoto–inspired proposals to make capitalists out of the poorest shack-dwellers by titling their shacks to laborite projects to "organize" petty street hawkers into labor unions). Such projects are a diverse lot, and some may have their uses in specific situations. But they seem to have in common a sense of being a bit out of touch with the actual realities of survivalist improvisation, since they so often start not with what people are (or can reasonably hope to be) but with productionist ideas of what they ought to be yet inexplicably are not (that is, proper business owners or properly organized workers).

The more optimistic accounts see in the so-called informal economy not an inert reservoir of poverty but a vast potential for "creating jobs" (as they say). I come to such accounts with a considerable fund of skepticism, deriving from my experience on the Zambian Copperbelt. There, a disastrous downturn in the mining industry produced massive unemployment. Former mineworkers (who had enjoyed relatively well-paid and secure employment) were reduced to trying to eke out a living on the streets. One man I knew, for example, tried to survive by buying each day a pack of cigarettes and then standing on a street corner trying to sell them one by one to passers-by. As I was observing such things, a celebratory policy literature was praising the "informal economy" for its ability to "create jobs" at an unprecedented rate. One had to wonder: if putting a mineworker on a street-corner selling cigarettes was "creating a job," what did "losing a job" look like?

A second scene from the Copperbelt is perhaps equally telling. On a certain street corner that I knew well, two women were in the habit of sitting and selling vegetables, mainly tomatoes and onions. By the time I completed my research, the same corner had at least ten women selling the same limited set of goods, to the same limited set of passers-by. What boosters of the virtues of "the informal" might describe as an impressive expansion of employment (ten small business owners instead of two) was, on inspection, something quite different. For the fundamental dynamic here was not one of creating new services or tapping new markets but of splitting an already small market into ever smaller slivers—raising the denominator, in effect, below a more or less constant numerator.

As argued in the section below ("A Distributive Political Economy"), a great deal of what counts as "informal" activity is fundamentally fractional in this sense—less about creating new goods and services than about raising the denominator in a distributional process. A good part of such activity, too, involves ways in which people who do not have access to wage labor endeavor to capture a piece of the wages earned by those who do. This is one of a number of reasons why it is misleading to speak of a "second economy" as if it were separate from the "first" (cf. Du Toit and Neves 2007); it's also one of the reasons why it is misleading to simply merge improvisatory survivalists with workers as if they formed a single class. The tendency to see production everywhere one finds people "working" means that the perception of a particular livelihood activity as productive (or not) often ends up depending more on the common sense of the analyst than on any inherent property of the activity. Are garbage pickers, for instance, engaged in "production" (as we might readily say if they were foraging in a wild landscape and not a dump)? Or "distribution" (as we would more likely assert if they were asking for scraps at the back door instead of taking them out of piles of discarded trash)?

Many of those who emphasize the productive element in informal improvisatory labor, of course, do so in order to defend the moral and economic virtue of the urban poor. The improvisers are not idle, they insist, but in fact highly productive—therefore (it is implied) they deserve our respect and help, not our disdain. Modern ideas of democratic citizenship have long relied on the dignity of wage labor as a kind of moral credential, authorizing social and political membership (Barchiesi 2011). Where large proportions of the population are left out of the world of wage labor (as they are in most African cities, and in many other places as well), it is understandable that those who would make claims for social inclusion and membership should be eager to argue that the urban poor are, in fact, highly productive workers and that we would see that if only we would look a little more closely.

Of course, work in the (so-called) informal sector, even at the lower, survivalist end of it, is indeed often productive in an economic sense, just as it is often integrated with (or functional to) the celebrated productivity of the (so-called) first economy. My point, however, is that even where it isn't, there is no cause for disdain, and no reason to ignore the fact that even the unproductive are both engaged in labor and entitled to social membership. The woman begging on the street may not be producing a good or selling a service, but she works all day. To say that she is not productive is not to denigrate her labor. It is, instead, to underline the importance and value of distribution.

In this perspective, it is significant that a great deal of what the improvisers actually do, in a day-to-day way, in fact has as much to do with distribution as with production. I emphasize that this is not a matter of a merely quantitative process of income distribution but rather involves (just as production does) a set of social relations, social institutions, and social processes. The concept I propose for grasping this key fact is "distributive labor."

Consider the following four examples of survivalist improvisatory labor (which one might easily observe in any African city today):

1. *A windshield washer:* A haggard older man hops up at a street corner when the light turns red, aggressively providing unsolicited windshield washes to motorists as they wait for the light to change. His hope is that he will receive a few coins as a tip before the driver speeds away.

2. *A panhandler:* A familiar sight in most cities today, the panhandler enacts in one way or another a picture of need while waiting, hour after hour, for the generosity of a passer-by. Male or female, he or she may have (or affect) a disability.

3. *A pickpocket:* The epitome of street hustling, the pickpocket is engaged in one of the many petty criminal pursuits that sustain uncounted masses of urban survivalists. The prototypical "lumpen," he is typically young, male, and despised by law-abiding folk.

4. *A mother making a family visit:* An older woman who perhaps comes from an impoverished rural area to visit her employed urban son.

She expresses through her visit her love and commitment to her son, while explaining to him the problems and hardships of people back home, perhaps returning home with money and gifts enabled by his wages.

If analyzed in conventional terms (where distributive dynamics are relegated to the background and productive labor is radically separated from other sorts), this list shows four quite different sorts of activity:

1. The window-washer is vending a service; he is a self-employed member of the service industry—some will perhaps even see him as a micro-entrepreneur.
2. The panhandler, in contrast, is unemployed, idle, and seeking charity.
3. The pickpocket is a predator committing a crime.
4. The rural mother is performing a kinship role and invoking traditional morality.

Seeing these four figures as different forms of distributive labor, in contrast, allows us to recover their fundamental unity. For all four of my examples involve people engaged in a form of labor, one that seeks to secure a transfer of resources from those who have them to those who don't. The indiscriminate application of the label "service industry," on the other hand, obscures the distributive point. The window-washer is not really selling a service (doesn't the motorist really wish he would just go away?) but rather pressing a distributive claim. The pickpocket is neither producing a good nor performing a service, but he is also working hard at the job of distribution—just like the others. The mother is not just being a mother—she is also working hard to press a distributive claim. Now, to be sure, distributive labor is not necessarily morally virtuous or ethically well justified. The young thug who beats up his grandmother and steals her pension is (in my terms) engaged in distributive labor, but there's certainly nothing commendable about his actions. Broadly, though, distribution (especially in a spectacularly unequal society) is a necessary and valuable social function, and it should be recognized, named, and valued as such.

Our mental habit is to do the opposite. We readily oppose productionist virtue to distributive vice, as the honest worker stands in contrast to the moocher, the layabout, the parasite, and the leech. Indeed, in our usual way of speaking and thinking, it is a denigration, almost an insult, to say that someone is "unproductive." But we seem much less ready to fault someone for being "undistributive" (indeed, the closing off of distributive channels may even be praised as "thrift" or "saving"). A truly "unproductive" person is not engaged in the great societal task of production. But almost inevitably, we will find that that person is engaged in the perhaps equally great societal task of distribution. Such forms of labor, I suggest, are important everywhere, but in southern Africa they are in fact central to the entire regional political economy. The next section seeks to demonstrate this in order to lay the groundwork for the analysis, in the chapters that follow, of the special issues of distribution that are raised by the growing role of social payments.

A Distributive Political Economy

The issue of distribution has long been at the heart of scholarly understandings of the political economy of the southern African region. As suggested above, this has largely been due to the highly developed and well-studied relations of interdependence between wage-earners and their rural communities of origin, especially in the context of the so-called migrant labor system. Such relations have been central to my own work. In my first research in the region, in highland Lesotho, I encountered an apparently rural people whose basic livelihood in fact derived from industrial employment that was geographically located hundreds of miles away, in South Africa's gold mines. Villages of what appeared to be peasant farmers were in fact, as Colin Murray memorably put it, a proletariat that "scratched about on the land" (Murray 1981, 19). But the scratching about was all the same crucial to maintaining livelihoods— not so much because it produced a robust agricultural income (in most cases it did not) but because it established the rural homestead as a viable home base, to which labor migrants would plan to return. A relation of dependence and mutual obligation between migrant mineworkers and their rurally based wives and kin was at the center of both the social and the economic system.

In later research on the Zambian Copperbelt (Ferguson 1999), I found that a key issue for urban mineworkers was how they would manage their retirements. With high and rising costs of urban living and meager employment options after leaving the mines, retiring to "home" villages was very much on the agenda, even for workers who did not relish the idea of rural life. But "going home" meant, first, having a rural "home" and, second, being welcome to "return" there. Relations with rural relatives were often tense and conflictual, and those who had not adequately attended to the needs and demands of kin "at home" during their working years could encounter social rejection and even violence in their own time of vulnerability and need. Even those who had kept close relations with a home community encountered distributive demands that they regarded as overwhelming, and a common strategy was to plan one's return to the village for the middle of the night, in hopes of avoiding a kind of public inventory of one's goods that would provide the basis for later distributive demands. Relations of generosity and sharing were in some sense obligatory for those anticipating a return to rural life. Mutualities of this kind, indeed, were often based on (as Bähre [2007a] has usefully put it) a "reluctant solidarity" often enforced through violence and other sorts of coercion; we should not suppose that such sharing ever emerged spontaneously out of some romantic and conflict-free communal unity. Yet fraught as such social solidarities undoubtedly were, rural communities, quite literally, lived on the distributive flows that they enabled.

Nor was this just a matter of Lesotho and Zambia. Across the region, the literature shows us that broad access to wage labor created streams of income that were rapidly channeled, via social processes of distribution, into a multitude of ramifying capillaries that spread it (unequally, to be sure) across geographical and social space. Through such processes, the resource streams embodied in wages, modest as they were, fed the needs not only of workers but of countless dependents of those workers—and, indeed, the dependents of those dependents.

So far, so familiar. But a sharp decline in demand for low-skilled and manual labor across the region has meant that access to wages is today no longer such a dominant route to income for poor people in the region (for South Africa, see Seekings and Nattrass 2005). Instead, other sources of income, especially social grants and the loosely structured improvisations of the "informal economy," loom increasingly large. Under such conditions, Lesotho can no longer really be termed a labor reserve, since there is so little demand for the labor that it still holds "in reserve." But relations of distribution, rooted in practices of sharing and dependence, continue to be crucial, as Turner has argued (2005). And while young men can no longer access migrant wage labor in the way that they did in the past, new streams of income have appeared, albeit usually much smaller. Women, for instance, have gotten some unstable, low-wage employment in a fragile, on-again, off-again textile industry. And old people now get pension grants (even if these are much smaller than those of other southern African states that have more elaborate social protection systems, such as Namibia, Botswana, and South Africa). Here, as elsewhere in the region, aging grandmothers no longer have much reason to think about how to make claims on the earning power of their sons and grandsons, since young men have so largely lost that power. Instead, relations of dependence are often reversed, as it is now young men who are likely to be dependent on others. Indeed as du Toit and Neves (2009b) have shown for South Africa, both social transfers and most forms of informal enterprise are bound up very tightly with social networks and the petty reciprocities that make them work. For this reason, it is increasingly the case that successful livelihood strategies for the poor hinge crucially on the distributive dynamics associated with these networks.

Social grants, in such a context, are not simply payments to individuals who are thus enabled to use small amounts of cash to meet their needs. Instead, those who are able to access resources as dependents of the state are themselves the *source* of income for others we might term "sub-dependents." The truly destitute household, on the other hand, is the one with no children nor old people nor disabled members and therefore no eligibility for state distribution.

But such distributive processes are not only a matter of those with regular cash incomes such as wages or grants and those who directly depend on them. Instead, a much broader domain of social practices is implicated, comprising nothing less than an entire distributive political economy, cutting across what are commonly thought of as distinct social domains. Here I consider six such domains, summarizing the distributive practices that the literature has shown to be central to the livelihood dynamics that unfold there. The six domains are land and landholding; kinship and sharing; migration and movement; work and business; sex and love; and death and funerals.

Land and Landholding

As noted above, in a regional political economy long dominated by an extensive system of migrant labor, the ability of land to support at least minimal agricultural livelihoods has historically also provided a crucial distributive resource in that rural dependents of absent laborers could expect some measure of material support from those who would one day return "home" to fields and cattle as well as to wives, kin, and loved ones. For many in the region, such a dynamic continues to this day, enabling at least some portion of wages earned in distant cities and mines to be circulated within the (typically poor) rural communities that depend upon them.

Today, however, far fewer rural households have a member employed in wage labor (migrant or otherwise). What is more, in much of the region smallholder agriculture itself seems to be on the decline. In parts of the former "reserves" of South Africa in particular, it is reported that fewer fields are being cultivated, and those that are are cultivated with less intensity, even by those who do have land rights (see, for instance, Aliber et al. 2005). The percentage of people farming "seriously" (as they say) seems to be shrinking, while the dreams and ambitions of young South Africans focus less on smallholder farming and more on urban living, consumer goods, and the ever-elusive "business." As Mudhara (2010) has put it, rural smallholders today "only derive a minuscule proportion of their livelihoods directly from agricultural sources. In its place, non-agricultural sources such as remittances, off-farm work, and government transfers have all been gradually strengthened in light of the demise of agriculture" (2010, 1). Yet even as rural holdings have become less productive in agricultural terms, they have hardly ceased to have their value. As I have argued at some length elsewhere, the reasons for this are largely distributive (Ferguson 2013).

While cities in southern Africa have long been defined as the place of work, rural settlements have historically served as refuges for the supposedly "non-productive" (the old, the sick, the disabled, young children, etc.). But nowadays it is precisely the "non-productive" who are, as state dependents, likely to be key sources of income. To have a piece of land where an elderly parent or grandparent can stay (typically with much lower living costs than in town) today often means having access to that elderly person's pension money. If children are sent to the countryside to be cared for, the child care grant likely goes with them.

Such distributive payments flowing into rural households form a key resource for rural households seeking to find non-agricultural livelihoods in today's "informalized" economies. As du Toit and Neves (2009b) have shown, petty retail trade is a shoestring operation, operating on the margins of the huge supermarket chains that have now spread across the region. And in pursuing such trade, the small but regular payments provided by social grants are often key. The month's pension money, for instance, may provide a trip to the supermarket and a small bag of "essentials" that can later be sold slowly over time in one's own neighborhood. The effect of this, of course, is principally distributive, in that it involves not creating new goods and services for the market but taking a fairly static retail trade and chopping it into smaller and smaller slivers. And this, what we might think of as an urban pattern, seems increasingly to be at work in the countryside, too, even when it comes to trading in agricultural goods and foodstuffs. A vision of rural smallholders as farmers would lead us to look for small producers bringing their produce to town to sell it (and no doubt there are many contexts within which this happens). More characteristic of the times, though, is a very different scenario, in which the smallholder packs up money (not crops) for the trip to town, and where cash (obtained via circuits of distribution rather than agricultural production) is transmuted into food via the magic of the supermarket. Landholding here helps put food on the plate, not by growing it but by providing a support base for the non-agricultural distributive activities that end up enabling a trip to the supermarket. In this way, the possession of small plots of land can catalyze distributive flows and associated economic activities, even where remittances of wages have diminished. Land, long understood as a "factor of production," may today be equally important as a "factor of distribution."

Kinship and Sharing

Kinship has always been a key vector of distribution, and kin-based distributions of cash and other resources are one of the main ways that those excluded from the circuits of wage labor and social payments in fact survive. This should not be romanticized: as noted in chapter 2, visions of unlimited generosity on the part of African "extended families" were always overdone, and the claims that poor people can make on their kin are nowadays probably even more restricted than in the past—generally directed at a tighter cluster of relatives (and increasingly concentrated on the maternal side), as Sarah Harper and Jeremy Seekings have shown in a recent Cape Town study (2010). As Bähre (2007a) has emphasized, the solidarities of kinship do not unfold in opposition to conflict but in the midst of it; they involve "small bonds fraught with social tensions" (2007a, 52). But distributive claims based on such "small bonds" continue to be extremely important to day-to-day survival strategies, especially among the poorest.

Indeed, sharing among kin should be seen as part of a larger set of phenomena that du Toit and Neves (2009b) have termed "horizontal philanthropy," on which, as they note "the survival of the poor . . . crucially depends" (2009b, 23). A national survey in South Africa (Everatt and Solanki 2008) revealed that huge numbers of respondents reported giving money or goods to those in need. Some 45 percent had given money to a poor person within the last month, and a similar percentage reported having made in-kind gifts such as food or clothing. Even larger numbers (55 percent) reported having given money or goods to "members of their family not living in their household" in the month preceding the interview. Tellingly, percentages were even higher in the provinces with the greatest concentrations of poor people, such as the Eastern Cape (75 percent) and Limpopo (73 percent). As the report authors noted, such "giving" was highest among those in low socioeconomic categories, suggesting that such practices lie at "a considerable distance from traditional notions of philanthropy" (2008, 64). Such findings come as no surprise to those who have lived and worked in poor communities in the region. Indeed, the entire ethnographic record can be read as a kind of documentation of the key role of practices of distribution in such communities.

This suggests the vital importance of being able to draw on the income and wealth of better-resourced others and (what must come first) of achieving the sort of social standing that would *enable* one to make claims on those others. Mere blood kinship brings no automatic ability to make such claims (as Seekings [2008a] rightly emphasizes), and a great deal of work goes into establishing the kind of social standing that might enable distributive claims. Dependence of this kind is not a passive condition—

it is a carefully cultivated status that is the result of long processes of building social ties and reciprocal obligations (cf. chapter 5). Here, too, the securing of distributive outcomes does not occur all by itself but only as the hard-won outcome of a kind of distributive labor.

Movement and Migration

Southern African political economy has long been characterized by high levels of mobility. But why do people move? The old story gave a central place to labor—the "migrant labor system" induced or coerced the movement of massive numbers of workers to industrial sites such as mines while failing to accommodate their permanent presence; hence an endless (and socially damaging) churning from rural to urban and back again. Today, as is widely agreed, the declining availability of manual-laboring jobs combined with the growing possibilities of urban settlement has resulted in a marked decline (though not an end) to this sort of labor-based migration. But there is still a striking amount of spatial movement (including movement back and forth between rural and urban areas), much of which can only be understood in the context of the sorts of social dependencies and distributive pressures I have discussed here. Moving today may be less about getting or losing your job and more about finding a place where you have people who can care for you. A person lacking an adequate income may no longer find work by moving but may instead find a place to live at a lower cost, or an opportunity to move in with a relative with some sort of an income.

Anthropologists have long commented on the dynamic composition of households in the region, with people moving in and out of various domestic arrangements in ways that confound attempts to identify static entities like "families." Yet as Seekings (2008a) has argued, movements are not random, and it would be useful to go beyond simply pointing to "fluidity" and to arrive at a better account of exactly who moves from one household unit to another, when, and why. Much of this research has not yet been done, but Seekings (2008a) points out that much of the shifting membership of households derives from the movements of children and elderly people in and out of them, largely in the service of managing distributive claims and distributive flows. As he suggests, it is "very likely that children are moved between households not simply to facilitate access to school but also to facilitate access to care and food" (2008a, 43). And the same is probably true of other movements between households.

> Older household members might also move to access food, care or other resources. Furthermore, people may move in order to provide care or to bring resources into a "household." This might be true not only for adults, but also for children—who might be sent, for example, to a rural area to care for an elderly grandparent at the same time as benefitting from the grandparent's access to pension income." (Seekings 2008a, 43)

A special case of this general process of moving people within a field of distributive flows involves the movement of the ill when they are in need of care. This has, of course, become especially crucial in the light of the region-wide AIDS/HIV epidemic, which has stricken millions. This has placed extraordinary burdens not only on clinics and hospitals but perhaps even more on the vernacular systems of care that have, to an extraordinary extent, accommodated the needs of the sick and the care of the orphaned children left behind. A place to go when one is sick is not just a place to live but a place to access care and social support in one's time of need, and it is crucial to recognize the often unspoken solidarities that have enabled the vital but unwaged work of care, nursing, and support (see Henderson 2012). This is a reminder that it is not only wealth that is "distributed" across social bonds; so too is suffering. The same social relationships that underlie the practices of distribution of such things as income also do the essential work of distributing the burden of illness and suffering.

Work and Business

In addition to the remuneration of wages, employment in the region has characteristically involved other sorts of transfers of goods and services, often under the ideology of a paternalistic or kin-like relation of dependence and obligation. The best known example comes from farm labor, where an informal compact governed relations between farmer and farmworker, according to which very low wages were balanced with a range of other goods and services provided in terms that glossed such obligations in quasi-familial or "paternalistic" terms (see Van Onselen 1992; du Toit 1993; Rutherford 2008). But such distributive flows are hardly confined to the farm, while such practices have come under pressure in recent years, they remain widespread, and constitute another arena of distributive practice, albeit under starkly unequal and sometimes humiliating terms. Regular gifts of clothes and other goods, for instance, are widely understood to come with the job for the huge number of domestic and household workers in the region. These goods are themselves distributed within the social networks of the employee, generating an even larger penumbra of distributed goods (see Cock 1990; Ally 2009). Even outside of the home, employers are often still expected to help out with a range of needs (for an account of the long history of such relations of dependence via labor, see chapter 5). Such practices are presumably reflected in the finding (cited above) that fully 45 percent of South Africans reported having given food, goods, or clothes to a poor person or "someone asking for help" within the previous month (Everatt and Solanki 2008, 60).

Similar distributive pressures are at work even among the "self-employed" purveyors of "business," such as small retail traders. Such trade is itself a form of distributive labor, insofar as it provides a means of engineering tiny diversions of value from those with at least some resources to those who lack them (this is often the case when "survivalist" traders eke out livings by selling tiny quantities of basic goods to neighbors or passers-by). But even more-successful "informal" traders are bound up with reciprocal distributive circuits and not just the "business-like" pursuit of profits. As Neves and du Toit (2012, 139) have observed, a key requirement in such pursuits is the need to negotiate a complex landscape of social claims and expectations of fairness and non-exploitation, "keeping them at bay while nonetheless engaging with them." Skillful management of such claims and expectations is necessary to ward off the theft or violence that might be visited upon a merchant considered to be "stingy," indifferent to people's needs, or overaggressive in the pursuit of profit—and to maintain a client base among people with whom one has a social relationship, and for whom reputation and social loyalty may be more important than price. Indeed, Neves and du Toit noted in their field-sites something that is commonly observed across the region: that petty traders refused to consider competing on price. This is, of course, at odds with the usual economics textbook understanding of trade, but it is explicable in the light of the sort of social pressures reviewed here. Traders, like others who negotiate the region's elaborate distributional economy, need to pay close attention not only to such things as prices and profits but also to (as Neves and du Toit put it) "managing socially redistributive claims and practices" (2012, 145).

Sex and Love

Across the region, policy papers and tabloid newspapers alike appear fascinated with a sensational figure: the "sugar daddy." The term refers, of course, to a wealthy older man who seeks out, and generously rewards, much younger partners in sexual relationships. The offender is usually depicted, in popular accounts, as a powerful government official or businessman, while the underage victim is figured as a young (often underage) girl (stereotypically a schoolgirl) seeking money to buy desired consumer goods. Press coverage inevitably combines prurient fascination with the erotics of the situation with themes of moral outrage and humanitarian and/or medical concern both for the girl and for society at large.

There is no doubt that empirical examples of the "sugar daddy" phenomenon are easily located in ethnographic reality, some of which are every bit as outrageous as anything in the popular press might suggest. Yet the much-rehearsed figure of the "sugar daddy" is in the end a caricature that conceals more than it reveals. The elaboration of such a plainly pathological figure, after all, enables both universal disapproval of a moral breach and the rendering of that which lies on the near side of that figure as normal and approved. What is obscured is the fact that social and economic dynamics quite similar to those denounced in the "sugar daddy" relations in fact characterize a much broader range of relationships than are generally reckoned to be captured in that phrase. Indeed, the uncomfortable truth is that it is not only in the disapproved "sugar daddy" relationships that quite direct economic transfers from men to women are understood to be a normal and proper part of intimate sexual relations. As has often been noted, a discrete "prostitution" category is often difficult to locate in poor and working-class communities, and a range of short- and longer-term sexual relationships typically involve regular, undisguised transfers of cash and other gifts to the woman in ways that are regarded as normal and even proper.[8] (The relations between money and sexual intimacy are discussed at greater length in chapter 4.) But it is not only a matter of money for sex. Well-resourced men are understood to have a proper moral duty to provide for, and to provision, those under their care and protection. In such circumstances, a deep material dependence in the context of sexual intimacy may be understood, as Hunter (2010) has suggested, not as contradicting or compromising a relation of "real" love but on the contrary as a key attribute of a certain form of love—what he terms "provider love." Similar dynamics have often been observed to be at work within the marriage relation. At the same time, reciprocities of the economic and the sexual are linked with the deeply conflictual gender relations that are also well documented in the regional ethnography. In my own work on the Zambian Copperbelt, I found that profound economic asymmetries (in which men controlled both wage labor and housing) accounted for deeply conflictual relations between men and their wives and girlfriends, relations within which distributive questions were central. Women found themselves, I noted, "obliged—by the economic rules of the game that they encountered as given—to work tirelessly at extracting favors, gifts, and payments from the men they were attached to," while men, suffering from a contracting economy and declining earning power, and beset by demands from all sides, were "bound to resent it fiercely" (Ferguson 1999, 194).

Today, with wage labor both less available (in many cases) and less likely to be restricted to men, and with women enjoying more possibilities for supporting themselves in more autonomous ways, the situation is significantly transformed. The improvised livelihoods discussed in this chapter (such as petty trade) are often more open to women than the stereotypically male forms of labor such as mining that once dominated the labor market, while social grants (especially child care grants) have given millions of women independent sources of income. Under these transformed conditions, more women are able to live independently of a male "head of household," and rates of marriage have declined sharply (Hunter 2010; Kumchulesi 2011). But recent ethnographic accounts such as those by Hunter (2010) and Swider and Watkins (2007) make it very clear that sex and love continue to be tightly bound up with distributive flows (even if the sources of the resources so distributed have changed). And as the moral panic over "sugar daddies" shows, there is both a widespread public awareness of, and a considerable amount of anxiety over, the extent to which distributional considerations permeate intimate relations today.

Finally, it is important to remember that a transfer of resources from a man to his lover is not the end of the distributive story. Just as the dis-

tributive flows that are social grants themselves enable a host of subsidiary distributive practices (so that pension recipients can take in orphans
or buy clothes for a struggling adult child), so too do the recipients of
various forms of "provider love" often put a portion of the resources they
receive into their own channels of distribution and social obligation.
Through the distributive genius that is so characteristic of the region, a
"sugar daddy" may thus end up supporting not only his several mistresses
but also each of those mistress's own network of dependents as well.

Death and Funerals

Death has long provided a key occasion for distributive practices, via both
inheritance and the range of practices surrounding funerals. The importance of funerals is a striking characteristic of the region. Historically, it
has long been noted that even migrants living many hundreds of miles
from their regions of origins have felt the need to be buried "at home"—an
often-enormous cost willingly borne by even the poorest families. Hylton
White (2010) has recently described the durable and highly valued cluster
of practices surrounding burial in ancestral ground as a "necrocultural
complex" that has long linked lineages to land via practices surrounding
death, burial, and the care of ancestors. As Henderson (2012) has noted,
illness and death are occasions for the activation of the most profound
commitments of care and kinship within rural communities, commitments that are as powerfully material as they are emotional.

Today, urban burial has become more accepted (Lee 2011). But the
funeral continues to be a strikingly important social and economic institution, and the nexus of a host of important distributive practices. As anyone familiar with the region cannot have failed to notice, a vast funeral
economy looms large in the economic life of poor and working-class
people, a long-standing social reality that acquired a whole new level of
visibility and importance with the surge of deaths that has accompanied
the regional HIV/AIDS epidemic. And, as has long struck observers across
Africa, surprisingly large sums are mobilized for funerals, even by what
appear to be very poor people. Given how important funerals are to local
political economies in the age of AIDS, it is remarkable that we do not
have a better ethnographic understanding of the distributive issues they
raise.[9] Erik Bähre's rich study of migrants in Cape Town, however, gives

us valuable insights into the kinds of processes that occur in such settings (Bähre 2007a, 2007b). He demonstrates that funeral expenditures rely on a vast social infrastructure in which a vital role is played by mutual associations that provide for an insurance-like pooling of funds.[10] As he emphasizes, it is such vernacular practices of distribution and mutuality that enable the staging of what are often, in local terms, almost unbelievably expensive events. Against romantic depictions of "communities" that unproblematically care for all, Bähre shows that practices of financial mutuality are always embedded in complex and often conflictual fields of sociality. The solidarities that are expressed in marking deaths are for this reason riven by the strains of bad reputations and broken relationships that inevitably loom large in poor communities, meaning that quarrels and ill-will are quite as much a part of the social dynamic as are respectful love and generosity. Yet as ambivalent as these solidarities undoubtedly are, there is no doubt that funerals provide key points of collection and reallocation of substantial amounts of money. One recent study of a district in northern KwaZulu-Natal (Case et al. 2008) found that households spend the equivalent of a year's income for an adult's funeral, while also noting that some 45 percent of those enormous costs were covered by gifts from other households (2008, 5). It is evident that very important distributive dynamics occur at funerals, even if we do not as yet have a very complete picture of what they are and how they work.

"I Live on Handouts": Distributive Livelihoods at the Top of the Heap

The reliance upon distributive channels for accessing resources is not unique to the poor. This was recently illustrated by the remarkable way that the populist politician Julius Malema responded to critics of his accumulation of wealth. Such critics, he said to interviewers, failed to understand that (in a phrase that was instantly taken up by his many detractors across the country) "I live on handouts most of the time." He went on to reflect:

> If I don't have food to eat, I can call Cassel Mathale [Premiere of Limpopo province] and say: "Chief, can you help me? I've got nothing here." I can call Thaba Mufamadi, I can call Pule Mabe [ANCYL trea-

surer general] or Mbalula. They all do the same with me. That's how we have come to relate to each other. That's why at times you can't even see our poverty because we cover each other's back. As comrades, we have always supported each other like that.[11]

For many, this was simply a ridiculous statement from a corrupt and clownlike politician—a "tenderpreneur"[12] playing poor while looting the public treasury. But upon reading more carefully, an important sociological truth emerges, and it is a very serious one. For the fact is that many of South Africa's emergent new elites are like Malema in owing their new economic standing to political appointments. These appointments bring relatively high incomes, but they also come with new lifestyles that entail high demands for consumption and high expenses. Money sometimes runs out for a while. Those in such new circumstances can quickly find themselves on both the giving and the receiving ends of requests that take the form, "Chief, can you help me?" Indeed, it is a common observation that it is not only newly enriched elites but a huge range of ordinary salary-earners who are besieged with such demands. As one university-trained activist in Namibia recently told me, "I have three children. I pay school fees for eight. Every Namibian with a decent job will tell you the same story."

Then, too, anthropologists have long known that there is a fine line between "corruption" and things like friendship and loyalty (see, e.g., Smith 2008). The new forms of accumulation that have been facilitated by political connections with the ruling party (sometimes under the cover of state programs promoting "Black Economic Empowerment") are like many other forms of accumulation in that they occur via networks and connections, which bring with them both the opportunity to make distributive withdrawals from resource flows as well as a host of reciprocal obligations. The tenderpreneur, too, is a seeker of distributive flows, and Malema was probably right that such a life entails no simple luxury but a quite demanding and more or less continuous social performance that entails both the giving and getting of a complex range of "handouts." This is to say only that distributive livelihood strategies are not simply a product of poverty and deprivation but instead rest upon a deep social logic that finds application at all social levels.

This kinship between the vernacular distributive practices of elite and subaltern may help explain the appeal of Malema-ism (this is a topic that is discussed at greater length in chapter 6). Many have wondered why township youth seem attracted to Malema's political program, which critics see as a more or less undisguised program for black elite enrichment that would seem, on its face, to have little to offer to the poor and unemployed.[13] Are not the class interests of Malema and those of his township youth followers sharply divergent—even diametrically opposed? But as documented in chapter 6, Malema begins his political analysis with fundamentally *distributive* questions that connect in a very visceral way with the life conditions of the poor. South Africa is a rich country, he says. To whom does it belong? Is the right answer to this question not, he asks, that it belongs (or ought to belong) to us, the (South) Africans?[14] And if it's ours, then why do we not see any of the benefits? In the existing system, benefits are not properly divided and shared, and the few (especially, the whites) are taking far more than their share. Thus the familiar call for such things as land reform and nationalization of major industries, understood not as *taking* by the state but as *restoring* what was stolen to its rightful owners.

The appeal of this sort of argument does not derive from any clear demonstration that such policy measures would in fact benefit the unemployed youth of the townships (a point on which critics have sound reasons for doubt). It is instead rooted in the attraction of a moral language of ownership and rightful shares (see chapter 6) that speaks to those excluded from the world of production in a way that languages of civic rights and fair wages do not. Such arguments respond to a palpable hunger for distributive economic demands—a hunger, in effect, to be cut in on the deal. Given the analysis provided in this chapter, it should also be clear that such political sensibilities fit well with the actual livelihood practices of unemployed young people, which rest so fundamentally on getting a cut, a piece, a crumb, or a share. And while Malema's reactionary chauvinism is rightly deplored by South Africa's polite political society, the power of a politics that starts with the promise of directly sharing wealth with those unjustly excluded from it is evident. Whether such a politics can transcend the sort of spoils system that Malema-ism at its worst seems to promise is an issue that is taken up in a later chapter (chapter 6). For now, it is enough to have demonstrated that livelihoods based on practices of distribution are not some sort of scheme waiting to be introduced by social policy experts but are the mundane and established reality for vast numbers of southern Africans today, rich and poor alike.

Distributive Policy in a Distributive World

In the context of this book's larger purpose, this chapter has meant to demonstrate that state programs of distribution are inserted into a world in which distribution is already both a pervasive process and a concrete set of activities. Distribution, that is to say, is and long has been a key foundation for livelihoods—both for those who receive grants and for those who do not. It is not a question of "dependence" for those who receive state payments versus "independence" for those who do not. Poor southern Africans have long secured their livelihoods by accessing a multitude of channels through which distributive flows water the social field. And today, as has long been the case, those who receive distributive allocations are themselves subject to claims from their own dependents. Distributive flows, that is, are themselves distributed. The implications of this for thinking about state programs of distribution are pursued in the following chapter, which explores how the distributions and dependencies associated with social protection transfers are articulated with the other distributions and dependencies that are so vital to the actual livelihoods of the southern African poor.

4. The Social Life of Cash Payments

Money, Markets, and the
Mutualities of Poverty

Recent years have seen the emergence of new kinds of welfare states in the global South, a trend that a recent *Newsweek* article described as Welfare 2.0.[1] Advocates have sung the praises of new programs that directly transfer small amounts of cash to the poor. An impressive policy literature has documented the considerable achievements of such programs, among the most famous of which are Brazil's Bolsa Familia program and (an instance I will discuss at some length here) South Africa's system of pensions and grants. While narratives of a triumphant neoliberalism might have led us to expect a retreat from programs of social assistance, or even an end to the welfare state, the fact is that new welfare programs are proliferating and expanding across much of the world, most of them based on the appealingly simple device of directly providing poor people with monthly cash payments. There is much that is unclear about these programs, but it does seem evident that they are associated with an important new kind of politics, focused, at least in part, on the distributive claims of those excluded from the world of waged labor.

It is easy to see why those on the political Right, who generally oppose redistribution and disdain state programs of social assistance, would be hostile to the idea of "just giving money to the poor." But proposals to transfer cash into the hands of the poor are often criticized with equal vehemence from the Left. Indeed, in making presentations on these issues to a range of audiences in recent years, I have been struck that most objections to cash transfers, in an academic setting, come from those who position themselves on the Left. In an earlier era, such objections might perhaps have been traced to the old antipathy of the revolutionary Left to all forms of "reformism." But few on the academic Left today are still waiting for the revolution, and my sense is that the real resistance here is based on a more visceral distaste for the very idea of poor people receiving cash.

The concern seems to be that programs of cash transfer ultimately serve the cause of "commoditization," and thus capitalism, since people who receive cash are at the same time being "drawn into" a "neoliberal" world of market exchange. The underlying worry, which has a long pedigree in socialist thought, is that such participation in markets will "break down" social relationships, while the pursuit of money will upend long-established relationships based on meaning and moral obligation in favor of mere egoistic calculations of advantage. Cash, in such a view, is conceived as a kind of universal solvent that dissolves the social glue: "the cash nexus" erodes or displaces all other forms of social and moral relation.

The earliest reference to such a "cash nexus" may be Thomas Carlyle's 1839 essay on Chartism, in which he painted a rather sentimental picture of the social bonds formerly linking the old aristocracy with the lower classes and lamented their destruction, insisting that "*cash payment*" (he italicized the phrase) had become, thanks to capitalism, "the universal sole nexus of man to man" (1840, 58). Marx and Engels would famously extend the argument in the *Communist Manifesto*, charging that the bourgeoisie, in replacing feudalism with capitalism, had "pitilessly torn asunder the motley feudal ties that bound man to his 'natural superiors', and has left remaining no other nexus between man and man than naked self-interest, than callous 'cash payment' " (1998, 37). Small wonder, then, if the heirs to this tradition regard with almost instinctive skepticism any social policy, or any substantive politics, that would be based precisely on the form of the "cash payment." Cash payments for the poor, in this view, may well alleviate some misery in the short term. But in a longer perspective, they are just another channel through which the corrosive force of money and markets creeps into people's lives, in the process inevitably destroying a richer and more meaningful world of social connections and obligations. Cash transfers, in this view, may in fact be a kind of Trojan horse. The unsuspecting poor may be quick enough to welcome such payments, thinking only of cash's evident capacity to help them meet their most pressing needs, while they are really being seduced into "the cash nexus" and thereby drawn in to a capitalist system of monetized exchange that ultimately works against their interests.

Actual studies of how poor people engage with the cash economy, however, reveal a very different sort of relation between money and social relationships, one in which money, meaning, and mutuality are entangled rather than antagonistic. To make sense of this entanglement, we need to rethink the relation between "the cash nexus" and various forms of social connection and mutuality. And this rethinking will entail challenging a whole series of conventional oppositions (interest versus obligation, feeling versus calculation, altruism versus selfishness, etc.) that ground the traditional Left's phobic antipathy (as I am increasingly inclined to call it) toward both cash payments and market exchanges.

The southern African poor, as a rule, are both highly social and highly cash-oriented. Here, I will review a rich literature on this topic, drawing conclusions about the way social relations rely on both honoring ties of dependence and obligation and pursuing the acquisition of cash and the things it can buy. These empirical observations contradict the common tendency to oppose the "logic" of the market to the "logic" of communal solidarity, along with the related view that resources are accumulated in the cash economy (according to one set of rules) and distributed in the moral economy (according to another).

The deeply rooted hostility of the Left to markets and processes of commoditization is usefully illustrated by Marxist theorist G. A. Cohen's recent eloquent articulation of the first principles of socialism (2009). Cohen exemplifies the virtues of socialism, and the moral shabbiness of capitalism, by inviting us to consider the way that a group of people might organize themselves when undertaking a camping trip. The campers have a range of talents and interests, and various facilities and equipment will be used on the trip, but the whole enterprise is structured by a set of mutual understandings and goals in pursuit of which the campers freely agree to cooperate. Goods are shared, and chores distributed, in an equitable way. "There are plenty of differences, but our mutual understandings, and the spirit of the enterprise, ensure that there are no inequalities to which anyone could mount a principled objection" (2009, 4). Nearly everyone would agree, he suggests, that norms of equality and reciprocity should apply to such a common venture. And he then goes on to invite the reader to imagine situations in which individual campers seek to make egoistic property claims to various talents and discoveries that emerge in the course of the trip. Imagine, he says, if a camper who catches fish ("Harry") comes back to camp and tries to claim a superior share of the catch on the grounds that he "owns" them? What if another ("Sylvia") finds some apples, and then tries to exchange them for having fewer chores to do? Would not the others regard such egoistic attempts to profit via exclusion and exchange as outrageous and unacceptable? Such behavior would be seen as greedy, selfish, and contemptible, and would quickly be condemned by the other campers. Greedy Harry, for instance, would be rebuked as a "schmuck," and instructed (in language that could only come from a camper who has been dreamed up by a philosopher), "You sweat and strain no more than the rest of us do. So, you're very good at fishing. We don't begrudge you that special endowment, which is, quite properly, a source of satisfaction to you, but why should we reward your good fortune?" (2009, 7). Repelled by such selfish advantage-seeking, the group insists on dividing tasks and distributing resources equitably and cooperating in the shared purpose of an enjoyable common experience.

The camping trip, then, is based on a communal solidarity in which sharing and cooperating are accepted as normal, natural, and good. And if we accept such values in the context of small-scale social interaction, as most of us do, Cohen claims, we should also strive for them at the level of society as a whole. He acknowledges that organizing social cooperation and sharing at a large scale is much more difficult than it is at the scale of a camping trip. But that is a practical obstacle to be worked on, not a reason to abandon the socialist principle of communal solidarity that we rightly value when it comes to small-scale ventures like the camping trip.

An anthropological response might begin by talking about actual camping trips (instead of the made-up kind preferred by philosophers), where one would quickly find that inequalities characterize intimate relations of "communal solidarity" quite as much as they do market situations of exchange. Cohen's analysis is strangely silent about the ways that chores on camping trips are commonly divided unequally, often according to gender (for instance, men catching the fish and women doing the dirty work of cleaning them), or the ways that relations of authority are defined by generation (with parents bossing around children until someone says something like "I wish I had never come on this stupid trip!"). In fact, the campers in his example seem strangely to have no structured social relations at all with one another. (No established relations of kinship, affinity, or occupational hierarchy appear to shape the relations of "Harry" and "Sylvia.") This is hardly a likely scenario for any actual camping expedition and surely an utterly implausible model for communal and cooperative relationships in general, since such relationships, in real life, normally unfold within well-defined institutional settings and social roles.

But Cohen is not really arguing that non-market relations are unproblematic or wholly benign, only that they spring from motives that are less base than that of seeking monetary advantage. This is because market relations, in his account, unlike those of communal reciprocity and solidarity, are fundamentally based on the seeking of a "cash reward," as he puts it (2009, 39). The market motive to productive activity is therefore "typically some mixture of greed and fear." It is true that people can engage in market activity for other reasons, but "the motives of greed and fear are what the market brings to prominence." These are

> horrible ways of seeing other people, however much we have become habituated to them, as a result of centuries of capitalist civilization. (Capitalism did not, of course, invent greed and fear: they are deep in human nature. But, unlike its predecessor feudal civilization, which had the [Christian or other] grace to condemn greed, capitalism celebrates it.) (2009, 41)

It is true, for Cohen, that socioeconomic systems of great productivity can be built by nourishing and harnessing such human motives. But we should not forget that "greed and fear are repugnant motives," and "market socialists" who think markets can be harnessed to socialist ends must remember the essentially and unalterably ignoble and destructive nature of markets (2009, 77–78). In certain contexts, markets may be a necessary evil, but Cohen is quite clear that they are indeed evil, and necessarily so: "Every market, even a socialist market, is a system of predation" (2009, 82).

At this point, it is difficult not to recall the long, unhappy history of regimes of the Left trying to destroy these so-called systems of predation. State socialism became notorious, of course, for its non-market regimes of bureaucratic rationing and queuing for basic goods. But such policies were not some sort of Stalinist distortion, for the socialist antipathy to markets runs far deeper and longer than the Soviet-style central planning state. From the beginning, many early socialists imagined that the revolution would bring with it the end both of market exchange and of money itself, and that economic life would be organized through either spontaneous non-market cooperation or centralized planning.[2] And, of course, even late into the twentieth century, avowedly socialist regimes and movements repeatedly pursued disastrous policies that are only explicable in the light of a conviction that markets are a form of evil—the most notorious examples perhaps being the Khmer Rouge's systematic killing of "merchants" or the Peruvian Shining Path guerrillas' policy of violently attacking rural peasant markets as manifestations of "capitalist exploitation." Less spectacularly but more recently, we have seen Robert Mugabe's regime in Zimbabwe responding to the rising bread prices caused by runaway inflation by vilifying "exploitative" bakers who dare to sell their bread at a market price and ordering them to reduce their prices below their production costs, thus effectively driving most bakers out of the business of baking bread, and even imprisoning some (BBC 2006).

Anthropologists have often shared traditional socialism's antipathy to market sociality and have sometimes invoked Marcel Mauss's famous essay on the gift in support of a moralistic and nostalgic dualism. As Keith Hart has noted, the idea that modern Western capitalist societies have an asocial "commodity economy" while other, radically different societies feature morally inflected "gift economies" has come to be widely circulated, "routinely reproduced in introductory anthropology courses everywhere" (2007, 11). Starting with such a binary, it is only too easy to tell the familiar anti-market story, arguing that whereas pre-capitalist, traditional societies were built on virtuous things like giving, sharing, and human connection, capitalism and its cash economy have increasingly replaced this full, meaningful world with the cold and inhuman hand of the market.

But as Hart has usefully pointed out, such accounts attribute to Mauss "the very ideology his essay was intended to refute" (2007a, 11). In tracing the ways that the circulation of objects, across a range of different societies, is always bound up with both social meaning and personal interests, Mauss aimed to show that "human institutions everywhere are founded on the unity of individual and society, freedom and obligation, self-interest and concern for others" (Hart 2007a, 9). His famous examples of the Trobriand *kula* ring and the Kwakiutl *potlatch* showed that "traditional" gift-giving was, in fact, always highly interested and often involved motives that were both competitive and antagonistic, just as his closing discussion of Western society and its emergent welfare-state institutions (including cooperatives, social insurance programs, and social norms around employment) insisted on the continuing relevance of the "prestation" (and related considerations of honor, caring, and solidarity) in the midst of a complex market system.

As David Graeber (2004) has suggested, the essay on the gift should be read with an appreciation both of Mauss's active lifelong commitment to socialism and of his critical response to the Bolshevik experience in the early years of the Soviet revolution. He wrote the gift essay (published in 1924) following his visit to the Soviet Union, and it is best read in conjunction with his extended evaluation of the Soviet "experiment" (Mauss [1924] 1983). Mauss's critique of the Bolshevik experience was based precisely on his conviction that markets were both desirable and necessary. Among the Bolsheviks' chief mistakes was their attempt "to destroy the essential constituent of the economy itself, i.e., the market" ([1924] 1983, 353). This was an elementary error, since a modern society without market exchange (i.e., without a system in which people have a right to buy and sell goods via "alternative prices freely 'supplied and demanded'") is "inconceivable" ([1924] 1983, 353). "Freedom of the market," he wrote, "is the absolutely necessary precondition of economic life," and socialist ideas about dispensing with money were deeply misguided ([1924] 1983, 353).[3] "Statism and bureaucracy, or the authoritarian direction of industry—the legislation of production, on the one hand, administrative rationing of consumption on the other—in a word, all of what Herbert Spencer would have called 'military' economics, are opposed to the 'exchangist nature' of modern man," and cannot succeed ([1924] 1983, 354).

Crucially, Mauss made these criticisms as an advocate of far-reaching socialist transformation, not as some sort of capitalist opponent of it. What the Bolsheviks had missed or ignored was the fact that socialism had to be founded in society itself, not on abstractions such as the state or the individual. And society itself was organized by a host of mutualities and free associations that money and markets enabled (including things like producer co-ops, professional associations, friendly societies, and so on that Mauss took to be the most advanced and promising manifestations of socialist transformation). Since markets were themselves social institutions with a central role to play in actual forms of social solidarity and common purpose, socialism would have to work with them, not against them. "For the moment and for as long as one can foresee," he wrote, "socialism—communism—must seek its path in the organization and not the suppression of the market" ([1924] 1983, 353).[4]

Following this line of thinking, we may say that market exchange is not the negation of sociality; on the contrary, it forms a vital—indeed, irreplaceable—part of the coordinated social life of any modern society. And any socialism worthy of the name must build on, rather than destroy, such actually existing forms of collective life. Indeed, it is the fact that markets, morality, and sociality are inevitably brought into practical relation in actual social life that surely explains why Peruvian peasants failed to see their cheerful local market days as part of "a system of predation" (as Cohen would have it) but instead recognized them as both a vital sphere of sociality and a valued mechanism of distribution. (And for them, of course, it was not the market vendors seeking a good price for their fruit but the self-righteous guerrillas who were machine-gunning them who appeared as the predators.)

Non-market relations, meanwhile, are, as Mauss demonstrated, never based simply on altruism or kinship-based sharing, but themselves contain powerful elements of egoism, self-interest, competitive striving, and antagonism (as he reminded us, the old German word Gift means "poison"). In contrast to Cohen's imaginary camping trip, actual "communal solidarity" is not built solely out of egalitarian relations of cooperation and altruism but just as much out of interested and often competitive relations of exchange. Both a wholly disinterested sharing and a purely asocial calculation are fantasies; real sociality always unites sharing and self-interest in a single act. This state of affairs is sometimes glossed as "reciprocity" but might better (given the unfortunate economistic tendency to reduce complex reciprocal dependencies to tit-for-tat transactions) be expressed as mutuality.[5] This mutuality is found in the kula, the potlatch, and the peasant marketplace; and it is found just as surely in the annual meetings of the modern corporation and the competitive frenzy of the stock market trading floor.

Indeed, in the years since Mauss wrote his groundbreaking account, anthropological scholarship has given us an even clearer picture of the deeply social nature of market-oriented economic action. It has long been understood that markets are social institutions and that market activity—as Harrison White (cited in Zelizer 2005, 44) once put it— is "intensely social—as social as kinship networks or feudal armies." Nor are passions and sentiments, solidarity and caring, absent from such behavior. A rich recent literature shows that the motives of market participants—even of business professionals in the act of doing business—are suffused with sentiment, affective rationality, social expectations, obligations, and so on.[6]

But it is not only that ostensibly "market" spheres of action reveal social and emotional motives and attachments; it is equally the case that relations of intimacy, including those of care, love, sharing, and attachment, are themselves deeply bound up with market transactions and exchanges. While an ideology of what Viviana Zelizer (2005) calls "hostile worlds" implies that cash exchanges must contaminate or erode real intimacy, we need only look around our modern societies to see how routinely intimate social relations are combined with monetary transactions. As Zelizer observes (2005, 27):

> Parents pay nannies or child-care workers to tend their children, adoptive parents pay money to obtain babies, divorced spouses pay or receive alimony and child support payments, and parents give their children allowances, subsidize their college educations, help them with their first mortgage, and offer them substantial bequests in their wills. Friends and relatives send gifts of money as wedding presents, and friends loan each other money. Meanwhile, immigrants support their families back home with regular transmission of remittances.

The presence of cash in these relationships does not render them merely commercial or prevent them from being sites of caring, affection, cooperation, and sharing. Indeed, one of the main reasons people value money in the first place (and try so hard to acquire it) is precisely so they can carry out such acts of caring and support for others—sending money home to relatives, saving for a child's education, and so on.

But the insistent linking of a kind of asocial self-interest with the very presence of money or market transactions persists. This linkage is especially pernicious when we deal with questions of distribution and social assistance, since crudely associating markets and "the cash nexus" with things like selfishness and greed prevents us from seeing two key realities that are central to understanding the contemporary politics of distribution among the southern African poor. The first such reality is that markets are social sites of distribution and coordination, and not only of "predation." Recovering the fundamentally social nature of markets helps us to recognize ways that market mechanisms can potentially be turned to progressive distributive ends. The second crucial reality is that, in the everyday lives of southern Africa's poor, participation in a cash economy and participation in social relations of care, dependence, and obligation are in practice not contradictory "logics" but mutually enabling practices. The actual solidarities and mutualities that sustain rich lives under adverse circumstances are in fact conditioned on, rather than in contradiction with, "the cash nexus," and monetary transactions themselves may often be viewed (as Clara Han has argued in a Chilean context) "as affective enactments of relations, gestures of care toward others" (Han 2011, 25). The following two sections take up these two themes in turn. A final section will draw conclusions for thinking about "cash payment" in the context of social assistance.

How to Do Things with Markets

The traditional Left's suspicion of "cash payment" tends to be coupled with a general hostility to markets, as I noted at the start of this chapter. This hostility has often been shared by anthropologists, who have tended to see market activity as promoting egoistic calculation and destroying or weakening relations of mutuality and community (as noted by Hart [2005, 2007]). Yet if Mauss was right that markets are vital mechanisms of social integration, social coordination, and organized distribution, then those who wish to find ways of reorganizing society to better meet the needs of those who are currently most marginalized or excluded ought to be asking how markets can be used to accomplish this task. It is not a question of replacing markets with something else (which Mauss convincingly argued would be both unworkable and wrongheaded) but of using markets to do socially useful things that would be difficult or impossible to do without them.

What sorts of socially useful things? For one thing, markets make it possible to aggregate and make visible great masses of information—including (something that socialists, of all people, ought to recognize as important) information about the needs of others. G. A. Cohen, for all his hostility to markets, clearly recognizes this capacity. In a complex and highly differentiated economic system, he acknowledges, it would be difficult to know "what to produce, and how to produce it, without market signals: very few socialist economists would now dissent from that proposition" (2009, 60). As he puts it, prices do two things at once. They provide a "motivation function" (people seeking advantage in their transaction, which Cohen finds morally objectionable). But they also provide an "information function," in which prices send signals about where demand lies and how much people are willing to give for what; in this way, "they show how valuable goods are to people, and thereby reveal what is worth producing" (2009, 61). In this way, markets can collect and synthesize information about the wants and needs of huge numbers of consumers. Prices that reflect "how much people would be willing to sacrifice to obtain given goods and services" (Cohen 2009, 61) in this way allow goods to be distributed in a way that takes people's own preferences into account.

In principle, as economists like to point out, this "information function" of markets makes it possible for markets to provide a socially coordinated allocation mechanism that takes account of people's own needs and values in ways that even the most well-intentioned centrally planned systems of allocation could never manage. Julian Simon (1994) has presented an especially clear example of such a mechanism: the introduction by airlines of a voucher system for handling overbooking.[7] The old system of arbitrarily picking passengers to be "bumped" was unable to distinguish between different passengers with very different situations. One passenger might be a businessman who flies every week and would just as soon wait for the next plane; the next might be a mother racing to get to her daughter's wedding for whom any delay would have heartbreaking consequences. Being bumped would have very different "values" to the two passengers, but the officials making the decision lacked the detailed contextual knowledge to make a good (i.e., informed) decision, leading to arbitrary decisions about who would and would not be bumped. A simple regulatory solution (banning the practice of bumping) would give passengers security but at the less-than-optimal cost of airlines flying with more empty seats, which would lead to significantly higher flying costs for all consumers. Instead, by offering a small monetary reward (say, a $200 coupon), the airlines were able to recruit volunteers and avoid bumping those for whom the inconvenience would have the highest "cost." A consciously constructed "market," in this example, allows a group of people, via a kind of self-organization, to identify whose need is greatest and to allocate a good in a way that takes this need into account. As Simon (1994, 323) put it, "the people who care least about waiting for the next plane select themselves to get a benefit that they prefer to flying as scheduled."

This example is the kind that economists love, of course—the famous "win-win" scenario, in which everyone is better off (all flyers do better, in this system, than they would in either the case where bumping is arbitrary or where it is outlawed). Since the fliers in the example can freely take or leave the $200 coupon, no one is unjustly forced to give up their seat, and those who do not get seats are those who, being most willing to give them up, presumably needed them least. Thus, we arrive at a kind of collective decision-making, even perhaps a kind of justice (where allocations are, as Simon [1994, 323) puts it, "fair, rather than arbitrary"). Indeed, one can even see here how such a market mechanism can enable a kind of sharing, a way of achieving an equitable allocation of a limited good.

But, of course, markets do not just allocate a good based on how much it is needed or desired by the buyer; they also allocate based on the consumer's ability to pay for it. And, in a world of huge inequalities, those with the greatest needs are often those with the least ability to pay. So in the airline bumping example, we might imagine a scenario in which somehow, among the passengers whom the example seems to presume to be economic equals, a small subclass of desperately poor fliers exists for whom the value of even a very small voucher would exceed their annual income. The specific personal circumstances of such flyers (such as being in a hurry that day) would immediately pale beside the economic value of the coupon, with the less satisfying result that the one who gives up the seat is now not the one who is least inconvenienced but the one who is poorest. In such a system, it is the members of one class of passenger who will, time and time again, give up their seats for the convenience of the members of the other class (albeit via the mechanism of "free choice"). Critical scholars attentive to such problems of inequality will insist that real-world markets often, or even usually, produce such effects, yielding an allocation principle that is brutally simple and has little to do with either information or justice: the rich get whatever they like, and the very poor get nothing. In the extreme situation of famine, for instance, the "market signal" of high price ensures that all the available food is routed to those who can afford to buy it, leaving the rest to die. For this reason, markets are often bypassed in times of famine, as governments move to hand out food directly to those in need—justice, not prices.

But new thinking in famine relief questions this reasoning, and suggests ways of combining the "information function" that Cohen acknowledges with the egalitarian goals he advocates. As I have pointed out elsewhere (Ferguson 2010), recent critics of the conventional use of food aid in response to famine argue that hunger is often best dealt with by boosting the purchasing power of those at risk rather than by distributing food. The current international food aid system involves taking excess grain (produced under subsidized conditions in rich countries) and transporting it to places (largely in Africa) where people are at risk of hunger. Following Amartya Sen (1983), critics have long noted the perverse effects of this system: depressed producer prices for local farmers and damage to the local institutions for producing and distributing food crops. Once food aid has arrived, local food production often fails to recover, and the "temporary" crisis becomes permanent. As an alternative, Sen's followers have pushed for cash payments to be made directly to those at risk of food deficit.[8] People with money in their pockets, Sen points out, generally do not starve. And the economic chain of events that is set in motion by boosting purchasing power leads (through market forces) to increased capacity for local production and distribution; recipients can use cash flexibly not only to buy food but also to restock or preserve productive assets like livestock and seed (Sen 1983; Dreze and Sen 1991). Of course, direct distribution of food will also have its role in situations of acute famine, but the thrust of the argument is to show that providing cash in context of food deficit can work with markets (not against them) to allow recipients to achieve relief while deciding for themselves what their most pressing needs are. Such an approach allows the information function of markets to operate, even among the desperately poor.[9]

Water provision is a similarly challenging case for markets, and critics of privatization have rightly pointed out that simply treating water as a commodity yields the politically and ethically unacceptable result that poor people are unable to access what ought to be a basic human right. (For a stimulating recent analysis of the South African case, see von Schnitzler 2008; on the limits of the "rights" construct, see Bond 2013.) But simply being against privatization is not an answer to the allocation question. Is everyone, in an undoubtedly water-scarce context such as South Africa, simply supposed to take as much water as they like? A well-known anti-privatization activist at a public meeting in Durban in 2009 made the argument very effectively that metering water is in fact a necessity for any progressive public policy: "We don't want the bosses filling their swimming pools at no cost with the public's water." Although a basic minimum allocation of free, or "decommodified" water for the poor, has been a key progressive demand in South Africa's water wars, prices also have their place in this politics—for how else will it be possible to soak the overconsuming rich to help cross-subsidize the poor in a context where water is a scarce good to which everyone must have some minimal level of access? Here, a progressive pricing mechanism that charges high rates to the rich to cross-subsidize the consumption of the poor can function not as an "instrument of predation" but precisely as an instrument of solidarity.[10] Again, markets are revealed to be potential tools for coordinating collective affairs and distributing resources in ways that can (by recognizing the artifactual and constructed nature of markets) be brought into accordance with social aims.

Socialists have too often confused cash transactions and market exchanges with the historically much more recent system of production that is capitalism. But markets have no essential attachment to capitalism and have existed (as they undoubtedly will continue to exist in the future) under a much wider set of social and economic systems. If we keep this fact in mind, we may be able to better recognize how markets, as social institutions, can be articulated with other social institutions to produce specific, desired social effects. In addition, it may become easier to see the value of some emerging political initiatives (including programs for cash transfers in southern Africa) that rely, as Mauss ([1924] 1983, 353) put it, on "the organization, and not the suppression, of the market." I return to this point in the final section of the chapter.

Money and the Mutualities of Poverty

Notwithstanding a rich anthropological literature on the subject,[11] "most anthropologists," as Keith Hart (2005, 1) has observed, "don't like money." It symbolizes "the world they have rejected for something more authentic elsewhere"—and "every anthropology student knows that money undermines the integrity of cultures that were hitherto resistant to commerce." In this rather nostalgic spirit, anthropologists and others engaged with contemporary poverty in Africa still sometimes tell a slightly too familiar story. Once upon a time, the story goes, Africans lived together in an organic unity, bound by shared values, moral obligations, and ties of kinship. Today, however, capitalism (neoliberalism, modernity, commodification, the world system—the villain changes with the times) tears apart these bonds and replaces them with the heartless logic of "the market." This familiar communitarian framing, tired and clichéd though it is, continues to shape many discussions of the problems of the southern African poor. A recycled modernization theory here conspires with an equally indestructible vernacular critique of "greedy youth" who "nowadays only care about money," and so on. Generosity, in the tragic account that each generation seems determined to tell about the next, has given way to calculation, selfishness, and greed (cf. Cole 2010).

Such moralized accounts, which cast "the market" in the role of demonic arch-villain, are increasingly out of touch with the empirical research on the lives of southern Africa's poor, research showing clearly that poor people's livelihoods are bound up with forms of sociality that cut across the divide between non-market and market, between social obligation and commoditized exchange. For this reason, understandings of the relations of dependence and mutual assistance with which people are engaged (and on which they depend for their survival) must take account of what David Neves and Andries du Toit (2012) have termed "the sociality of money." Far from being antithetical to relations of sociality and mutuality, the "cash nexus" turns out to be integral to such relations as they actually exist. People seek money, and engage in exchanges, within the context of dense social relations of mutuality, just as they tend their relationships by fully deploying the powers and potentialities that access to money can enable. Such observations, as Neves and du Toit note, "challenge meta-narratives of a 'great transformation' toward socially disembedded and depersonalized relationships in relation to money" (2012, 131).

To understand the way that social relationships and cash exchanges are intertwined, one must return to the old anthropological point that mutuality is not simply altruism, cooperation, or generosity—and not just egoistic advantage-seeking either. As Mauss repeatedly insisted, mutualities normally involve antagonism and generosity at the same time.

And such forms of sociality involve people, inexorably, in both moral relations of obligation, care, generosity, and obligation and various forms of interested exchange. It is not a question of a historical transition from one to the other—the Maussian point is that solidarity and exchange depend upon each other. And this observation is as true in a capitalist market society as it is in any other.

Such mutualities have been the subject of a large body of high-quality research in the southern African context.[12] Here I offer only a very schematic review of some of the main findings. For the sake of brevity, I discuss just two key sites of intimate sociality where mutualities and the cash economy are constitutively intertwined.

First, the domain of kinship is decidedly not a sphere set apart from money and markets. Kinship, after all, is not really something you have—it is something you do. And to do it (or at least, to do it right), in today's southern Africa, requires cash. Southern Africans have long been in the habit of using monetary cash payments to mark marriages and have long recognized that bridewealth "cattle" come in two kinds: those "with legs" and those "without legs" (i.e., cash) (Sansom 1976; Murray 1981; Ferguson 1985; Comaroff and Comaroff 1992).[13] Cash is equally central to that other key ritual passage, the funeral—on which households typically spend the equivalent of a year's income, according to one recent study (Case et al. 2008). And the multiple reciprocities and solidarities with which kinship bonds have long been associated also unfold within (not against) the world of cash. For it is not only that those with money are expected to honor certain claims; it is equally true that needy kin often require access to cash to be able to make strong claims in the first place. Traversing space, for instance, is often key to making successful distributive claims, which means that money for transport is crucial. Attending and appropriately participating in funerals (both of which require money) is often a condition of being able to claim full membership in kinship groups. And the ability of a potential beneficiary to reciprocate (even in very small ways), research has shown, often makes the difference between the sort of kinship claim that will be attended to and the kind that can be ignored (see Turner 2005; du Toit and Neves 2007; Seekings 2008a; du Toit and Neves 2009a, 2009b; Harper and Seekings 2010; Neves and du Toit 2012).

Second, let me mention a very rich recent literature on the mutualities of sex, love, and money. The topic is, of course, haunted by the specter of prostitution. As Zelizer has noted of discussions of commoditization in general, "the relation between prostitute and patron looms as the ultimate triumph of commercialism over sentiment" (2005, 124). But the best scholarship on southern Africa is agreed that sex, love, and money are in fact bound up in ways that the opposition of "real love" versus "prostitution" does more to misunderstand than to clarify. Sexually intimate relations between men and women, in poor and working-class settings across the region, are widely assumed to properly involve relations of economic dependence, and women normally expect their lovers to provide them with a range of gifts, payments, and other forms of material support (Ferguson 1999; Leclerc-Madlala 2004; Swidler and Watkins 2007; cf. Cole 2010). Even the most apparently commercial relationships of this kind are normally not without social and emotional content, while relations explicitly based on romantic love, and undoubtedly entailing deep emotional attachment, typically also entail trade-offs involving money that Western observers have long found disturbing. Mark Hunter (2010) has recently developed the useful concept of "provider love" to capture the way that economic provisioning is often understood not to contradict romantic love but to confirm it. Real love, in this conception, should be combined with, and given substance by, real material care (just as in that other case of provider love—the relation between parent and child). It is not a question of love versus money; both the providing and the love are absolutely real (indeed, it is the providing that proves the love is real). To ask whether a woman in such a relationship is motivated by money or love is therefore to ask the wrong question. The conventional opposition of the material to the sentimental makes no sense since the material is meaningful precisely as the embodiment of sentiment.

What all of this shows is that, contrary to what generations of social theorists have supposed, intimate social bonds are not eroded or destroyed by the presence of money and markets. On the contrary, what we find is that the most important and highly valued forms of sociality, reciprocity, solidarity, and care among the southern African poor are precisely those that are facilitated by the use of money and participation in markets. Those who are most successful at building social networks of support and care are those who are able to obtain money, while many of the most important ways of obtaining such funds themselves depend on webs of sociality and mutual dependence. The truly isolated and alienated are those who really are, by virtue of utter destitution, outside of the "cash nexus"; for the rest, having cash is precisely what enables the myriad mutualities that sustain (what Elizabeth Povinelli [2006] might call) the "thick life" of the southern African poor.

The Social Life of Cash Payments

What are the implications of this discussion for social assistance? Recent research on cash transfers (as briefly reviewed in this book's introduction) has emphasized that even very small streams of cash income can both catalyze and stimulate a range of social and economic activities and enable people to better meet their needs as they themselves define them. Recognizing that planners cannot have very good knowledge of the precise nature of poor people's problems nor of the varied resources they draw on to solve them, new thinking in social policy places new emphasis on cash payments as a way of enabling low-income people to access goods, and participate in livelihood strategies, in ways that are more responsive to their actual circumstances.

Whereas older thinking saw social assistance as a kind of substitute for "real" economic activity like wage labor, the new research emphasizes that cash does not so much compensate for *inactivity* as complement and enable a range of *activities*. Andries du Toit and David Neves (2009b; see also 2007, 2009a, and Neves et al. 2009), for instance, have provided vivid descriptions of the way that access to social grants enables poor South Africans both to engage in economic activities (from petty trade to searching for work) and to participate in what du Toit (2007, 14) has called "the dance of the relational economy." A major pilot study in Namibia that provided a small, unconditional "basic income grant" to each member of one community found that the insertion of cash not only improved indices directly related to consumption, like nutrition and health (as one might have expected), but also yielded a surge of new social and economic activity. Grant recipients were enabled to start businesses and look for work; they also engaged in new forms of community organization and collective projects and did a better job of caring for their sick (including many suffering from AIDS) (Haarmann et al. 2009).

In contrast, the literature paints a very dark picture of those who are so unfortunate as to lack cash entirely. The key to relations of solidarity and mutual assistance, du Toit and Neves have argued (2007, 2009a, 2009b), is an ability to participate in at least a minimal way in the petty reciprocations of the "relational economy." Those who are unable to re- ciprocate are also unable to be properly social. Those who are unable to move through space (through lack of money for transport) are at the same time unable to activate and refresh the social relationships they might otherwise be able to depend on. Those who are unable to purchase basic consumer goods (through lack of money) are at the same time disabled from coherently marking their social location in a field of signification. If having "style" is a major asset in modern township life (as I have argued elsewhere), then lacking it is a distinct social disability, implying a withered and diminished sort of personhood (Ferguson 1999). If there is isolation and alienation here, it is not a product of being "drawn into" a cash economy but of having no standing or capacity within it.

The impact of cash transfers needs to be understood in this perspective. Advocates of cash payments are right to insist that such payments can address not only nutritional and physical needs but also social ones. Indeed, the more radical new thinkers about social policy advocate, for just this reason, a universal guaranteed income (or "basic income") for all (see, e.g., Standing and Samson 2003; Haarmann et al. 2009). Some minimum level of ability to engage in consumption and exchange, they argue, should be conceived as a citizenship right. Just as modern systems of water distribution normally recognize a need to provide some minimum amount of "lifeline" water to the poorest citizens (independent of their ability to pay), advocates of basic income insist that some minimum quantum of income must be provided to all citizens—and for the same reason. In a world where cash is nearly as basic to life as water, the provision of at least some basic minimum becomes both a potent political demand and a compelling ethical obligation.

Whatever one might make of such claims, the advocates of basic income are surely right that cash, like water, is more than just a desirable consumer good; it is, under modern conditions, a need so basic that it must be in place before a range of crucial forms of social action and social being can even exist. For, as we have seen, cash in the pocket is related—in a constitutive rather than antagonistic way—to multiple socialities and mutualities that are (quite literally) a matter of life and death.

Implicit in this view is a realization that spending is a socially constructive form of activity. An older conception of social assistance saw in spending only a kind of waste, or at best "consumption." In this view, there really was (as was often insisted) "no point" in giving money to people who would (as they said) "just spend it!" The idea was that the poor person would, having spent the money, be right back where they were before. And worse, they would have become "dependent." Instead of active and hard-working laborers building something real, they might become, through the hazard of "dependency," passive, demoralized, and inactive. Such conceptions are being displaced, however, by a new view of social assistance that has a much more ethnographically informed view of what it means to spend. As one of the innovative "policy intellectuals" working in this vein has put it, it is not welfare that makes poor people dependent (Meth 2004). The poor are *always* dependent, and the poorer they are, the more dependent they become. Cash transfers, in this perspective, do not introduce "dependency" into a social world that had been innocent of it; rather, they enable less malevolent sorts of dependence to take root and a circuit of reciprocities to unfold within which one-sided relations of dependence can become more egalitarian forms of interdependence (cf. du Toit and Neves 2009b, 20). In this perspective, expenditure by the poor is not waste but a potent form of *activity*, one that stimulates and enables a host of others.

 It is true, of course, that the social policies based on cash transfers that are sweeping the globe do not go nearly as far as the basic income concept would suggest they should. Both the small size of existing transfers and the conditionalities normally attached to them limit the extent to which they can be associated with far-reaching social transformations. But these policies do have the virtue of beginning both to accept that people pursue multiple livelihoods that are largely illegible to state planners and to seek governmental strategies that aim to enhance, rather than ignore or demolish, those livelihoods.

I hope to have shown that such policies do not destroy or erode sociality or mutuality. But what about the charge that they help draw people "into" capitalism? In the first instance, the objection seems both naive and anachronistic—as though, if only people were left alone and without any money, they would somehow remain outside of capitalism. If there are any places in the world where such a view remains plausible, southern

Africa is surely not one of them; any real possibilities of dwelling outside of capitalism and the cash economy were extinguished already in the nineteenth century.

But if it is clear that new welfare schemes do not draw people into capitalism (as if from outside it), it is also true that existing cash transfer programs do seem to take the capitalist system as given and concentrate on ameliorating (rather than overturning) the conditions of extreme poverty and inequality that it produces. One can easily argue, for instance, that a new Oxfam-funded cash transfer scheme in Malawi is making a real difference in the lives of the poorest households there. But it is hard to think of this as much more than bread crumbs from the table when the cash benefit on offer is just $3 per person per month.[14] Are cash transfer programs the beginning of a new and promising sort of distributive politics? Or just a cheap way of managing the most outrageous of capitalism's deprivations while leaving the system that produces them untouched? This is an issue that is discussed at length later in this book (see especially chapter 6 and the conclusion). Here, I can suggest only that it is worth considering the possibility that moves to create guaranteed incomes, however mild and even feeble they appear in their present form, may indeed have the potential to begin to help open up new forms of politics that might take us far beyond the limited, technocratic aim of ameliorating poverty that dominates existing cash transfer programs.

It is significant, in this connection, that the program of basic income is linked not only to pragmatic discussions in the world of social policy but also to an interesting radical politics (see also this book's conclusion). At the Left-most end of the "distributive justice" tradition, for instance, philosopher Philippe van Parijs has long advocated an unconditional basic income as a mechanism for achieving what he once called "a capitalist road to communism" (van der Veen and van Parijs 1986; cf. van Parijs 1993, 1995, 2013). Among autonomists, arguments have recently emerged lodging the source of value in society (rather than in labor) and insisting on basic income as a key element of a new socialist politics (see, e.g., Hardt 2009). Such approaches have their problems (as briefly discussed in this book's conclusion), but they do point to new sorts of politics that have been willing to leave behind the widespread Left nostalgia for the politics of the proletariat (see Barchiesi 2011) and embrace new kinds of politics rooted in the needs and demands of those who are marginal to the world of wage labor (sometimes understood as comprising "the precariat") (Frassanito Network 2005; Saul 2011; Standing 2011; cf. this book's conclusion).

Other authors have pointed out that cash payments can catalyze a range of economic strategies that people are already engaged in to escape capitalist relations of production. J. K. Gibson-Graham (2006) have emphasized the importance of what they call "economic heterogeneity" and the extent to which non-capitalist relations in fact *pervade* economic formations we too easily conceptualize as simply "capitalist" through and through. In the South African context, Franco Barchiesi (2011) has provided a rich recent account of workers' attempts to exit the capitalist world of work by pursuing projects in the "informal" domain that take us far beyond that traditional horizon of conventional Left politics, "full employment." Such approaches, by displacing the assumed centrality of wage labor, suggest possibilities for a new politics centered on distribution.

In all of this, it may be possible to identify potential points of traction for a radical politics that would start from what people do instead of from some theorist's idea of what they ought to do. Prejudices derived from theoretical deductions (whether the heroization of proletarian wage labor, the disparagement of the "lumpen" classes, or the stigmatization of the "cash nexus") have not served the Left well in recent decades. Instead, we might do better to work inductively, watching and listening to what the world's disadvantaged actually do and say, and seeking political strategies and social policies that can enhance the forms of cooperation, mutual aid, solidarity, and care that are already in play. Looking to build upon, rather than destroy or disparage, such actually existing mutualities, as Mauss long ago urged us to do, we may arrive at new ways of thinking about both money and markets and the role that they might play in any socialism worth wishing for.

5. Declarations of Dependence

Labor, Personhood, and Welfare
in Southern Africa

In the 1820s, in the midst of a period of grave political disorder and violence, a band of Nguni-speaking refugees (scattered from their original homes in what we today call the KwaZulu-Natal province of South Africa) headed north, raiding their neighbors as they went.[1] They soon coalesced into an entity we know as the Ngoni state and eventually roamed northward as far as Zambia and Tanzania, where Ngoni communities can still be found to this day. Like the better-known Zulu state, the Ngoni state was a fearsome military machine that terrorized and preyed on its unfortunate neighbors. And as the Ngoni state moved northward, it was in a near-constant state of war with whatever groups it encountered, decimating its enemies, taking captives, burning out villages, destroying or plundering scarce food, and appropriating livestock as it went.

J. D. Omer-Cooper (1966, 83–84) described the Ngoni invasions as "a terrible disaster for the peoples of East-Central Africa" which left "famine and desolation" in their wake. And indeed, nineteenth-century observers noted the grim consequences of the Ngonis' brutal raiding that resulted in (as one observer described it) "hundreds of skeletons lying about everywhere" (E. D. Young, quoted in Thompson 1995, 17) and often left the surrounding countryside completely emptied out. What is more, such bloody raiding was not episodic or occasional but a more or less continuous way of life, giving the Ngoni, as the medical missionary Elmslie put it (1899, 78), "a reputation for war and cruelty . . . wherever they were known." Those who managed to flee the Ngoni incursions resorted to extreme measures to escape the fearsome raiding parties and to conceal their own presence, hiding themselves in caves or retreating in desperation into fetid and disease-ravaged swamps (Thompson 1995, 17; Elmslie 1899, 70–90; see also Wiese [1891] 1983, 153–55).

So it is a little startling, as we read John Barnes's classic account of this extraordinarily violent and predatory polity, to hear of a number of instances in which people from neighboring chiefdoms actually sought out the Ngoni state and voluntarily surrendered to it. Indeed, according to Barnes, some came of their own volition from great distances specifically with the goal of being taken captive by the Ngoni (Barnes 1967, 27).[2] I shall return to this curious fact in a moment.

But let us first fast-forward to the much more recent past. A few years ago, an American acquaintance of mine was sent to Johannesburg for several months by his employer. He was not an academic or scholar, but he did have progressive political commitments and had therefore followed with interest and sympathy the struggle against apartheid and the advent of non-racial democracy in South Africa. But his experiences in Johannesburg were not what he was expecting, and he found them very troubling. What he found most disturbing, he told me, was the steady parade of out-of-work black South Africans offering themselves in one or another form of service to him. A regular stream of supplicants came to the door, begging to work in his kitchen or garden, calling him "baas" (master, boss), and so on. The terms of employment were not really the issue ("Just pay me what you want!" the job-seekers would say). And leaving the house offered my friend no escape. When he went to the supermarket, a swarm of young men and boys appeared, trying to help him put the groceries into his car (in hopes of a small tip). And so on. At every turn, the message sent by poor black South Africans to this white, foreign, would-be egalitarian seemed to be "Let me serve you! Be my boss! Exploit me!" And this, my friend wondered, is "the new South Africa"?

His reaction was typically (and perhaps parochially) American, in that it presumed a valuation of individual autonomy and self-sufficiency that is cross-culturally far from universal. But it was also founded on a perception of a real irony that is genuinely troubling (and not only, I think, to individualistic Americans): that is, the irony of what we thought was a liberated people voluntarily offering themselves (often in embarrassingly eager and abject terms) in servitude.

What these two tales have in common, I think, is that they are discomfiting to what we might call the emancipatory liberal mind. Rather than seeking autonomy and independence—which we have come to associate with dignity and freedom—we have, in both cases, the disturbing spectacle of people openly pursuing a subordinate and dependent status. Rather than striving to escape, cast off, or struggle against relations of hierarchical subordination (as the emancipatory liberal mind would expect and approve), they are putting extraordinary energies into seeking them out. What are we to make of these pursuits of subordination, these (as I will call them here) "declarations of dependence"?

There are good historical reasons why the spectacle of people seeking out their own subjection and dependence makes us so uncomfortable. The long, noble history of antislavery and anticolonial struggles makes it easy (perhaps too easy, I will suggest) for us to equate human dignity and value with autonomy and independence. A will to dependence therefore seems sad—even shameful. In this optic, dependence is a kind of bondage, a life in chains—the very opposite of freedom.[3] It is thus no accident that declarations of independence loom so large in the emancipatory liberal imagination, where such proud declarations are linked both to key Enlightenment motifs (as in the U.S. Declaration of Independence's linking of political independence with such things as individual freedom and equality) and to twentieth-century postcolonial ideals of liberation (as in the once-obvious linking of African independence with African freedom—an association that today seems perhaps less obvious than it once did) and development (long seen as precisely a struggle against economic "dependency"). In all these cases, progress is seen to lie in the triumphant elimination or reduction of dependence. Indeed, in the influential conception advanced by Amartya Sen (1999), development is actually defined as an increase in individual freedom, rendering dependence and bondage the very opposite of developmental progress. In such a worldview, to declare for dependence, to wish for it, to seek it, seems to be a wish for one's own devaluation and even dehumanization.

To understand (and, in important ways, to overcome) our discomfort with dependence, I will review a regional history here. The empirical historical material I will present is well known. But I want to retell familiar facts in order to take a perhaps *too-familiar* history (of labor and capitalism in southern Africa) and narrate it a little differently. My aim in doing so is to draw some conclusions that may help us to see the historical novelty of some of our political challenges in the present (in particular in relation to questions of poverty and social assistance).

So let us start by going back to the early nineteenth century, and the Ngoni state. Why would one wish to subordinate oneself to one's enemy—and especially to such a violent and terrifying one? We can easily understand the motives of those who fled the Ngoni state. But what of those who sought it out and even traveled hundreds of miles—not away from but toward this mobile wrecking machine?

Such a choice becomes less mysterious when we start to understand the social logic of the Ngoni expansion. For the Ngoni state was most fundamentally not about killing its enemies (though there was admittedly a fair amount of that) but about incorporating them. Women and children and often men as well were taken captive and thereby became members of the Ngoni social system. The process was often horrifically violent, physically and (one presumes) psychologically (as Delius [2010] has observed; cf. M. Wright 1993). But the reward was often a quite full-bodied social membership. To be sure, captives entered the social system as inferiors. But they also entered as distinct social persons, ascribed specific kinship roles. Captive women became wives, and captive men and children became the children of Ngoni military leaders. New social segments were formed on a lineage model, and in a rapidly expanding system, with new members coming in with each fresh battle, new segments (and with it new opportunities for leadership) were being created at an astonishing pace. Captured men, in such a system, came in as dependents, at the bottom of the pecking order. But with new captives constantly entering the system, they could quickly end up founding new segments of their own and acquiring social and political influence by building up large followings of quasi-descendants (including those they managed to capture in battle). Powerful men had large numbers of wives, who were divided into groups that Barnes (1967) called "bevies." The senior wife of each "bevy" enjoyed authority over the segment formed by the sons and captives of all the women of the bevy.[4]

The result was something like a classic segmentary political system on amphetamines, which Barnes famously dubbed a "snowball state." As he put it (1967, 60):

Segmentation in a lineage system [normally] depends basically on the unalterable processes of human reproduction and maturation. Until a man's children become adults his agnatic segment cannot split. The Ngoni, by recruiting many of their members when they were already grown up, were able to increase their population at a prodigious rate and with it the degree of segmentation of the State. As the Ngoni army increased in size, so it became easier for them to capture more people, so that what we may describe as an inflationary spiral in population was set up. The Ngoni State was like a snowball which grows larger and larger as it is pushed from place to place, but still remains uniform throughout.

This was a highly exaggerated form of a political logic that was broadly characteristic of most precolonial southern African societies. While political contestation in Europe was largely about controlling land, in much of Africa land was abundant and political power derived from controlling what Suzanne Miers and Igor Kopytoff (1977) famously called "wealth in people" (see also Vansina 1990; Guyer 1993). In such systems, political leaders became powerful by building up their polities via bringing in followers. As Barnes put it for the Ngoni (1967, 30), "The principal index of power was the number of a man's dependents. Political struggles were essentially not struggles to control wealth but to enjoy the support of followers."[5]

But these same leaders were always at risk of losing their power if followers left to join their rivals, or to found their own polities. As has often been noted, this need to retain followers often acted as a check on the powers of chiefs and kings. These societies were certainly not democracies in the usual sense, but they were strikingly dynamic and open social systems characterized by very high levels of mobility and a profusion of exit options that could swiftly penalize leaders who disregarded the needs and desires of their followers.

In such a world, dependence was not simply bondage or unfreedom (as the emancipatory liberal mind tends to assume). On the contrary, in a social system put together around competition for followers, it was actually the existence of possibilities for hierarchical affiliation that *created* the most important forms of free choice. Where many such possibilities for affiliation existed, dependents could enjoy considerable agency, and dependence itself could become (following Bayart's memorable phrase

[2000, 218]) "a mode of action." Such freedom as existed in such a social world (and it was not inconsiderable) came not from independence but from a plurality of opportunities for dependence. (I will return to this point shortly.)

It is important to note that this was a way not only of structuring society but also of constructing persons. In the people-centric social systems of early colonial southern Africa (as anthropologists have long recognized), persons were understood not as monadic individuals but as nodes in systems of relationships. While modern liberal common sense often universalizes an ideologically conceived liberal individual and sees society as composed of transactions among such individuals, anthropologists of Africa (from Radcliffe-Brown onward) have long insisted that relational persons do not precede relations of dependence; they are, instead, constituted by those relations.[6]

The Ngoni system worked according to just such a logic, in that society was founded not on relations of exchange between liberal, transacting individuals but on relations of dependence and respect among relational persons. Relations of hierarchy and obligation here did not diminish or fetter the attainment of full personhood but rather constituted and enabled it. Hierarchical dependence here, as throughout the region, was not a problem or a debility—on the contrary, it was the principal mechanism for achieving social personhood. Without networks of dependence, you were nobody—except perhaps a witch. With them, you were a person of consequence. As Barnes put it, "Every man was a potential lord, and every lord, except the Paramount Chief . . . , was a dependent of some other lord higher in the hierarchy" (Barnes 1967, 10). And every woman, we might add, was the potential head of a new bevy whose social personhood was constituted by the web of kinship and quasi-kinship dependencies in which she was enmeshed. Ngoni captives, we can now understand, were not simply subjected. They were *incorporated*— incorporated into a social system within which they had a recognized and valued social position and within which significant opportunities existed for improving and enhancing that social position. We can now perhaps understand better why acquiring membership in such a social system might have been something worth seeking out, especially in times of widespread insecurity and hardship.

Colonial Transformation—and Continuity

Colonial conquest and the subsequent rise of capitalism have generally been treated as a more or less comprehensive break with the world I have described. In the familiar narrative, the old institutions either were wholly displaced or were retained in ways that subordinated them to the new system of industrial capitalism, as social systems based on kinship and wealth in people gave way to radically new logics—the political logic of racial domination and the economic logic of capitalism, commodity production, and wage labor.[7] Supposedly "traditional" institutions like chiefs and cattle-keeping, for instance, might have continued, but analysis revealed that chiefs had really become colonial bureaucrats and cattle a form of investment and savings for proletarian wage-earners.

The breaks introduced first by colonial conquest then by capitalist industrialization are obviously massive, and I have no wish to minimize them. But even amidst such epochal social and economic transformations, I want to emphasize a continuity that increasingly strikes me as a crucial one. It is this: even as capitalism shattered the old social systems and drew the entire subcontinent into a world of wage labor and commoditization, *people* continued to be struggled over. For the century following the discovery of mineral wealth in South Africa, as has often been observed, the entire region was characterized by a labor scarcity economy (van Onselen 1986; Seekings and Nattrass 2005). Many of the harsher aspects of South African capitalism have been traced to this root, as state coercion was applied to break the black peasantry and force people into low-cost wage labor. But, for all its harshness and cruelty, this was a social system hungry for people. And people were brought into it by the millions. Often, it is true, they were brought in by force. But it is impossible to ignore that very significant numbers of people voluntarily travelled many hundreds of miles (from places as far away as Zambia and Malawi) in order to submit themselves to a notoriously violent and oppressive socioeconomic system.

This was a different kind of snowball state—drawing people in (from within South African territory as well as far beyond) and hierarchically incorporating them (now as laborers rather than as political followers) into a larger whole. Race exclusion meant that those drawn in no longer had the opportunities for mobility that systems like the Ngoni state provided (no longer was "every man a potential lord"—far from it). But colonial racial capitalism in South Africa, whatever else it was, was unquestionably a voracious consumer of wealth in people (now in the form of labor). And, as in the case of the Ngoni, we scratch our heads (and perhaps squirm a bit) when we read of people who traveled great distances in order to subject themselves voluntarily to such a brutal system.

The continuing competition over people had some important implications for indigenous conceptions of personhood. Wage labor (as a rich ethnographic literature has shown) came in the twentieth century to be an important foundation of male personhood. Relations between senior and junior men were radically transformed by young men's access to wage labor (and the full social personhood it bestowed). The claims to social status that came from education were similarly transformative, as Zolani Ngwane (2004) has pointed out. Marriage came to be intimately linked with wage-earning capacity (through the transformed institution of bridewealth), and the subordination of women acquired new mechanisms and justifications. A crucial distinction also emerged between rural and urban social membership, and urban membership (or at least the stunted version of it that was available to blacks) became tightly linked to wage labor.

But a logic in which personhood was achieved through relations of dependence often continued to apply.[8] In many domains, in colonial and apartheid southern Africa, *being* someone continued to imply *belonging* to someone. The importance of ideologies and practices of paternalism has often been remarked on, of course, for rural farm life in the twentieth century (even if, as van Onselen [1992, 130] has noted, it always remained in a racially truncated, stunted form), and Rutherford (2008) has convincingly argued that a system of what he calls "domestic government" established both social hierarchies and highly valued forms of incorporation that explain much about contemporary land struggles in the region (see also van Onselen 1996). But such personalistic relations of dependence were also central to workers' identities in urban and industrial settings. The culture of work on the mines, for instance (as convincingly described by such authors as Donald Donham [2011] and Dunbar Moodie [1994]), was hardly less paternalistic and personalistic than on the farm.[9] And it is important to note that this is not only a matter of hypocritical white rationalizations (as in the notoriously self-serving formula "we treat our blacks like family"). For it is clear that (in spite of the often appallingly abusive conditions of work) African workers themselves often understood managerial authority in familistic and quasi-kinship terms.[10]

Again, there has been a tendency to tell a transition story here, where these supposedly "premodern" forms of socially bound, kinship-idiomed labor were gradually displaced by the purely commoditized purchase of labor power that idealized models of capitalism imply. Yet we now know that twentieth-century South African capitalism, through a century of more or less constant "modernization," did not do away with personalistic and dependent relations between employer and employee. Andries du Toit has shown that even on Cape fruit and wine farms (generally reckoned the most "modern" and fully capitalist agricultural sector in the country), capitalist agriculture continued to depend on paternalistic relations of authority with deep continuities with the past (1993, 315). In a more recent article (with Joachim Ewert), du Toit shows that paternalistic values continue to be central even in the latest rounds of "modernization" of labor relations, and even on what are termed the most "progressive" farms (Du Toit and Ewert 2002, 91–92). Mining labor tells a similar story, where Donald Donham (2011) has shown that supposedly premodern paternalistic relations of authority continued to be central to the management of labor right up through the 1990s on some mines.[11]

Capitalists, farmers, and supervisors seeking to capture human wealth in the twentieth century, then, used some of the same devices (of personalistic and quasi-kinship-based social inclusion) that kings and chiefs seeking the same had used in the centuries before. And as in the old social systems, sought-after persons (even those recruited by force) retained some measure of recourse via exit. Employers' competition over labor, like chiefs' competition over followers, provided ordinary people at least some room to maneuver and thereby set some limits to domination. There were, of course, notoriously brutal coercive attempts to limit such options. But the extraordinary resilience and mobility of workers meant that such attempts never met with more than partial success. As in precolonial times, the ability to exit and move on provided crucial limits on the most despotic abuses of power and vital lines of potential relief for the most disadvantaged. To the extent that such exit options existed, I emphasize, they were largely premised on a generalized situation of labor scarcity.

Having suggested that the phenomenon of labor scarcity created some continuities (alongside the more often noted breaks) between precolonial- and colonial-era social systems, let me now briefly consider how social membership was constituted in colonial- and apartheid-era South Africa and, in closely related (if sometimes less extreme) ways, the other settler colonies of southern Africa.

One system of membership from this period is, of course, the most discussed and analyzed—that is, race membership. The colonial color bar separating settlers from "natives" was in South Africa famously elabo- rated into a baroque and fetishized categorical system of ranked member- ships that increasingly scandalized international liberal opinion as the twentieth century wore on. And, of course, race membership was always complicated and to some extent cross-cut by class membership, leading to such familiar phenomena as the so-called poor white problem and the increasingly important differentiation between more and less educated black urbanites.

Alongside these more familiar systems of membership, though, was another, which we might call "work membership." Urban society in par- ticular was structured not only by the privileges and penalties of race and class but by a legal and social distinction between urban "belongers" with recognized waged employment and "hangers-on" who lacked it. The linking of a kind of urban membership with work left women (legally and culturally barred from many forms of wage labor) in a precarious posi- tion. But the same was true of many men who lived in the city, but without the formal waged employment that would have given them the truncated but significant set of legal and social rights enjoyed by the recognized "worker." As in contemporary China, the urban masses were divided by a legal mechanism that created different sorts of membership rights to the city based on membership in officially recognized work groups (Zhang 2002). Through the notorious pass laws (but also through housing policy and other means), those lacking this crucial form of urban membership were systematically disadvantaged but never effectively removed from the urban environment.

While analytically separable, both the race system and (what I am call- ing) the work system of membership came to be called into fundamental question at more or less the same historical time. For during the same time that South Africa's notorious apartheid race laws (which legally separated white from black) were being dismantled, so were such things as pass laws and housing restrictions (which fundamentally acted to separate black from black—i.e., those possessing work membership from those who lacked it). This coincidence (for that is what it is) has meant that the decline of the system of work membership has tended to be obscured by the more visible (and upbeat) story of the overthrow of official race membership. Yet the breakdown of the old system of work membership, I want to suggest, has profound consequences for understanding the current impasses in southern African politics and social policy alike.

The Era of Labor Surplus: An Era of In-dependence?

For several decades now, the economy of southern Africa has ceased to be characterized by labor scarcity. Raw manual labor, for so long competed over by employers, now goes begging in the marketplace. Mass unemployment (in economic theory and economic history) tends to be associated with economic decline. But South Africa shows that even what economists call "healthy" economies in these times often end up pushing people out of the labor market, not drawing them into it. As Seekings and Nattrass (2005) have shown, in both the late apartheid period and the years since then, economic growth in South Africa has coexisted with rising numbers of unemployed, many of whom are now locked out of the labor market not temporarily but more or less permanently. This is not economic decline but a perverse sort of ascent. The picture that emerges is of what we might call a "snowball state in reverse"—rolling along nicely, but throwing people off (rather than picking them up) as it goes along.

This expulsion of whole sectors of the population from the workforce is not unique to southern Africa, as Tania Li (2010) has recently pointed out in her important treatment of "surplus populations" in South and Southeast Asia. Nor is it a terribly recent turn of events—it has been going on for several decades at least. Indeed, apartheid's Bantustan experiment has been analyzed as a way of dealing with what officials saw as "surplus people" (Platzky and Walker 1985), while Seekings and Nattrass convincingly argue that mass unemployment was already unquestionably in evidence by the mid-1970s (2005, 166–77). It is, nonetheless, a huge transformation, one that has exploded into its fully visible and unmistakable form only in the last twenty years. After centuries in which people were scarce and sought-after (first as wealth in people, then as labor), the last few decades have introduced a fundamental break. We are so used to seeing industrialization and the rise of capitalism as the macro-historical break that we have perhaps not allowed ourselves to see that the shift from a people-scarce system to a people-surplus one is in some ways just as radical.

What does this shift mean for social personhood? Rather suddenly, unclaimed men (formerly fought over and eagerly claimed—first as chiefly subjects, later as scarce wage laborers) have become at the same time without commodity value and truly independent—a terrifying predicament given the importance, as I have argued, of relationality for personhood. Women and children often bear the brunt of the male rage that this predicament provokes. At the same time, women's old vital role as social and biological reproducers of the workforce is hugely devalued when the wider economic system no longer needs an expanded workforce. But women may also sometimes manage to retain a sense of personhood based on relations of dependence that men often lack. I have in mind here not just familial roles such as mother and grandmother but also the social role (for that is what it is) of grant-recipient—most of all, of the widely distributed child support grants. I will return to the question of social grants shortly.

Analysts of southern Africa's migrant labor system used to decry the way that a system of racial capitalism pulled apart black families (which they tended to regard as naturally cohesive entities), sacrificing family unity on the altar of cheap wage labor. What we see today, however, is that the "freeing" of a whole generation of young men from the demands of wage labor seems to be fragmenting (rather than uniting) families—and even making the conventional notion of the male-headed household obsolete—in ways that leave many men (and some women) ironically nostalgic for the bad old days of apartheid migrant labor (as Hylton White, for instance, has shown [2004]; cf. Dubbeld 2013). The freeing of young men from the "dependence" of wage labor has led to a radical decline in the institution of marriage (Kumchulesi 2011), while women and children have been swept up into a new system of dependence centered on old age pensions and child support grants that is giving rise to new "matri-focal" (or even "granny-focal") forms of domestic structure.

The grim consequences of the severing of the ties that once bound people to the "snowball" of southern African industrial capitalism are perhaps most vividly illustrated by the extent to which the disadvantaged today (as in the troubled and insecure days of the old Ngoni state) in fact aspire to dependence—as in my reference at the start to the visiting foreigner's shock at encountering citizens of the new, free South Africa who called him "baas" and begged to serve him.[12] The perilously insecure and unattached will accept (now, as then) subordination in exchange for membership (see also Rutherford 2008). Their problem today is not that they are being subordinated and subjected—it is worse. The real problem is that they have become not worth subjecting, cast off from the societal snowball. For those thus abjected, subjection can appear only as a step up.

Those rendered "independent" of the wage labor system, then, do not remain happily independent but rather seek (with more or less success) to build up new dependencies. This, of course, was what my American acquaintance was observing. But the manifestations visible to this sort of middle-class observer (people coming to the door, begging in the street, or hoping for coins at the supermarket) are only the tip of the iceberg, for most claims and requests for assistance are made by poor people on other poor people. As recent surveys of giving behaviors in South Africa show, "giving is more common among the poor than the rich"; not only is poverty not a deterrent to giving, "giving within poor communities is crucial to their very survival" (Habib and Maharaj 2008, 26, 38). More generally, ethnography reveals the key role of distribution in poor communities. Indeed, as I argued in chapter 3, much of what goes on in the (misleadingly named) "informal economy" is less about producing goods and services than it is about finding opportunities for what I have termed "distributive labor." Such activities facilitate a kind of day-to-day survival on the part of the unemployed, but they are left in a very precarious position—hanging (as the literal meaning of "depend" suggests) by a thread (or perhaps, in the better case, by a frail network of threads).

Such dependence, though, is not the worst of outcomes. To be dependent on someone is to be able to make at least some limited claims on that person. A poor person who is enmeshed in networks of dependence with others in a similar condition thus has at least some people on whom he or she can make such claims. And the desirable alternative to such claim-making is normally not independence or autonomy (indeed, that would be possible only under truly exceptional conditions). Rather, the realistic alternative to dependence on other poor people is more often an ability to become a dependent of (and thus to be able to make claims on) an actor with a greater capacity to provide and protect (whether this is an individual, a firm, an NGO, or indeed a political party or the state).

This is a major theme in recent ethnographic work on local politics in southern Africa, much of which seems to show that liberal emancipatory models of mobilization are often less successful than non-liberal ways of binding people together via hierarchical dependencies. Steven Robins, for instance, has done a fascinating study of the South African Homeless People's Movement and found that while the cosmopolitan NGOs that funded this organization advanced democratic and anti-hierarchical ideals of citizenship, the rank-and-file federation members, as well as the leadership, were "not always as committed" to this agenda (2003, 262). While funders and Left intellectuals promoted horizontal and egalitarian relations of trust and empowerment, the "grassroots" Homeless People's Federation (HPF) "seemed more concerned with housing delivery and the consolidation of vertical relations of patronage and dependency" (2003, 263). Indeed, the HPF slogan, "We don't collect money, we collect people" (2003, 245), could refer (as the metropolitan leadership may have interpreted it) to a process of conscientization and emancipation; but such an expression might even better describe the snowball-like accumulation of followers by political patrons able to disburse such favors as housing allocations.

Similarly, Kea Gorden's Ph.D. research (2008) showed that well-intentioned projects to build norms of democratic citizenship in Kwa-Zulu-Natal ran afoul of entrenched local expectations about hierarchical leadership and a stubborn (and, to the emancipatory liberal mind, scandalous) attachment to the personalistic and decidedly undemocratic authority of chiefs (see also chapter 8 in James 2007). For Namibia, John Friedman (2011) has described the importance of paternalistic relations of authority in the workings of the colonial Namibian state, as people pursued their aims less by asserting individual rights than by seeking the protection of chiefs and other political patrons. Today, he reports a kind of grassroots nostalgia for such relations and a critique of the contemporary state for failing to provide them—for failing, in his words, "to uphold its end of the paternal bargain." This is, he concludes, precisely "a critique of *non*-dependence" (2011, 247; emphasis supplied). Again, it is the apparent preference for, and active seeking out of, relations of dependence and hierarchy that is so striking here. It seems that for poor southern Africans (as for a great many other people in the contemporary world) it is not dependence but its absence that is really terrifying—the severing of the thread and the fall into the social void.[13]

Does this mean dependence is actually a good thing? Such a claim makes us uneasy. The fear is that valorizing or even acknowledging dependence may authorize or legitimate inequality. But this fear may be misplaced. Whether we approve of it or not, inequality must be confronted—it is unavoidable, as a matter of both practical politics and (as Amartya Sen [1997] has demonstrated) theoretical necessity. To be sure, it is vitally important to strive to reduce the massive inequalities that are so striking a feature of southern African societies (notably, those of income, wealth, education, and landholding). But at the same time, perhaps we progressive scholars would do well to do more of what our informants do, which is to deal pragmatically with (rather than just deploring) the social world we have got. And for the near to medium term (at the very least) that social world is one of massive and extreme inequality. Dealing with (rather than just denouncing) this reality means going beyond pious wishing for equality to ask how inequalities are socially institutionalized and whether some such modes of institutionalization are politically or ethically preferable to others.

The phrase "social inequality" perhaps rolls off our lips too easily—as if "social inequality" is simply a synonym for "inequality." But what is specifically "social" about it? The term *social inequality* implies a common membership within a "society," and relations of inequality among those members. But today we're seeing, all around the world, a shift toward what we might call "asocial inequality," where huge inequalities of life conditions and life chances are increasingly severed from those embarrassing experiential social relationships of inequality.

By "asocial," I mean here something quite specific. There are, of course, still identifiable and important links between the worlds of rich and poor, and if we insist (as social scientists tend to do) that every human relation is by definition a social one, then of course the sort of inequality I have in mind plainly is "social." But if we ask another question, namely whether inequalities are lived and experienced within the imaginary horizon of that nineteenth-century invention, "society"—whether inequality, that is, is conceived as a relation among the members of a morally binding membership group—then the answer, increasingly, is "no" (cf. Rose 1999, 101; cf. chapter 2).

Increasingly, then, those suffering from what I call *asocial* inequality actually seek out *social* inequality. A great deal of poor people's labor, in fact, goes into trying to turn asocial inequality into the social kind. And this becomes especially visible (at least to relatively privileged people like my friend in Johannesburg) when we encounter poor people trying to strike up—or assert, or reassert—a social and personal relationship (even a highly dependent one) with those better off than themselves.

Asocial Assistance?

Having discussed labor and personhood, let us now turn to the third term in this chapter's title: welfare. What is the future of social assistance where inequality is increasingly "asocial" and where labor no longer provides the sort of foundation it once did for the domain we call "the social"?

The intellectual and political challenge here is a formidable one. As I have noted (see chapter 2), traditional twentieth-century conceptions of social welfare took for granted an economic world in which waged labor was socially generalized and the domain we have come to know as "the social" was constructed on the foundation of the able-bodied male worker. Indeed, the list of those requiring "social" intervention (the elderly, the infirm, the child, the disabled, the dependent reproductive woman) traces a kind of photographic negative of the figure of the wage-earning man. Persistent and socially normal mass male unemployment is therefore a huge challenge to the social democratic worldview.

In this context, the recent southern African campaigns for a basic income grant (BIG)—especially in South Africa and Namibia—provide a fascinating example of new thinking about an old subject. In the briefest of terms, the main idea is for the state to deal with a crisis of persistent poverty by providing a small unconditional minimum monthly payment to *all* citizens (see Standing and Samson 2003 for an overview; see also chapter 6). In contrast to older forms of "welfare" assistance, the claim is that such grants rely on poor people's ability to solve their own problems without imposing the policing, paternalism, and surveillance of the traditional welfare state. The "social" of the social welfare state is largely discarded in this scheme. Assistance is largely decoupled from familistic assumptions and insurance rationality alike, while the state is imagined as both universally engaged (as a kind of direct provider for each and every citizen) and maximally disengaged (taking no real interest in shaping the conduct of those under its care, who are seen as knowing their own needs better than the state does).

Many attempts to enhance state social assistance these days have a backward-looking and even nostalgic feel about them, "defending" and "preserving" benefits won long ago but lately threatened by neoliberal pruning. And they remain wedded to the social democratic view of the world, in which labor is the foundation of the social order and social support is needed only to provide insurance against predictable sorts of individual and systemic risk (ranging from workplace injuries to dips in the business cycle).

The BIG campaign has been unusual in basing its arguments for social support on very different grounds. Facing squarely some uncomfortable economic truths, BIG proponents recognize that mass unemployment is not going to disappear anytime soon and that wage labor can therefore no longer serve as the main basis of social membership. Instead of the nostalgic workerism that one encounters in many other progressive quarters, BIG advocates take seriously the challenge of dealing with the fact that a substantial part of the working-age population, even under the most optimistic of scenarios, will not be absorbed into the formal-sector workforce any time soon. As Charles Meth bluntly put it, "There is little hope that economic growth can rescue the poor—except among propagandists, there seems no doubt that the economy simply cannot grow fast enough" (2004, 9). Indeed, the South African state committee (the Taylor Committee) that originally proposed the BIG went so far as to speculate that a world of full employment, in the usual sense of the term, may *never* come to countries like South Africa. "In developing countries, where stable full-time waged formal sector labour was never the norm, it is increasingly unlikely that it will become the norm (DSD 2002, 38)."

What is more, BIG proponents boldly dispense with the usual fetishizing and moralizing of wage labor and the exaggerated fear of so-called handouts and dependency.[14] Would the BIG promote "dependency"? Meth suggests this is the wrong question. With or without state transfers, he argues, the poor are dependent. And the only real alternative (even for those with decent incomes) is interdependence (not independence). It is not a question, then, of introducing the snake of dependency into a garden that had been innocent of it. Dependence is rather, Meth insists, "an empirical matter," and debates around social policy must accept that the real questions are not about whether people are or should be dependent but rather about which forms of dependence are to be promoted and which discouraged (2004, 23).

The BIG campaign has also had the great virtue of identifying the need for new forms of socioeconomic membership. Recognizing the demise of "work membership," BIG promoters see a pressing need to give both social recognition and economic support in a way that would not be tied to labor. Significantly, they see the BIG not just as a "grant" but as a "citizen's income" that acknowledges a kind of nationwide membership and solidarity that would go beyond such (often empty) political rituals as voting to include rights to subsistence and consumption.

Part of the conception, too, involves a move to create economic rights that can be accessed by even the poorest citizens without the obstacles of bureaucracy or the potential corruption and abuse of a patronage-based system of distribution. Proponents place great hope in technical devices that might shorten the route between state coffers and poor people's needs. In some versions, for instance, the BIG might be accessed by any citizen at any automatic cash dispenser; biometric markers could make sure that funds are transparently dispersed to all the right people and none of the wrong ones (see chapter 2). Like most anthropologists, I am skeptical of attempts to solve political and social problems with technological fixes. But I must say that the prospect of social assistance being dispensed with the ease and efficiency of a routine withdrawal from a cash machine does sound appealing to me—especially after years of watching desperate pensioners try (and mostly fail) to collect their retirement money from Zambia's corrupt and mismanaged National Provident Fund.

Yet as thoughtful and compelling as the BIG campaign has in many ways been, there is no avoiding that fact that it has, after an initial flurry of interest, stalled politically (especially in South Africa; the Namibian case is a bit more mixed). Why, with all that's so attractive and forward-thinking about the BIG, has it not managed to get more political traction? It cannot be not due to any general hostility to social grants—the

South African state currently spends an impressive 3.5 percent of GDP on grants, which are now paid to fully 30 percent of all South Africans (notably via old age pensions and child support grants—see this book's introduction). Yet neither ruling officials nor impoverished masses seem to have rallied to the BIG cause.[15] No doubt there are many reasons (for a recent analysis of the South African case, see Seekings and Matisonn 2010). But one wonders whether one underlying weakness of the campaign may not be that while social payments address quite directly (if minimally) the material needs of impoverished citizens, they offer far less by way of dealing with their social and moral needs. In a world where social position has for so long depended on a kind of exchange of labor for membership, an unconditional "transfer" of cash may seem dangerously empty—a way of preventing the worst, in material terms, but without the granting of any sort of meaningful personhood or social belonging.

This is especially the case for men, for whom social membership and adult masculinity alike have long been linked to a highly valorized capacity for wage labor. Unlike the BIG (which remains only a proposal), grants for women, children, and disabled people have been long established in South Africa and Namibia (as discussed in earlier chapters). These grants are widely accepted and generally popular, but they are specifically targeted at social categories conventionally recognized as legitimately "dependent" and for whom the state can be imagined as taking on the metaphorical role of husband/father. But for able-bodied adult men in the prime of life, the receipt of a grant may seem inappropriate, and it is still the promise of jobs that beckons (even if that promise remains, for many, illusory).

Is this, then, a matter of men refusing the humiliation of dependence and instead insisting on an autonomous independence? Hardly: as I have noted, the sort of employment for black men in South Africa that is nowadays nostalgically longed for was hardly ever a vehicle for independence. On the contrary, it constituted precisely a form of dependence, albeit a highly valued kind of dependence that brought with it a kind of unequal incorporation that I have termed "work membership." Men's desire for employment of this kind cannot be figured as a yearning for autonomy; it is on the contrary precisely a desire for attachment—for incorporation, even under highly unequal and often dangerous and humiliating terms, into a social body.

If this is the case, then it may be that the real problem with the BIG is *not* that it would (as neoliberal critics tend to assert) "create dependency." If anything, the danger may be that it can provide only a shallow and impersonal sort of dependence instead of a richly social one—for a mere grant, at least as such grants are presently conceptualized, cannot provide the sort of full social position that comes with employment or other forms of socially "thick" incorporation. (Note, however, that the issue of possible emergent alternative conceptualizations of social payments is the central theme of the next chapter.) In place of the social personhood and membership long associated with a job, a cash transfer may appear to offer only a notional national membership and a cold and impersonal relation with a technocratic state.

Social membership implies what political theorists call "recognition." But recognition can come in many different forms. Here, we might usefully contrast two sorts of recognition that figure in contemporary South Africa. First, consider the sort of recognition that occurs when a person is approved for receipt of a social service by being "recognized" by a local traditional authority. Here the technical task of recognition (making sure it's the right person) is combined with the political *act* of recognition (a chief recognizes his subject as such and vice versa), together with the social familiarity that comes from long acquaintance, entangled family histories, and so on. Contrast the visit to the automatic cash dispenser envisaged by the BIG advocates. Here there is also a form of "recognition" at work: the machine scans the grant recipient's iris and fingerprints, "recognizes" him or her as the rightful recipient, and dispenses the money. But this is recognition only in the most technical and socially minimal sense. In this technocratic utopia, functional "recognition" is stripped free of the person-to-person social relationships that have historically accompanied it.

The attraction of doing this is evident: BIG advocates aim to avoid the patronage and potential corruption associated with old-style handouts and to allow poor people to receive what is due them without having to kowtow to local bureaucrats and minor despots. But one wonders whether, for some, these technical advantages might not be offset by the "social" attractions of a more familiar sort of claim-making, where the socially "thick" recognition that comes from being looked after by the local party-state is after all preferable (for many) to the frighteningly "thin" recognition of the iris scan—if only because it implies a humanly social (rather than technocratically asocial) and actively affective bond between state and citizen (cf. White 2012).

This suggests the need to revisit the fraught issue of "paternalism"—a bogey of contemporary social assistance discourse and more generally a kind of specter haunting the liberal imagination across postcolonial southern Africa. The dangers and dysfunctions of states based on kinship-idiomed patronage politics are well known from studies of African states that lie to the north (see, e.g., Berman 1998; Bayart 1993), and worries about the potential for such dynamics to erode state capacities and democratic norms (in southern Africa or anywhere else) can hardly be dismissed as unwarranted. But if, as I have suggested, claims of belonging via personalistic dependence are taking on new urgency in a world where "work membership" is simply no longer available to much of the population, then simply ruling such claims out of bounds in the name of a liberal teleology of progressive emancipation may, in fact, turn out not to be very "progressive" at all.

A few years ago, a major political opinion survey provoked consternation among liberal political scientists and other right-thinking people when it revealed that an embarrassing majority of South Africans agreed with the statement "People are like children, the government should take care of them like a parent" (Afrobarometer 2009, 4).[16] For those seeking to build a culture of rights, this apparent yearning for parental authority could only appear a dangerous reversion to the logic of the bad old days of colonialism and apartheid. South Africans, in this view, ought to be equal citizens proudly claiming rights, not childlike dependents seeking the protection of a parent. But in styling the people as "like children," the statement can also be read as making a very strong assertion not just of inequality but of a social obligation linking state and citizen. In that sense, indeed, sentiments of this kind can provide a basis for powerful political claims based on an obligation so fundamental that it precedes any right (Englund 2008). After all, southern Africans (from the days of the Ngoni and long before) have always known that kinship relations such as descent are precisely *political* relations, just as anthropologists have always known that such relations are central to structures of distribution in every society.

Citizenship has often been imagined as a domain of equality and rights, to be contrasted with the Ngoni-like hierarchical and clientelistic relations of rural "traditional authority"—thus "citizen" versus "subject," as Mamdani (1996) would have it. But where social assistance looms so large in the state-citizen relationship, the state may well appear to the citizen not principally as a protector of equal rights but as a material benefactor or even patron, while the positive content of citizenship itself may increasingly come to rest precisely on being a rightful and deserving dependent of the state. For such a relationship, a parent-child metaphor can be both politically and analytically powerful. In place of the temptation to see such thinking as proof of a stunted or undeveloped culture of democratic citizenship, we might better see it as an indication both of the real limits of the formal equalities of citizenship under substantive conditions of extreme inequality and of the real likelihood that demands for social inclusion and protection may be, under present circumstances, more relevant to many people's circumstances than any abstract equality of individual rights. Perhaps, that is, instead of waiting for some evolutionary logic to make people give up their "backward" ideas, we should begin taking these ideas seriously and recognizing the way that they address the very contemporary needs for care, moral connection, and responsible obligation in ways that emancipatory liberal rights talk often does not (cf. Englund 2008, 2006).

Declarations of dependence are a challenge to liberal common sense. Like the forms of Islamic piety analyzed by Saba Mahmood in Egypt (2005), they present us with the theoretical and political challenge of a form of agency that seeks its own submission. Their very existence poses a challenge to liberal ideals of freedom, autonomy, and dignity. But however uncomfortable it may make us, an ethnographically informed approach to the political challenges of the present will need to take such forms of agency seriously. The aspiration to dependence is not just an embarrassing holdover from the bad old days of colonial paternalism. On the contrary, it speaks eloquently and urgently to the radical specificity of the present. Declarations of dependence can tell us much (if we will listen) about what the real needs of poor southern Africans are today and how they might be better met in the years to come.

For more than a century in southern African, labor provided the most powerful foundation for subaltern social membership (especially in domains marked as urban and modern). Today, with work decentered and underemployment a durable and widespread reality, we must rethink both the grounds for social membership and the meaning of work.

With respect to social membership, we must come to terms with the declining significance of both work membership and race membership. But it would be well not to be too quick to unconditionally embrace the obvious alternatives. In particular, a recent history of xenophobic violence across the continent should remind us of the dangers of relying on national citizenship as an unproblematic alternative to the exclusions of past systems of membership. It is worth pondering, for instance, how proposals for a "citizens' income" can deal with the problem of the impoverished non-citizen (an issue discussed in this book's conclusion).

With respect to the culture of work, the need is to follow the BIG campaigners in challenging the moralizing attitudes that stigmatize those excluded from the labor market. Wage labor is not the only way of contributing to the society, and various forms of dependence (including caregiving and care-receiving) must be recognized as necessary building blocks of a healthy society.

Social policy, in particular, should not treat "dependency" as a disease—the task is not to eliminate dependence but to construct desirable forms of it. We still don't know what those are. But the goal should be not an end to dependence but a plurality of opportunities for beneficial forms of it. Seeking such a goal may be obstructed by an exaggerated fear of "patronage" (and the racialized fear of an "Africanization" of the South African state that is often associated with it). The dangers of patronage-based state forms (with their associated corruption, inefficiency, and all the rest) are real enough, and ought not be taken lightly. But forms of political mobilization that "don't collect money" but "collect people" instead may offer badly needed new forms of belonging, attachment, and care. In a context where material inequalities are staggering and social obligations binding the haves to the have-nots are being rapidly shed, we may be wrong to worry so much that those with resources will extend patronage to those who lack them. The greater danger may be that they will not.

A social policy, and a politics, that takes maximizing independence and autonomy (and minimizing dependence and patronage) as its ultimate goal may not be able to address the crisis of personhood that, I have argued, is at the heart of the region's contemporary predicament. New thinking now emerging in the domain of social policy, though, offers some hope that we may find ways of approaching the question of dependence in a more rewarding way, a way that would be able to credit and respect the vernacular aspirations to social relationality that are so puzzling to an emancipatory liberalism. We still have a great deal of work to do if we are to develop intellectual tools and political strategies adequate to these difficult times. But if we are willing to keep our ears to the ground and take seriously what we hear there, we may yet learn to think, and act, in new ways. If we can do so, it is perhaps not too optimistic to hope that we just may, one day, manage to find ways to restore value in people (and not just their labor) and to build a new dispensation within which people could truly count, once again, as the most precious form of wealth.

6. A Rightful Share
Distribution beyond Gift and Market

The people shall share in the country's wealth!
—The Freedom Charter of South Africa

Of all the promises that sustained the anticolonial struggles for liberation across southern Africa, perhaps none has been as elusive as the one expressed so economically in the fourth proclamation of South Africa's Freedom Charter.[1] The ringing declaration has inspired generations with its clear assertion that liberation must entail not just new political rights but also a new distribution of resources. Yet how such a result might be obtained remains underspecified. What exactly does it mean for "the people" to "share in the country's wealth"?

This is, of course, a key question of this book as well as an animating theme of the emergent "distributive politics" that it seeks to identify in a range of developments across the southern Africa region and beyond. This chapter discusses the limitations of the ways that this question has been approached in traditional Leftist politics and seeks to show that different and perhaps more politically promising approaches to wealth-sharing may be emerging out of the distributive practices of what I have termed the region's new welfare states (especially South Africa and Namibia). In the wake of the conjunctural collision of new and expanded programs of cash transfer with fierce populist demands for the sharing of national resources,

I suggest, it may be possible to spot the seeds of what could become a potent new form of political mobilization and claim-making.

In its day, the Freedom Charter's demand that "the people" should "share in the country's wealth" was generally understood to refer to nationalization. The paragraph that follows the declaration goes on to state that "the national wealth" (including "the mineral wealth beneath the soil") "shall be transferred to the ownership of the people as a whole." This key formulation was widely interpreted as calling for state ownership of at least the "strategic sectors" or "commanding heights" of the economy (within which the mining industry inevitably looms large).[2] But South Africa's ruling ANC party never took that path, and most of the regimes in the region that did nationalize major industries have since rethought the issue. While the state-owned mining company remains an internationally reputable model for natural resource extraction,[3] the region's history has made clear that such nationalization by no means automatically leads to ordinary people "sharing in the country's wealth," and the ANC today insists that it has no ambition to nationalize major industries such as mining.[4] Yet there continues to be a vigorous distributive politics in the region, and the old dream of a liberation in which "the people" might "share in the country's wealth" remains very much alive.

A recent wave of strikes in the South African mining industry (with associated violent repression) reminds us of the continuing intensity and vitality of struggles around the division of the production pie between capital and labor. Yet while such spectacular clashes over distribution at the point of production command massive media attention, the prospects for such actions bringing about a comprehensive sharing of "the country's wealth" with "the people" seem quite limited. Where higher wages have in fact been obtained, employers have tended to respond by employing fewer workers, limiting the overall distributive effect. And with the share of the population in a position to make such distributive claims shrinking, higher wages for organized, formal-sector workers can at best allow only a sharply limited (and, in relation to the masses of un- and underemployed "poor," better off) subset of "the people" to "share in the country's wealth" (Seekings and Nattrass 2005).

Struggles over wage labor, though, are very far from exhausting the domain of distributive politics in the region. Indeed, those excluded from the world of wages are making increasingly vocal claims to other sorts of distributive shares, often based on criteria such as specific histories, identities, and experiences that make them rightful recipients of national resources. In many southern African countries, for instance (most notably Zimbabwe and Namibia), we have seen the state honor the strong claims made by "veterans" of the anticolonial struggle in the form of regular cash payments.[5] Perhaps more visible, and equally politically charged, have been claims involving land and its distribution. Here, the key dynamic has involved populist economic demands made in the name of a politically empowered but economically marginalized majority. Often the landless masses are invoked as the holders of an implicit property claim—not simply as a political majority but as autochthons, the original and real *owners* of the country (a claim that brings with it both echoes of anticolonial armed struggle and sometimes overtones of racist and xenophobic animus toward "foreigners" or "settlers," as in the case of Julius Malema discussed below).

Such demands for land have (with the exception of the much-discussed case of Zimbabwe) generally yielded little in the way of concrete results,[6] even as the position of organized labor has mostly deteriorated across the region (Pitcher 2007; for South Africa, see Barchiesi 2011). At the same time, though, a more rewarding field of distributive struggle has emerged around what is called "service delivery"—a phrase that today evokes a broad package of goods and services the provision of which (often on highly subsidized terms) is increasingly understood as a state responsibility to a deserving citizenry. These include such things as housing, electricity, sanitation, water, and social assistance. Claims to these services tend to be based not on labor but on such things as citizenship, residence, identity, and political loyalty. Indeed, in discussions of this kind, jobs themselves sometimes seem to be conceived as simply another kind of good that the state ought to "deliver."

Ability to access services of this kind has been patchy, and failures are as notable as successes. South Africa, particularly, has "delivered" millions of state-furnished houses—but equally evident are the millions more still living in shacks and the widespread demonstrations over failed service delivery (Alexander 2010). Yet in the midst of this fiercely contested landscape, there is one sort of service delivery that has indisputably had a major distributive effect: the programs of direct social assistance via cash grants that now directly reach 30 percent of South Africans (and indirectly far more than that) and are also an increasingly important part of poor livelihoods in other southern African countries (especially Namibia, Botswana, and Lesotho—see this book's introduction).

At first glance, militant political demands for state appropriation of land and industry would seem to have little connection with the sedate administrative world of social policy and cash transfers. Descriptively, certainly, the chauvinistic blood politics of racial ownership discussed in the following section hardly resembles the grey technocratic machinations of the social security apparatus. And analytically, one is tempted to see radical challenges to the system of ownership of the means of production as quite fundamentally different from the merely ameliorative politics normally associated with social assistance. But I want to suggest that these two forms of politics are not as separate as they seem and that bringing the two into relation raises some intriguing political possibilities. In particular, the existence of powerful political claims to ownership of a national wealth, when juxtaposed with a remarkably elaborate and effective apparatus of direct distribution, allows us to imagine (and perhaps see some preliminary flickers of) a different kind of distributive politics, one that has affinities both with fundamental social principles of allocation familiar to anthropologists and with some of the most challenging recent thinking of philosophers and social theorists. That is a politics of what I call "the rightful share."

First, I describe the way ideas of shares have figured in recent resource nationalism (especially in South Africa) and then reflect on the limits of such a politics. Second, I assess the achievements of the new programs of social assistance and note the way they are limited by certain fundamental and persistent conceptions concerning the nature and purpose of social payments. Finally, I consider a case (the basic income grant campaign in Namibia) in which social transfers are being reimagined in ways that allow the idea of a "rightful share" to take on a quite different significance than it does in traditional discussions of nationalization of natural resources.

Resource Nationalism and Its Limits

Southern African politics has recently seen a burst of public debate around natural resources and the question of who rightfully owns them. Powerful assertions have been made of a "people's" right to, quite directly, "share in the country's wealth," and even of a right of "the people" to literally *own* such wealth. I will explore these lines of populist assertion using the recent public statements of the South African politician Julius Malema. Malema has accumulated a legion of detractors, who see him as a kind of clown or petty criminal at best (a "tenderpreneur" who has enriched himself via his personal links with ANC cronies) and a dangerously illiberal demagogue at worst. And there is no doubt that Malema's undisciplined and ethically questionable conduct has led him into very serious political and personal setbacks (the loss of his post as ANC Youth League president as well as legal problems that may yet lead to his prosecution and conviction for serious crimes). But the crowds of enthusiastic supporters that he and his new political party (the "Economic Freedom Fighters," or EFF) have attracted in recent years among the poor and working classes, together with the level of alarm and anxiety thereby provoked among the propertied, suggest there is more going on here than just buffoonery or criminality. Instead, I suggest, the Malema phenomenon provides a particularly clear window into a powerful strand of vernacular thinking about property, ownership, and justice. And whether or not Malema's personal political star is now rising or falling (few seem to be sure), we have surely not seen the last of the sensibility to which he has given such alarmingly unfiltered voice.

Press coverage of Malema has tended to focus most of all on his tendency to play on (if not actively to incite) sentiments of racial resentment and score-settling (as when he told a crowd, to "deafening applause," that in the South Africa he envisioned in ten years, domestic servants would be white) together with his weakness for loose and irresponsible threats of violence against white landholders (most famously in his deliberately provocative use of the old struggle song "Kill the Boer").[7] There is no doubt that a crude and demagogic racial politics is a key part of his populist appeal as well as a key reason for the disdain expressed toward him by many pundits and mainstream politicians. But our understanding of the passions to which Malema gives voice will be incomplete if we see in them only a negative resentment and not also a positive aspiration. And that aspiration is not simply to democracy or political equality but to something even more explosive and difficult to realize. It is an aspiration to ownership. "How," he asks, "does South Africa belong to all of us when the majority of our people do not own anything?"[8]

The most powerful symbol of such ownership, as it has been for generations across the region, is land. Land, with its indissociable link to place and ancestry, is readily associated with an "original" ownership. Malema likes to taunt whites on this very point, asking how much land they brought with them when they came from Europe.[9] The Landless People's Movement makes a similar, populist argument (echoing the restitution campaigns in Zimbabwe), saying simply "The land that was stolen from us must be returned! Give us our land now" (Landless People's Movement 2001). Malema taps into this widespread sentiment, using the plain and forceful language of the natural provocateur: "This is our grandfathers' land, taken by force. We want that land back. We constitute 90% of the country and the ownership . . . should reflect that."[10] "If you have 1,000 hectares of land, we want 800 hectares of it. And we are not going to pay for it because we haven't got money."[11] "They have stolen our land. They are criminals and must be treated like that. We want our land back and we want it for free."[12]

But it is not just land that Malema demands. Just as the settlers did not bring land with them, neither did they bring minerals, which properly belong to the nation.[13] "These are our mines and we must fight until we benefit from these mines," he told an enthusiastic stadium audience in the platinum-mining town of Rustenburg.[14] "The coloniser" continues to exploit mineral resources while the people suffer; only nationalized ownership can remedy this.[15]

There is more going on here, however, than mere "us versus them" claims of historical priority and original ownership. For Malema also deploys a powerful language of universalism, in which "*everyone* has the right to benefit from wealth in South Africa."[16] What he calls "economic freedom," he insists, does not exclude whites. "We never said they must be sent to sea. We just want to share the cake."[17] South Africa's wealth should properly belong to all South Africans—*all* should be owners, and *all* should receive a share. And equality must mean not just political equality but economic equality, which he understands as an equality of ownership, ownership shared equally.[18] As he told the Rustenburg crowd, "Never apologise for demanding an equal share."[19]

But Malema moves very quickly from a diagnosis that calls for universalistic sharing among a vast plurality of owners to a remedy that calls for just a single owner: the state. Nationalization appears as the obvious, almost self-evident solution in this line of thinking. If "the people" rightfully claim the resources, then "the nation as a whole" should own them, in the form of the state. History has shown the cost of this slippage. By a sleight of hand with which students of socialism (African and otherwise) are only too familiar, the moral claims of "the nation" are appropriated by a state that turns out to be not the transcendent embodiment of the spirit of the people but just an ordinary bureaucratic institution controlled by small numbers of very fallible mortals. And as even casual observers of African political economy know, "the state" can only too easily end up serving the private interests of those powerful elites who control the state apparatus. In this way, "the people's" claim of rightful ownership quickly becomes attached to the property claims of the state and those who control it. The empirical "people" become nominal owners of all, but actual owners of precious little. For Malema's critics, it is all too easy to visualize the path that would lead from nationalization to the looting of putatively national assets by a clique of well-connected cronies.[20]

National ownership, of course, need not have such an outcome. Many successful, well-governed national industries are organized around corporations owned entirely or in large part by the state, including that of Norway (often cited as a model for socially responsible mineral extraction), and different models of national ownership are found across the world and even within southern Africa (World Bank 2011). Experiences with nationalization present a huge range of different distributive outcomes, and South Africa surely enjoys much stronger governmental institutions than many of the other African countries whose experiences with state-owned mineral industries are sometimes invoked as "nightmare" cases meant to stop nationalization arguments in their tracks. But if it is reasonably objected that South Africa is not, after all, the Congo, it must also be pointed out that it is not likely to be confused with Norway, either. In reality, the wide range of possible outcomes shows only that nationalizing an industry like mining does not necessarily imply *any* particular distributive consequences for the ordinary people in whose name it is proposed. In fact, specifying national ownership, in itself, tells us *nothing at all* about the key allocation questions: Given that a certain stream of value is being produced here, where will it go? Who will get a piece of it? How big a piece for each, and via what mechanisms? And in the context of Africa's long engagement with mineral extraction, the answer, worked out in practice, has too often been that a small group of rich powerful white foreigners is replaced or (more often) supplemented by a small group of rich and powerful black nationals (as Fanon long ago foresaw ([1961] 2005). Angola is an especially clear example—a state whose vast oil riches, and the state corporation that is granted the rights to them, are proudly declared to belong to "the people" even as a tiny elite divvies up the spoils with transnational corporations, leaving the majority to struggle in abject poverty (cf. Ferguson 2006, 194–210). One can, if one wishes, think of this as "black economic empowerment," but those thereby empowered are very few, and the majority of the population may find little in it to celebrate.

As appealing as popular ownership is as a rhetorical demand, then, nationalization, in itself, does not begin to address the real distributive question: How can what is claimed to be commonly owned wealth be actually shared in common—in fact and not just as an ideological proclamation? How is the formidable stream of value produced by such "national wealth" *in fact* to be distributed—to whom and by what mechanisms? And where can the powerful distributive demands channeled by a figure like Malema lead, if not to the Angola-style dead end of state capitalism and elite enrichment? To answer these questions, we must consider in greater depth another, apparently quite different, sort of distributive politics.

Ameliorative Welfare and Its Limits

As noted in this book's introduction, southern Africa's new programs of social assistance have been a rare success story in the world of development and poverty policy. A substantial body of solid research demonstrates that programs of direct cash transfer (especially old age pensions and child support grants) have had real and impressive positive effects. In the midst of massive economic restructuring that has resulted in the shedding of many of the low-skilled jobs that once sustained poor and working-class communities across the region, social grants (in those countries that have such systems) have been hugely important in enabling children to be fed, retirees to be sustained in dignity in their old age, and destitution to be reduced. In a region that has for decades been littered with failed development and anti-poverty schemes (cf. Ferguson 1990), the demonstrated successes of these new and expanded systems of cash transfer are genuinely impressive. (See this book's introduction and the literature cited in it.)

But as Andries du Toit has recently pointed out in a stimulating critique of South Africa's remarkably extensive array of post-apartheid state social programs, such interventions directed against poverty have tended to "avoid confronting head-on the structural and systematic constraints that keep poor people marginalized" (2012, 8). Instead, what he terms an "anti-poverty consensus" has settled on a depoliticized understanding of poverty as a simple lack experienced by individuals and households rather than an aspect of a social structure that has to be understood as a system of relations. The result is a framing of poverty that tends to sidestep the social clashes and vested interests that are integral to its production and "a process of depoliticizing poverty and disconnecting it from questions of social conflict, inequality and antagonism" (7).

The danger here, as Akhil Gupta has pointed out in his analysis of Indian anti-poverty programs, is that programs of limited redistribution, if disconnected from more far-reaching processes of political mobilization and economic transformation, may only "shore up the legitimacy of ruling regimes" without posing any fundamental challenge to the entrenched inequalities to which the programs are supposed to be a response. Indeed, he asks whether it might even be the case that programs that prevent the very worst outcomes for the poor may have as their main effect to "inoculate us to the political possibility of their death becoming a scandal" (2012, 278).

In addition to the danger of depoliticization, there is another problem with the existing systems of cash transfers in the region. As pointed out in earlier chapters (the introduction and chapter 2), southern African programs for addressing poverty via social assistance continue to be modeled on the old, European social democratic conception of "the social," a conception that presumes a "normal" situation of widespread and near-universal wage employment. For this reason such programs have mostly avoided (or evaded) addressing the millions of healthy working-age men who are durably excluded from the world of employment. Payments of social grants therefore tend, in practice, to go largely to women who provide child care and retired older people and can respond only in a very limited and indirect way to the crisis created by the disappearance of the low-skilled, manual labor jobs that once sustained much of the country.

While programs of public works and community-based employment have provided some low-wage labor, especially in recent years,[21] it remains the case that social payments flow chiefly to those caring for children (who are mostly mothers and grandmothers), the elderly, and the disabled. With "able-bodied men" still anachronistically presumed to be "workers," social protection continues to be implicitly styled as a sort of kindness shown to those who are in some way diminished, a framing that brings with it implications of incapacity, charity, and help for the helpless. These long-standing meanings attached to social payments contribute to the depoliticized character of the system and may lead the receipt of "grants" to be associated with feelings of shame and (especially for men, for whom wage labor has been such a foundation of personhood—see chapter 5) diminished personal worth.

In view of the continuing prevalence of this form of social assistance, it is hard to avoid the conclusion that the political possibilities raised by existing social programs are indeed quite limited—perhaps as much so, if for different reasons, as those raised by militant resource nationalism. Most progressives would surely agree that, flawed as they are, these redistributive social programs are far better than nothing. But most will struggle to see in them anything approaching a genuinely radical or transformative politics either.

Yet, as du Toit himself acknowledges, there may be more possibilities implicit in this vast and contradictory system of distribution than we have yet been able to appreciate. Discourses of social justice and social solidarity, as he points out, "can play an important role in forging frameworks for understanding and dealing with poverty that are not so depoliticized and limited," while deeply rooted traditions of giving in the region "may have significant and as yet untapped political potential" (du Toit 2012, 10).

How might that potential be realized? Could a social apparatus that has proven admirably effective in delivering cash payments to the poorest be repurposed into something more transformative than a depoliticizing device for ameliorating poverty and helping the needy? Perhaps at least some significant part of an answer to these questions might start with a rethinking of the meaning of such payments—in particular, the idea that a social payment might be understood not as aid, assistance, gift, or charity but instead as a kind of share. The next section develops this conception, and the following one makes the argument more than hypothetical by showing how an idea of a rightful share is being put to use in one specific empirical context.

Beyond Gift and Market: The Promise of the Share

Social assistance is specified in the South African constitution as a right. But it is, in practice, widely understood as fundamentally motivated by a kind of generosity. In this way, it is often implicitly styled as a kind of unreciprocated gift—"assistance" or "help," "granted" to the needy and unfortunate, motivated by such things as kindness and compassion. With social payments construed as generous gifts, questions arise (as they generally do with asymmetrical gifts) about failed reciprocity (what does the recipient of a social payment owe, "in exchange," to society?) and about dependence (is it healthy or dignified to be dependent, to get "something for nothing," to receive "handouts"?). The reliance here on a quasi-anthropological paradigm of "the gift" is generally left implicit, but it was made explicit by one of the foundational thinkers of the British welfare state, Richard Titmuss, in a way that is useful for the argument that I wish to make here. Titmuss's influential study of blood donation ([1970] 1997) contrasted a system based on altruistic giving with a "market" one based on cash compensation, proposing the "gift"-based system of blood donation as a kind of paradigm for the sort of non-market, altruistic morality he believed was at the heart of the welfare state. The book has been a touchstone in a wide range of discussions about the relationship between markets and social policy (see Wilding 1976 and Busby 2004 for discussions); indeed, one recent commentator described it as "the only socialist classic of the last fifty years" (McLean 2010).

Titmuss explicitly grounded his account of blood donation in ethnographic studies of gift exchange, but he slid quickly from the anthropologists' analysis of gift-giving as interested, obligatory, and reciprocal toward a moralistic valorization of giving as a manifestation of a "biological need to help" ([1970] 1997, 279). In this, he misunderstood the anthropological literature by which he claimed to be inspired (as has been noted by those few anthropologists who have entered this debate [see Douglas 1971; Leach 1971; Busby 2004]). But he also erred, perhaps more fundamentally, in seeing "the gift" as an encompassing category for the whole domain of non-market sociality, merging small-scale, kinship-based systems of reciprocity with kindness to strangers and state welfare and social service institutions, all under the sign of "the social." As he once wrote, "the grant of the gift or unilateral transfer . . . is the distinguishing mark of the social (in policy and administration) just as exchange or bilateral transfer is a mark of the economic" (cited in Paul Wilding 1976, 147). For anthropologists, of course (or at least for those who are careful about their analytics), the gift has never been thought to capture the whole of non-market sociality any more than it has been seen to be opposed to exchange. But this has not prevented a certain image of "the gift" from providing a key point of imaginative reference for understanding what is happening when a poor person receives a social payment.

Perhaps anthropology can furnish a more suitable concept. Students of non-market systems of distribution, from Bronislaw Malinowski to Elinor Ostrom, have documented the existence of complex systems for the allocation of resources or valued assets to which an entire collectivity is understood to have rights (of access, use, or consumption). These systems, being governed by intricate social rules, are never a matter of free and unfettered use of "the common" (as is still sometimes imagined), but neither are they well conceived in terms of gift exchange. Rather, they provide ways of answering distributive questions (who gets what) in ways that typically have little to do with either market or gift exchange but rest instead on the principle of allowing to each a proper or rightful share. When chiefs lay down rules (as they have historically done all across southern Africa) governing the use of pasture land for grazing, for instance, or when a hunter returns with his prey and proceeds to allocate the meat to a range of others, the key dynamic is not gift and return but the proper and just division of a whole to which all have a claim.

Sharing has long been identified by anthropologists as a key feature of human sociality, especially within small groups. It was once common to assimilate these practices of sharing within the frame of reciprocity (e.g., Sahlins's "generalized reciprocity" [1974]), but more recent scholarship is adamant that (in Woodburn's fine phrase [1998]), "sharing is not a form of exchange." Attention to what Peterson (1993) has termed "demand sharing," in particular, has illuminated the need both to distinguish processes of allocation from the giving of gifts and to take note of the gap between Western ideas of sharing as a form of generosity and practices that in actuality operate according to another logic altogether.

In a revealing overview of sharing in foraging societies,[22] Woodburn (1998) insists that the much-discussed sharing of meat in these societies is organized not around gifts or exchanges but rather the aggressive demands of those who receive shares. "We often think of sharing as deriving from generosity. The emphasis in these societies is quite different. Shares are asked for, even demanded" (1998, 49). What we see as "donation," he points out, is in fact obligatory, and recipients feel themselves to be fully entitled to the meat they receive. Nor is there any expectation of reciprocity (men who never hunt, he notes, also receive meat, and this does not in any way affect their entitlement). The hunter who shares the meat is neither celebrated nor thanked, and in fact has little choice over who will receive the meat, which has to be given to everyone in the camp. Thomas Widlok has recently expanded this account, noting that "the ethnographic record shows that sharing takes place not only under conditions of scarcity, and that it typically takes the form of demand sharing rather than apparently generous gift-giving" (2012, 188). In contrast to gift exchange, sharing "is typically unceremonial" and is characteristically initiated by recipients, who "may be critical rather than grateful ('insulting the meat,' 'accusing the hunter')" (2012, 189).

Richard Grinker, in his work on forager-farmer interactions in what is today the Democratic Republic of the Congo (1994), has also noted the error of imposing an exchange model on processes of sharing. When Efe hunters come into farming villages with meat and other goods they have obtained from the forest, they transfer a portion of these goods to Lese farmers, with the farmers in this way obtaining meat and other valued forest goods, while the hunters take away grain and other agricultural products. But what Western observers have generally seen as an obvious situation of exchange or "barter" is in fact described by the participants very differently. Each hunter is linked to a family of farmers via shared membership in a "house," and the goods of both field and forest are understood to properly belong to the house as a whole. They must, therefore, be divided among its members. The process is described *not* as an exchange but by using a verb that refers principally to sharing or division; the rearrangement of goods is understood as a division or distribution of a commonly owned whole into shares. As Grinker puts it "those things circulated are transferred between people *who already have rights in them*. . . . The Lese-Efe relationship is founded not on exchange or purchase but rather on the distribution of common and shared goods" (1994, 133, 134).

Dividing a resource rightfully owned by a group into appropriate shares is not a process unique to foraging societies. As noted in chapter 1, the rightful share is also a very familiar part of modern capitalist societies, and corporate capitalism is in fact built not on "private property" (as is often ideologically insisted) but on property held in common by a membership group (a corporation), property which is carefully divided into shares. Indeed, given the prominence of the cultural and legal form of "the share" in modern corporate capitalism, the question our societies face is not really whether we will cooperate and share as members of groups or instead compete as individuals; it is who will have shares, who will be members of what corporate groups, and how will shares and dividends be divided.[23]

Given all this, perhaps the paradigm of the gift is the wrong place to start in thinking about social transfers. What if a poor person could receive a distributive payment neither as a reciprocal exchange for labor (wages) or good conduct (the premise of conditional cash transfers) nor as an unreciprocated gift (assistance, charity, a helping hand) but instead as a share, a rightful allocation due to a rightful owner?[24] At a stroke, many of the most troubling problems of social distribution vanish—stigma, humiliation, shame, the lack of self-worth associated with getting "something for nothing," and so on.[25] In fact, if payments can be conceived as rightful shares—that is, as allocations properly due to rightful owners—then there is no expectation of a return, no debt, and no shame. No one is giving anyone anything. One is simply receiving one's own share of one's own property. Is there any evidence that such a reconceptualization of social payments is under way? Let us consider some southern African material and particularly the Namibian basic income movement, which is a key case.

A Society of Sharing? Social Payments as Ownership Shares

The discussion so far suggests that a terminological caution may be in order. To speak of cash transfers as "aid," "grants," and so on is to impose a model in which property rights are understood in a very particular way. In this context, it is interesting that social policy experts around the world increasingly eschew the language of "aid" and "assistance" in favor of more neutral terms such as "social payment" or "cash transfer." We should take such terminological shifts seriously (in state bureaucracies no less than in the rainforest, the anthropologist should respect local uses). For there is, in such new languages of the social, a significant kind of minimalism. Against the rich particularity and personality of the generous gift, here we speak of simply "transferring" a sum from one account to another; neither asymmetrical assistance nor symmetrical exchange is implied. As in the systems of sharing discussed by Widlok, in the new world of cash transfers "both giver and recipient de-emphasize the position of giver and receiver" (Widlok 2012, 189).

In fact, what a social "transfer" really is today seems to be up for grabs. In some very substantial measure, of course, it still means "social assistance," with continuing connotations of charity, compassion for the unfortunate, and so on. The new language of "transfers" here competes with a still very vital older regional language of "grants" (which, the term implies, must be the work of a generous grantor). But there are also alternative conceptions at play. One classical anthropological diagnostic for distinguishing a share from a gift is that the response to a share may be critical rather than grateful (Widlok 2012, 189) and involve practices of complaint or derision such as "insulting the meat." There may be something of this in the social practices of receiving pensions and grants. From the anecdotal material I have managed to collect, at least, it seems that at the concrete occasions of distribution (when pensions and grants are received from government pay points), neither expressions of gratitude nor praise poems to the benevolent state are particularly prominent. Instead, the complaint is that the payments are too small, the government is stingy, there are administrative problems, the queries are too long, and so on. The "meat" is insulted, not praised. We may detect a hint here that social payments may be being seen (at least by some) not as gifts for which one should feel grateful but as something that one has coming—something that is delivered to you because it is your due.[26]

The most fully developed elaboration of the idea of social transfers as rightful shares, however, comes from Namibia. There, the strong language of ownership that one sees in discussions around the nationalization of minerals and land has also started to appear in at least some sorts of claims for social payments. In recent years, a vigorous campaign has been conducted for a basic income grant (BIG)—a minimum monthly state payment of N$100,[27] to be paid to each and every Namibian without condition or qualification. The campaign is innovative and interesting in a number of ways, as I have discussed at some length elsewhere (see Ferguson 2007, 2010; chapter 1 of this book). But my interest in it here is in the way arguments promoting it have invoked both a duty to share, on the part of the state, and a conviction that ordinary Namibians have a very specific and concrete sort of right "to share in the country's wealth." Like Julius Malema, but in a very different context, BIG proponents insist that citizens are also owners. For this reason, a social payment such as a basic income grant must be understood not as aid, charity, "safety net," or even "social wage" but as a rightful share—a share of what already, by rights, belongs to each Namibian: "the country's wealth."

Most bluntly, as one BIG activist put it, The state must take from the rich and support the poor. That is the model of sharing that we are proposing." In "a country that is considered the most unequal in the world," he argued, "that is the way to go"—to have the state intervene "to create a society of sharing." But this is not just a vague appeal for generosity. Instead, it is linked to specific distributive demands, grounded in specific moral and political arguments. Analysis of discussions about poverty, inequality, and social policy in Namibia reveals that there are several different models for sharing in play.

One such model is the familiar idea of the nation as a kind of family, and of a state duty to care for its people in the same way that a parent has a duty to care for a child. Leaders of the Namibian BIG campaign, for instance, spoke of a duty to care for the poor and unemployed specifically as a duty to care for "economic orphans," who should no more be ignored than other sorts of orphans. They also sometimes styled such a model of care as distinctively "African," invoking the African ideal of ubuntu (humanity) in ways that recall earlier "African socialist" arguments for "the African extended family" as a basis for modern socialist solidarities (see, e.g., Nyerere 1968).[28]

A second model for sharing is a specifically Christian one. BIG leaders often turn to the example of Christ in explaining the need for national-level sharing. This has especially been true of BIG activists associated with the Evangelical Lutheran Church in Namibia (which has from the start provided key institutional support for the BIG campaign in Namibia). When the longtime leader of the church, Bishop Zephania Kameeta, makes public arguments for the basic income grant, for instance, he often tells the biblical story of "the loaves and the fishes," explaining that the "miracle" that had enabled all to be fed was simply the act of sharing. The state, and those who lead it, must take Christ as their example by sharing out the national "loaves and fishes" to those in need. As with appeals to the-nation-as-family, such arguments have some commonalities with principles of solidarity that have been at the core of many Northern welfare states (especially in the "Christian Democratic" tradition, as Esping-Andersen [1990] has pointed out). But it is noteworthy that what is called for here is not the horizontal, comradely solidarity of the social democratic working man (cf. chapter 2). Instead, the solidarity envisaged in explicitly Christian arguments for the BIG is both distributive and reparative, invoking specifically the asymmetrical responsibilities of the rich toward the poor. A poster (with matching bumper sticker) distributed in support of the Namibian BIG depicts a young black Namibian child holding a Namibian $100 bill. Under the photo appear the words "Are you ready to share?" Clearly, the appeal here is to a certain ideal of sharing, but what is more striking is the fact that the appeal is directed not toward those who might benefit from receiving the grant ("Are you ready to receive your share?") but rather toward those who might be asked to pay for it ("Are you ready to share?"). Duty here is placed before right, and the key theme is that sharing must be understood as both obligation and virtue.[29]

But there is yet another model of sharing that is at work here. This model is perhaps less familiar than the first two, and it is, for my purposes here, the one that is most interesting. That is a model of sharing based on ownership (ownership precisely of a share). Here, the question of mineral resources and the rightful distribution of the wealth that they produce has been absolutely central. In a recent interview, for instance, one activist insisted that the national liberation struggle in Namibia was not yet complete, since that struggle had always been a struggle for a Namibia "where every Namibian has a decent life, a decent living." What is more, the country "*can afford* to give every Namibian a decent living because of the natural resources that we have been blessed with, the wealth we are generating." Social assistance, in the form of a basic income grant, is thus in the first instance a matter of *sharing* what is properly a national birthright. And this, he insisted, is not just a matter of sympathy, or even of good policy; it is a matter of right. "We argue that it is not just a benefit that people should get, but it's also a right that they should enjoy as citizens of this country."

Such claims regularly occur in the vigorous discussions over the BIG in the Namibian public sphere, as well. Letters written to the leading daily newspaper, for instance, illustrate well both the general link between social payments and a rightful share of mineral wealth and the specific theme of inheritance or birthright. One recent letter to the editor of the national daily newspaper, for instance, insisted that Namibia's rich resources should provide "a decent living for each of its citizens." For that reason, "it is the basic right of each Namibian to directly benefit from the resources of this country and in the same way, BIG is every citizen's basic right."[30] Another insisted on the BIG as part of a package of policies that would force the rich to give up their excessive wealth; rather than seeing the rich as people to admire or envy, the writer insisted, "We have nothing to be grateful to the rich about, in fact they should hang their heads in shame for being in that position."[31] A third insisted that "the problem is not that there are not adequate resources to go around for everyone. There is enough on this earth for everyone to live a sufficient life. The real problem is that resources are not fairly distributed. That is the main issue. It is all about distribution!"[32] Another letter insists that a BIG is due to all ("the mere fact of being a homo sapien or, if you like a Namibian citizen, should be sufficient to qualify") because "the historical situation is that the capitalist economy now only needs a small number of people in full-time employment." Those who object to giving money to people who do not work, the letter's authors insist, should look around and observe "the off-spring of the rich in Namibia. . . . They certainly do not work for a living. They inherit the wealth and do not have to lift a finger. Most of the wealth today is transferred through inheritance. This is one of the main reasons why the ideology of work is so false."[33]

Perhaps the most prominent public advocate of the grant, Bishop Kameeta, directly links the idea of basic income to a notion of citizenship rooted both in a moral model of "the house" and in a rightful entitlement to a material share of national wealth. Thanks to its rich mineral resources, he noted in an interview, Namibia as a country is rich. "We are living in a mansion. We are living in a villa!" But if a nation is a house, citizenship means being "part of the house. And if only some of the children are eating in the house, and some are starving, I think that is not fair!"

"What does citizenship mean?" the bishop asks. "Does it mean—well, you must be proud that you have an identity document? But that's more helpful to the police, to locate where you are!" Instead, "let citizenship not start with the official documents, but start with the sharing of the re-sources. . . . Citizenship should mean that I partake in the wealth of the country!"

Here it is possible to observe a kind of convergence, in which the mus-cular assertions of ownership that we see in Julius Malema-style resource nationalism are being harnessed to concrete and universalistic distribu-tive claims, claims that are made both plausible and practical by the new cash transfer apparatuses that deliver existing forms of social assistance. And while I have tried to illustrate this sort of reasoning by dwelling on one especially clear case (the recent Namibian BIG campaign), I empha-size that the idea that universalistic cash payments might be reconcep-tualized as a kind of share of a collectively owned mineral wealth is not unique to Namibia. Indeed, a recently launched region-wide campaign argues for a basic income grant scheme that would be funded by levies on mineral extraction, covering the entire Southern African Development Community. The campaign's argument begins by noting the regional fact of "poverty alongside mineral wealth" together with "evidence from countries such as India and Brazil" showing the effectiveness of cash transfers in fighting poverty and then seeks to mobilize support for uni-versal basic income precisely under the banner of the rightful share. (The slogan emblazoned on the campaign's logo reads as follows: "Our Right—Our Wealth—Our Share.")[34]

Conclusion: Toward a Politics of the Rightful Share

In all this, it may be possible to detect an emergent politics. Such a poli-tics is based on a kind of claim-making that involves neither a compen-sation for work nor an appeal for "help" but rather a sense of rightful entitlement to an income that is tied neither to labor nor to any sort of disability or incapacity. Like the claims to land discussed earlier, such claims are rooted less in legal rights, narrowly understood, than in a pow-erful encompassing sense of righteousness—a conception that, as noted in chapter 1, relies less on the liberal idea of rights "held" by individuals than on the principle (more moral than legal) that material distributions must answer to some idea of the proper, of the just, of the "rightful." At the most fundamental level, such distributive claims do not take the form of exchanges at all (neither market nor gift) but instead something more like demand sharing—a righteous claim for a due and proper share grounded in nothing more than membership (in a national collectivity) or even simply presence (cf. Widlok 2012; I return to the theme of "presence" in the book's conclusion). It is this (emergent, only partially realized) politics that I term the politics of the rightful share, and my claim is that, in a range of societies (especially where wage labor has lost the political and economic centrality it once had), it may be becoming a much more prominent and important form of political aspiration.

How are we to assess the potential of such a politics of the rightful share? Let us begin by considering where (and why) claims to rightful shares are politically potent and do manage to gain some traction. As noted in chapter 1, it seems to be the case that share-reasoning is most readily accepted when it comes to mineral wealth.[35] Why is this? If a small farmer works hard to grow a modest agricultural crop on some little patch of land, we readily accept the idea that the goods so produced belong to him or her, and not to us all collectively. But if the same farmer finds oil on that piece of land, installs a few cheap pumps, and starts earning billions, we easily conclude that at least some share of the wealth is or ought to be common. Why? Because, I think, the value is so out of proportion to the effort; in some sense, we recognize that the value was "already there"—stumbled upon, not created, by the farmer.[36] Immense value, that is, here emerges not from labor, but fabulously, almost magically, as if from nowhere.[37]

But mineral extraction is not the only place where the proportionality of wealth to effort we see in the case of the small farmer is absent; indeed, a disconnection of accumulation from such things as work, effort, and duration has been noted to be a distinguishing feature of the current era of "casino capitalism" (Strange 1997; Comaroff and Comaroff 2000). In fact, the morality of the unearned oil bonanza is not easily distinguished from similar "gushers" that nowadays spray torrents of money out of hedge funds, currency speculation, and executive compensation agreements. But, as pointed out in chapter 1, the same is true, in a different way, even of such pillars of the "real economy" as manufacturing, at least at the most up-to-date and capital-intensive end of things. In fact, a high-tech factory is today not so different from an oil rig—a huge piece of capital investment that, once in place, pumps out unimaginable amounts of valuable stuff with only small amounts of supervisory labor. The distributive claims that are plausible for mineral wealth thus become increasingly plausible for other forms of wealth as well—for they, too, now seem to appear fabulously, magically, as if from nowhere.

Distributive claims of this kind (i.e., grounded in membership rather than labor or misfortune) are, I have suggested, increasingly evident in certain new domains of social policy, both in southern Africa and internationally (the shifting international scene is briefly discussed in the book's conclusion). The legitimacy of such claims is a key theme, too, in much contemporary radical social thought, especially in a recent revitalization of thinking about what is an old topic for socialism: "the commons." David Harvey, of course, has in recent years revisited Marx's old discussion of "primitive accumulation," reminding us that the accumulation of capital via the appropriation of property formerly held in common is not an "original sin" that occurs at the birth of capitalism but a continuous process that carries through to the present as commonly held resources continue to be subject to private appropriation, especially in the latest, "neoliberal" round of capitalist restructuring (Harvey 2005). But more interesting for my purposes here are lines of thought that lie outside of the well-rehearsed verities of Harvey's traditional (and production-centered) Marxism and derive instead from alternative formulations of socialism that give a greater place to distribution—formulations to which it may be time to return. As discussed in chapter 1, for instance, the anarcho-communist Peter Kropotkin founded his critique of capitalism not on arguments about labor and production but on a fundamentally distributive claim—the claim that society's wealth properly belongs to all. Every member of modern industrial society, he noted, benefits from "an immense capital accumulated by those who have gone before him" ([1892] 1995, 11). And among those wealth-creating predecessors, he paid special attention to poor and working people and their sufferings: "Whole generations, that lived and died in misery, oppressed and ill-treated by their masters, and worn out by toil, have handed on this immense inheritance" ([1892] 1995, 14). Yet the descendants of those who paid this terrible price, instead of being treated as the inheritors of a vast richness, are denied any property rights at all. For all the vast wealth produced by modern railways, for instance, "if the children of those who perished by the thousands while excavating the railway cuttings and tunnels were to assemble one day, crowding in their rags and hunger, to demand bread from the shareholders, they would be met with bayonets and grapeshot" ([1892] 1995, 17).[38]

Importantly, Kropotkin does not say that such a person deserves a share of wealth because he or she works a certain amount. On the contrary, the entire production apparatus must be treated as a single, common inheritance. I therefore deserve a share of production not because I labor but because I own (via inheritance) a share of the entire production apparatus. Kropotkin appeals to labor, to be sure, but not just the labor of the present. Instead, it is past labor that is most fundamentally the source of the productive apparatus that we all inherit, so the heritage of labor is as important as its current condition. What is more, he grounds the right to a common inheritance not just in a long, shared history of work but equally in other historical accumulations such as inventions as well as forms of suffering, deprivation, and bloodshed (cf. Moore 2005). In this broad panorama, which encompasses the whole history of all of mankind, there can be no accounting of who produced how much or whose suffering was greater; the only practical as well as ethical conclusion is, as he famously put it, "All belongs to all" ([1892] 1995), 19).

More recently, autonomists have revitalized this old tradition of theorizing about "the common." Thus Michael Hardt (building on Virno 2004) has argued that value is really produced not by labor in the narrow sense but by society as a whole (2000). For instance, when an advertising campaign makes money using a hip-hop-themed jingle, where does the value originate? Not, he suggests, in the labor of the individual advertising employee, who is just repackaging creative musical ideas heard at a club the previous night—but not either in the individual performance of the hip-hop artist at the club (who has likewise borrowed and sampled from the prior creativity of others). It is society as a whole that produces such value, and society as a whole thus has a claim to appropriate the fruits of such production (2000, 27). (Indeed, Antonio Negri has recently suggested that, given the centrality of such social creativity in generating value today, the metropolis might properly take the place that the factory held for Marx as a principal site of struggle [Negri 2008, 211–30].) The key claim here belongs not to the wage laborers but to the members of society, the true originators of economic value; it is society as a whole, through the entirety of social life, that collectively produces wealth.[39] As in the case of Kropotkin, such arguments rooting value in the whole social process mean that rightful distribution cannot be reckoned as an exchange for labor and instead makes sense only on the scale of "society as a whole," which Hardt reckons in global terms (since "global society as a whole produces wealth collectively" [2000, 27]). As in the Namibian basic income grant campaign, an attentiveness to the social foundations and origins of wealth here grounds a specific argument for a guaranteed income independent of labor (Hardt 2000). Such attention to the claims of the "common" has also informed recent critical debates in South Africa, where specific struggles around service provision, labor, and natural resources have been linked to arguments for basic income (see, from a range of points of view, Tribe of Moles 2011; Barchiesi 2012; Bond 2012, 2013; Sharife and Bond 2013).

Here, too, we may also observe a new role emerging for the old idea of rent as a fundamental form of distribution. Already at the end of the eighteenth century, Thomas Paine had argued for universal cash payments as a "ground-rent" paid to owners (since the entire earth was properly, in his view, "the common property of the human race" [1830, 402–3]). The idea has some currency today, as sentiments of an (often vaguely defined) popular national ownership have risen to prominence even as labor provides an increasingly unreliable foundation for distributive claims. Brazil's campaign for basic income, for instance, is actually termed a demand for "basic rent" (*renta basica*)—a terminological nicety that, as Slavoj Žižek (2010, 233) has recently argued, should be taken very seriously. In a classical political economy, David Ricardo famously proposed to investigate how wealth is divided among the "three classes of the community": laborer, capitalist, and landowner. While some have implausibly sought to restore an economic role to those pushed out of the role of laborer by re-labeling them as micro-capitalists (e.g., DeSoto 2003), a demand for *renta basica* proposes a more convincing alternative solution, by reconceiving even those most marginalized from the circuits of labor and capital as *landowners* (in fact, the real owners of the entire country), who by virtue of such ownership are due, precisely, the payment of a rent. Such a formulation of course might also find some resonance with the highly contested southern African politics of land ownership, in which Julius Malema (as noted above) mischievously asks whites in South Africa how much land they brought with them from Europe, while the specter of Zimbabwe-style direct action land-occupation hangs over private landholding across the region.

It is not my purpose to attempt to assess or arbitrate these debates here. My intention, rather, is simply to point to their existence and to note that the intersection of new kinds of welfare states with new kinds of thinking about distribution has created a powerful conjunctural moment, one that I would like to suggest is as full of possibilities as it is of dangers.

My claim, in calling attention to these new developments, is not that they are unequivocally wonderful or that they solve all of our problems but only that they are important, and that they may be opening possibilities for new kinds of politics. In particular, I suggest that the new welfare states of the global South and the new kinds of political claim-making that are emerging within them may contain two linked potentialities. One is the possibility that the considerable political energies activated by Julius Malema's sort of resource nationalism might, under the conditions of the new welfare states, manage to find more effective outlets than old-style demands for nationalization. And the second is that programs of cash transfers might conceivably, in the years to come, be expanded and developed in ways that would take them far beyond the merely ameliorative and largely apolitical aims that govern current schemes and become instead sites for the development of a potent new distributive politics.

How much difference would this make? Potentially, a lot. Consider the difference between receiving "assistance" and receiving an ownership share, what I have here called a "rightful" share. What would change? First of all, social payments would become accessible to a much broader set of recipients (including able-bodied eighteen- to fifty-nine-year olds), casting aside age-old presumptions about who "deserves" to receive payments and severing the link between labor and income in a quite fundamental way. Equally important, those already receiving payments would also see a fundamental change, in that even an unchanged payment would bring with it a very different social significance. Framed as a rightful share, a transfer might bring with it not just some modest material resources but a new and powerful social identity: owner.

"The people shall share in the country's wealth!" The key unanswered question here has always been how—how a wealth of which all ought to have at least some share *can* in fact be meaningfully shared. Proponents of Malema-style nationalization have never managed to supply an adequate answer to that, and neither (it must be said) have socialist theorists of either the Marxian or the anarchist stripe.[40] But the intersection of a demand for rightful shares with a bureaucratic apparatus for direct payments opens up concrete new possibilities that are only now beginning to be explored. New kinds of welfare states, that is, may open up the possibility of imagining new kinds of politics—perhaps even new kinds of socialism.

Distributive claims, after all, may rest on the most compelling ethical and political rationales, but they can lead to actual distributive outcomes only to the extent that there exists an effective and universal apparatus of distribution. Without that, even the most assertive gestures of common ownership (such as nationalization) are unlikely to have genuinely distributive outcomes, as we have learned only too well. The new welfare states in places like Namibia and South Africa are in fact creating such apparatuses of distribution and thereby putting into place (unintentionally, I think) a precondition for a different kind of resource politics—one that could be socialist in a very different sense than traditional nationalization. That is hardly an assured outcome, and perhaps not even a likely one. But it is an intriguing possibility, and perhaps a hopeful point of aspiration on which to focus a new form of progressive political practice.

Conclusion.
What Next for Distributive Politics?

In the preceding chapters, I have reflected on the way that non-labor-based distributive allocations have come to play a significantly expanded role in a southern African context of entrenched and structural mass unemployment. But this is not only a southern African story. A worldwide set of developments has created massive new waves of urbanization even as the demand for low-skilled and manual labor has sharply eroded. In a host of different empirical sites spread across the far corners of the world map, those leaving the agricultural sector have found no industrial jobs awaiting them, while even communities formerly provisioned by labor have been obliged to learn the ways of what Michael Denning (2010) has termed "wageless life." When Guy Standing (2002, 7) declares "the end of the century of labouring man," we may find him guilty of a certain exaggeration, but any observer of the contemporary global political economy will recognize that his words speak to a certain reality.

It was long a fundamental assumption, shared by perspectives as different as Marxism-Leninism and modernization theory, that as poor, rural folk around the world exited subsistence agriculture, they would enter a new world within which wage labor would provide the normal form of distribution. Wages received by workers would now provide livelihoods for a new "industrial man," enabling at the same time new forms of consumption (thus the paradigmatic "Fordist" image of the worker/consumer who earns enough in wages to buy the cars he produces). Even in twentieth-century Europe, of course, waged employment was never really universalized in the way that many ideal-typical accounts would suggest (Yanagisako 2012), but that did not prevent wage labor from being anticipated, all across the world, as the "normal" modality of distribution for what was imagined to be a modern urban way of life in the making. In recent years, however, this vision has lost conviction, as new social groups lacking access to both land and regular employment have emerged, often "getting by" via the sorts of improvised livelihoods analyzed in chapter 3. In southern Africa, this has been driven by a continued exit from agriculture, but in the absence of what was long imagined as an "industrial revolution" (cf. Ferguson 1999) that would drive it. Instead, we have seen a process of, as Andries du Toit and David Neves (2007, 1) have put it, "simultaneous monetization, de-agrarianization, and de-industrialization." Under such circumstances, wage labor appears less and less capable of serving as a universal relay either between production and consumption or between capital and "the masses." Instead, regimes around the globe struggle to accommodate new populations (urban and rural alike) whose livelihoods are often starkly disconnected from both agriculture and wage labor.

As I have noted, such processes are hardly unique to Africa.[1] But there is a case to be made that the region may be serving as something of a pioneer here. While Africa has long been imagined as a developmental laggard, playing "catch-up," Jean and John Comaroff (2011) have recently suggested that we might better think of Africa as leading the way in certain domains. This may be one such area. Certainly, across the continent we have seen a remarkable pioneering of new livelihoods based neither on agriculture nor wage labor. And in southern Africa in particular, as I have emphasized, we have also witnessed the rising salience of state programs of direct distribution. Let there be no misunderstanding: my claim here is not that wage labor has somehow now become obsolete or unimportant (in Africa or anywhere else). The claim is only that it is becoming increasingly evident that such labor cannot fulfill the daunting distributive role that has so often been imagined for it—that it does not, and in the foreseeable future will not, in fact, deliver the distributive goods for large and (in many world regions) increasing proportions of the population.[2]

What other modes of distribution exist beyond wages and other sorts of market exchanges of labor? I have highlighted here state transfers associated with pensions and grants, as well as what I have termed the "distributive labor" of the so-called informal economy. But in concluding, I wish to go beyond this by briefly situating southern African distributive politics in a broader field of emerging distributive claims. I will very briefly review a range of innovative or experimental new ways of conceiving, applying, and justifying programs of direct non-market distribution. Some of these already exist in some form, while others are at this point only imagined or proposed. But all of them go in some significant way beyond existing systems of informal mutualities and state-provided social assistance to conventionally "dependent" categories such as children, the elderly, the disabled, or the temporarily unemployed.

The first example, which I have already discussed at some length, is the campaign for basic income. This is not a new idea and in fact has a surprisingly long and interesting history (as briefly noted in chapter 6).[3] Indeed, quite serious political campaigns had been waged over it (notably in Europe) long before it was ever raised as an issue in southern Africa.[4] But recent years have seen increasing interest in basic income, in the context not of what were not so long ago imagined as the "affluent societies" of the global North but of mass poverty and unemployment in the global South. A recent book (Murray and Pateman 2012) reviews some of the key basic income campaigns and documents the rising worldwide interest in the idea, and a scholarly journal (*Basic Income Studies*) is now devoted to documenting and analyzing the issue. Pilot basic income projects have recently been conducted and favorably evaluated in Namibia and India (Haarmann et al. 2009; Standing 2013), while significant headway has been made on the creation of nationwide programs in countries as different as Brazil and Iran (as discussed briefly below). A campaign for a region-wide basic income grant (BIG) has recently been launched for the entire southern African region (as discussed in the previous chapter), while a recent national campaign in Switzerland (culminating in a 2015 national referendum) shows the continuing attractions of basic income in the North as well. Followers of contemporary politics on the Left, meanwhile, will not have failed to notice the role that various versions of basic or "citizen's" income today play in discussions of radical politics. (Indeed, the philosopher Slavoj Žižek has recently described basic income as "arguably the Left's only original economic idea of the last few decades" [2010, 233].)

But our conception of the scope of the emerging new politics of distribution is altogether too narrow if we focus only on basic income. Indeed, recent years have seen a profusion of other sorts of policies, campaigns, and movements that also turn on direct distribution in the form of cash payment. And here, as I have suggested, the most fundamental new development may not be simply the payment of cash transfers but the development of new *grounds* for justifying or authorizing such distributive claims. Labor is still a crucial ground for distributive claims, to be sure, but one may also increasingly observe other sorts of reasoning grounding the allocation of distributive payments.

One such ground is provided in situations of humanitarian and emergency relief. A number of authors have noted the expanded role that humanitarian intervention plays in the contemporary world (see, e.g., Feldman and Ticktin 2010; Bornstein and Redfield 2011; Barnett 2013). In part this has meant that the grounds on which certain sorts of distributions of both care and material provisioning are made has shifted. As Didier Fassin (2011) has noted, in contexts of humanitarian care, distributions are often based not on the rights of nation-state citizens but on the compassion felt for those who suffer, especially those whose suffering is especially visible or "worthy." Insofar as such compassion-based distributions involve public claims, these are likely to depend, as Andrea Muehlebach (2012, 134) has put it, "on visceral feelings that wax and wane rather than on the sureties of social citizenship." At the same time, however, it seems significant that humanitarian interventions too are today caught up in the recent worldwide enthusiasm for cash transfers. As I have discussed elsewhere (Ferguson 2010), programs providing cash transfers in situations of food deficit and emergency relief have developed innovative ways of replacing paternalistic gifts of in-kind goods with cash incomes that recipients can use to cover a broad range of needs, taking advantage of their intimate knowledge of their own situations. As in the other systems of social protection that I have analyzed, the shift to cash payments here entails both a willingness to provide a need-based income that is independent of labor and a recognition that "the poor" may be trusted to look after their own best interests via their expenditure decisions.

Similar new developments can be observed in the world of philanthropic giving. Here, the payment of unconditional cash transfers has emerged as one of the "big new ideas" of recent years. A rising new organization, Give-

Directly, for instance, insists that the most effective, and even the most "democratic," form of philanthropy takes the form of unconditional cash transfers. Its programs therefore seek to link the donations of would-be helpers of the poor to particular households that are provided with small but steady no-strings-attached monthly incomes.[5] Such programs claim "robust" evidence of their effectiveness (in the form of randomized clinical trials) and respond to a new emphasis on transparency and accountability in philanthropy (with donors now seeking "hard evidence" that interventions are really "moving the needle" in measurable ways). For the most part, this is less a matter of the grounds for the allocation than of the technical adequacy and programmatic effectiveness of different ways of "giving." Unconditional cash transfers are here seen as simply the most effective and economical means to achieve concrete and measurable anti-poverty results. But in other domains, we have also seen surprising new arguments around "giving" to the poor that go directly to the question of the justification for such allocations. Pope Francis, for instance, has recently argued that the rich not only should, but (in Christian ethical terms) must "help, respect and promote the poor" via a "generous solidarity," with such solidarity understood as something like the acknowledgment of a property right: the decision of the rich to give generously, in his account, is simply "the decision to restore to the poor what belongs to them." In support of this argument, he cites the words of an early Christian father, Saint John Chrysostom: "Not to share one's wealth with the poor is to steal from them and to take away their livelihood. It is not our own goods which we hold, but theirs."[6] As in the Namibian arguments around basic income that I analyzed in the previous chapter, here one finds an argument that a transfer to the poor is both righteous and in accordance with a truer underlying state of ownership ("it is not our own goods which we hold, but theirs"). A similar position has recently been developed by Lucy Allais (2012), who concludes her analysis of Immanuel Kant's writings on begging by suggesting that it is possible to derive from them an alternative notion of charity, in which people given money after having been wronged by an unjust division of power "are only being given back what is rightfully theirs," "getting back a small amount of what they in fact have a right to." Perhaps, she concludes, " 'returning' is a better word than 'giving' here" (2012, 6–7).

A quite different sort of new "ground" for certain sorts of distribution appears in the rapidly expanding domain of the medical. Ramah McKay

(2010), for instance, has recently analyzed a complex set of interventions in Mozambique that amount, in her terms, to a kind of "post-social welfare." These include programs not only for the delivery of health care in the narrow sense but also things like the provision of minimum food entitlements. But this occurs in the guise of a medical ("nutrition") intervention and via institutional means that rely on NGOs and transnational foundations (such as the Gates Foundation) as much as on the national state. Here we may observe concrete forms of distribution that are not linked to participation in wage labor and that look in some respects like traditional "social assistance." But, as Tobias Rees points out (2014), this and other "global health" initiatives now being put in place in southern Africa and beyond by powerful transnational institutions such as the Gates Foundation seek to support not so much the members of a society as the members of a species ("humanity"), with no necessary regard for the nation-state boundaries that have traditionally defined "social" responsibilities of care. Again, we may be able to detect both a new rationality and a new ground for certain forms both of care and of material distribution.

Another sort of distributive principle is emerging around policy discussions of natural resources and the so-called resource curse—a shorthand way of referencing the fact that the wealth that comes from the exploitation of natural (and especially mineral) resources in poor countries is often diverted by governmental elites and typically fails to do much to elevate the positions of the great mass of ordinary citizens. Here, a bold set of policy proposals has recently emerged from the Center for Global Development (a Washington, D.C., think tank), urging that some major portion of the income from mineral extraction should be simply transferred directly to citizens in the form of cash transfers. Why, they ask, must mineral rents be swallowed up by national governments, when it would instead be possible "to distribute resource revenues directly to the true owners: citizens themselves." This is less of a leap of faith than it might seem, they suggest, since many countries already in fact distribute such rents to their populations—"just doing it badly via inefficient employment schemes or subsidies" (Moss 2012, 2). They acknowledge the existence of strong political obstacles, in that "politicians do not readily give up control over resource revenues," but they note that some programs already exist linking cash transfers directly to mineral income (including child care grants in Mongolia, elderly pensions in Bolivia, and the Alaska

Permanent Fund in the United States [Moss 2012, 3; on the Alaska case, see Widerquist and Howard 2012]). The idea has recently been elaborated by two World Bank economists (Devarajan and Giugale 2013).[7]

A related proposal has been made with respect to the problem of climate change and carbon emissions. While a carbon tax is generally regarded by economists as the preferred mechanism for reducing carbon emissions, those concerned with equity and social justice point out that a simple tax would disproportionately hurt the poor while allowing the richest to pollute at will. In response, a leading global warming activist, James Hansen, has proposed a scheme he calls "fee and dividend."[8] This would impose a steep tax on carbon, but remit *all* of the revenues thus raised in the form of equal cash payments to citizens. Here, low-income people would receive a significant new source of income, while strong incentives would both punish those producing large amounts of greenhouse gases *and* positively reward those who produce little. South African activists have made related proposals suggesting that environmental payments made under the United Nations "Reducing Emissions from Deforestation and Forest Degradation" (REDD) scheme might be used to provide basic income in the receiving countries (Sharife and Bond 2013). Here payment is understood as grounded in a principle of "climate justice," and receipt of a distributive payment is warranted not by labor but by national or ecological membership.

The point of this all-too-brief review is only to say that something is in the air with respect to the grounds and rationalities of distribution—or, to put it rather more precisely, many things are in the air. This leads to a sense of possibility about the present conjuncture, in which it seems that many are beginning to think in new ways about how the distributive claims of those excluded from a nostalgically recalled world of "decent jobs" can be realistically posed in terms of direct distribution. An old presumption has long had it that "handouts" and "welfare" must play a quietistic or even demobilizing role and therefore ultimately be linked to a conservative politics. But here we see the prospect of various forms of direct distribution linked to new kinds of arguments, and new kinds of claims, that hint at quite fundamentally different sorts of politics than those usually associated with "social assistance." Where, then, might the new sorts of distributive claims I have traced here lead, and how radical a challenge might such political claims pose to the status quo?

A Radical Politics?

Thinkers on the Left have not failed to notice the increasing displacement of labor and the diminished centrality, in so many settings, of formal-sector employment. But the most common response has not been (as advocated here) to give a greater analytical and political place to non-labor-based forms of distribution but instead to attend to the implications of this shift for labor itself, via a new attention to "precarity."[9] This allows the acknowledgment of a fundamental shift, even while keeping the focus on production and labor (even if it is now "immaterial labor") and continuing to see distributive claims as ultimately founded in contributions to production.[10] Through this maneuver, it is possible to posit an epochal transition to a new era, even while preserving, in a new form, the old labor- and production-centered conceptual apparatus of classical Marxism. Indeed, in some formulations of an imagined new political protagonist ("the precariat," "the multitude"), it is not difficult to detect a nostalgic yearning for some sort of new class (or class-like entity) that might take the place of the mourned vanguard proletariat of old.[11] But if we shift our focus, as I have urged, toward specifically distributive processes, we find that those who are excluded from wage labor, and who pursue what I have termed "distributed livelihoods" (chapter 3), do not much resemble any such "new class," precisely because the social relations that are constitutive of their position do not create a stable shared social and political standpoint but instead link, in the most intimate possible ways, those who have jobs and incomes with those who do not.[12] There is no reason to doubt that understanding the changing empirical conditions of labor is a vital part of the agenda for progressive thought today. But within the perspective I have been developing here, the greater challenge is to develop a radical politics rooted not in some new ("precarious") condition of labor (wasn't it always pretty precarious in most of the world?) but instead in forms of distribution grounded in principles other than labor altogether: in short, a radically distributive politics.

At some level, this would seem to be eminently logical. Distributive gains loom large in any realistic assessment of the accomplishments of radical and socialist movements in our recent past, and it is, after all, socialist-inspired forms of distribution more than those of production that are likely to form points of inspiration for today's social movements.

(It is the welfare state and the trade union, not the forced labor camp or the collectivization of agriculture, that most of us would prefer to take from the socialist tradition. Yet Marxism, the predominant form of radical social thought throughout the twentieth century, has been peculiarly ill suited to thinking through a radical distributive politics, committed as it has been to the primacy of production as a first principle and to the proletariat as history's protagonist. As I have suggested, both its devalorization of distribution and its denigration of non-productive livelihoods such as those of the "lumpen" pose major obstacles to the conceptual and theoretical tasks that we face.]

Other forms of radical thought have sometimes done better, as I suggested in chapter 6, as in Peter Kropotkin's bold arguments for the righteousness of universal distribution. Yet anarchist formulations such as Kropotkin's combined their radical insistence that "all belongs to all" with a principled hostility toward the only realistic available mechanism for achieving genuinely distributive outcomes (a state apparatus with the ability to do things like collect taxes and distribute cash payments). I have quoted at some length from Kropotkin's *The Conquest of Bread* ([1892] 1995) in the introduction and chapter 6. But it must be noted that the same text contains embarrassing extended discussions of how distribution will be organized "after the Revolution" that can only be described as sociologically very naive, wishfully imagining that a highly elaborate system for allocating goods to those in need would simply spring, fully formed, from the spontaneous will of the revolutionary masses, requiring neither a state nor indeed any sort of bureaucratic organization.[13]

Thus we are caught between a Marxism that denigrates and devalues distribution (in favor of production and labor) and an anarchism that denigrates and devalues the state and bureaucracy (in favor of spontaneity and the local). Neither can find its way to a form of politics that would combine the recognition that distribution is central (and not simply a derivative or a reflex of systems of production) with an appreciation of the political sociology that would be necessary to bring it about (within which the bureaucratic state remains a sine qua non). What might a radical contemporary politics look like if it were grounded in both a lively appreciation of the growing importance of non-labor-based forms of distribution and a strategy for turning the administrative capabilities of states more fundamentally toward that task?

I have suggested that the current conjunctural moment may be an especially auspicious time to be asking such a question. As I argued in the previous chapter, the southern African political scene today features both forceful populist demands for rightful shares independent of labor and, at the same time, sophisticated and effective "social" programs directly distributing income to citizens on a mass scale. While these discussions have remained mostly separate to date, their temporal coexistence, I have proposed, may be opening up possibilities for new sorts of distributive politics. Under these circumstances, is it conceivable that the distributive demands that have historically been channeled into things like nationalization of resources and state ownership of industries might take new and more promising forms?

The most ambitious contemporary manifestation of such a possibility, I have suggested, is found in the various campaigns for basic income. Yet as I have noted, it is not clear that the southern African BIG campaign is capable of achieving the sort of political traction that would be necessary to achieve its goals. The national BIG campaign has stalled in South Africa[14] (even if it still seems quite lively in Namibia and has recently been given new life by a region-wide campaign, as noted in chapter 6), and I have noted the limits of its current popular appeal, limits I have provisionally suggested might be linked to the relatively "thin" sort of social membership that it, in its current form, is able to offer (see chapter 5). One is also struck by the continued political power of a nostalgically productionist vision, within which an imagined return of "real jobs" for "real men" is magically conjured by skilled politicians, in what Franco Barchiesi has analyzed as "the melancholia of labor" (2011). Even in Namibia, where a pilot basic income project has been widely hailed as a great success, progress at the national level has stalled, and serious doubts have arisen about the sustainability of even the modest pilot project, lacking as it does any state support and depending instead on the uncertain funding and inconstant institutional energies and capacities of the NGO world.

Does this mean, then, that prospects for any more radical sort of distributive politics are grim? That would be much too hasty a conclusion. As intriguing as the basic income demand is, an undue preoccupation with this one modality of distributive politics (one whose promise, it must be said, remains at present almost entirely unrealized) risks remaining blind to the power and potential of other new distributive developments that exist not in some proposed future but right here and now, before our eyes. While many have seen the existing programs of grants in countries like South Africa as merely ameliorative of the worst poverty or a temporary stopgap until "real" improvement comes in the form of jobs ("until the doctor comes," as Charles Meth [2004, 24] has put it), both the scale of existing programs and certain emerging ways of thinking about them suggest that something more interesting may be going on.

In the introduction to this book, I quoted at some length a newspaper column by the South African political and cultural critic Jonny Steinberg in which he boldly asserted that it was a fantasy to suppose that the only "real solution" to widespread poverty was job creation, and argued that conditions approaching full employment are simply not on the horizon in countries like South Africa. Under such circumstances, he proposed, social grants should both be acknowledged as a necessary new form of distribution (for now and for the foreseeable future) and made universal by being expanded to cover not only children, pensioners, and the disabled but also all working-age adults, including men. In response to predictable reactions from readers who objected to "handouts" and the "dependency" they might provoke, Steinberg elaborated his views in a second column a few weeks later. While many who objected to his column seemed sure that "people need to work in order to be fully human," Steinberg suggested that such critics were clinging to an outdated worldview ("thriving working people on one side, rotting welfare recipients on the other")—one that had perhaps made some sense in Britain in the 1970s, when "full employment was a fresh memory and a living ideal," but one that "does not make sense here and now." Instead, he vigorously argued that "welfare" (in the form of social grants) encouraged "liberation, not dependence" and in fact brought to poor communities "life, not idleness." Reflecting on his extended stays in Pondoland during the time that social transfers were rapidly expanding in the early 2000s, he described the way that increased purchasing power in poor rural villages led to new enterprises, enhanced education, and even an increased ability to pursue work. The much-maligned "welfare" payments had in fact brought downtrodden and destitute communities back to life, bringing people "closer to the mainstream, closer to life." Pension payout days, he noted, "are not days of shame or resignation. They are festive and generous days, days of laughter and good spirits. With money to spend, people are feeling at their most human."[15]

This argument was extended by another commentator in the debate, the academic and activist Steven Friedman. Friedman noted that the critics of Steinberg's original column had included not only the usual Rightwing types (those who object to taking "our" tax money and giving it to "lazy" others—"those people") but also others who were much more sympathetic with the plight of the poor, and indeed actively supportive of ambitious state programs to fight poverty. For these more progressive critics, state intervention was all well and good, but simply "handing out money" failed to address the "root causes" of poverty. In this view, Friedman noted, the real need was not for more cash transfers but for programs such as community-based, government-funded employment programs and projects that might strengthen community capacity, address the problem of "low skills," and enhance self-esteem via employment. Friedman objected to these fairly standard liberal/progressive arguments in a forceful way:

> If we look beneath the surface, there is plenty of economic dynamism, many skills, and much "community capacity" among the poor—they wouldn't survive if there wasn't. But, because they don't operate out of air-conditioned offices, their economic activity is seen as a problem rather than an asset. Research that looks at what people do with their grants shows they know far more about what works than the designers of government employment schemes or the architects of the many other programmes policymakers come up with. And so [these arguments for state programs to transform the "capacity" of poor people and their communities] also express a prejudice—that "they" are not like us and so we must try to turn them into us. There is little difference between this attitude and that of the genteel Victorians who looked down on the poor and wanted them sent to workhouses to improve themselves.

Distributing cash grants, Friedman went on, is "just about the only antipoverty measure that works" because "it is the only one that relies on the decisions of the poor rather than on policymakers who believe they know what poor people want." For that reason, grants are disparaged by elites across the political spectrum, who "cannot abide the idea of poor people deciding for themselves" how to live. But social grants "are a success" precisely because "instead of trying to change the poor, they give poor people a lever that allows them to choose." New policy measures would accomplish more, both in helping people and in stimulating economic growth, if they offered people "the means to better do what they do instead of trying to turn them into people like us."[16]

To be sure, neither Steinberg nor Friedman thinks that South Africa's current distributional regime is in any way adequate, and neither would want to give up on looking for ways to increase employment. But it is striking, and encouraging, that one finds here—lucidly presented and in a mainstream venue—a vision of direct distribution not as charity but as liberation, and of the daily lives of the "unemployed" and grant-supported poor not as some lamentable warren of idleness, lack, and incapacity but as a domain of deeply knowledgeable, sometimes joyous, and socially and economically valuable activity. And it is perhaps even more encouraging to encounter arguments, articulated by members of the very propertied classes whose taxes support the welfare state, that combine a robust acknowledgment of a responsibility to one's fellow citizens with an explicit disavowal of that tired telos of generations of development and anti-poverty programs: the aim "to turn them into people like us."

Not only is the story of southern Africa's systems of grants and pensions more interesting than is sometimes realized, it is also unfinished and, in important ways, still in motion. Indeed, from the beginnings of the deracialization of social policy in the years approaching the end of apartheid, social protection in the region has continued to expand in both scale and scope. In South Africa, for instance, grants given to the poor majority were originally restricted to aid for the elderly and the disabled. At the time of transition to majority rule, a new program of state support for small children was introduced. Over the years the age of eligibility rose gradually from seven to eighteen, substantially expanding the number of households benefiting. At the same time, the amounts paid in elderly pensions rose significantly, while the age of eligibility for men was reduced to sixty to match that for women. As I have noted, this was a very substantial expansion of the social assistance system (both in terms of the numbers of people covered and the amount of money transferred to them), but it has remained within the horizon of a traditional "social security" paradigm (within which "dependent" elderly people, women, and children have some expectation of being provisioned by the state while men are presumed to be wage-earning "breadwinners").

But those who are working within the South African social protection system have a much more expansive concept. Interviews with personnel at the Department of Social Development revealed a quiet determination to place social transfer programs on a more universalistic basis. From the time that an official Committee of Inquiry first proposed a basic income grant in 2002 (DSD 2002), officials at the department have been broadly supportive of the aim of removing conditionality from social grants and reaching a larger population of beneficiaries. At the time of the interviews, they were in fact busy removing the means tests from established programs such as child support and pensions. What is more, they were actively working toward the creation of new social grants that would address what they described as the "huge gap" that leaves so-called working-age men without any protection. They hope to introduce in the near future a "job-seekers grant," for instance, that would provide cash transfers to unemployed "youth" between the ages of eighteen and twenty-four.[17] The idea of "job-seeking" fits well with prevailing societal ideas about what young men ought to be doing, but one official acknowledged that additional "seeking" was unlikely to produce many new jobs, and that "really, for 90 percent it will be income support by another name." Another idea being floated was a "pre-retirement grant" for unemployed adults between forty-five and fifty-nine (after which they become eligible for the old age pension). After all, as one official noted, "who will hire them?" Note that if these measures were to be implemented, only the residual category of non-disabled adults aged twenty-five to forty-four who are neither employed nor acting as the caregiver to a minor would remain without income. These would eventually be covered by another proposed grant targeting unemployed adults not covered by unemployment insurance schemes (something already proposed in an eye-opening Department of Social Development discussion document in 2008 [DSD 2008]).

A remarkable conception here emerges, from within the social grant bureaucracy itself, of income support as a universal social entitlement. The goal, as the 2008 discussion paper put it, is nothing less than the elimination of "income insufficiency"—"regardless of the cause" (2008, 9). As a top DSD administrator put it, the country is already committed to universal minimum standards for housing, electricity, water, and so on; "why this resistance to doing the same for income?" Through a gradual, inch by inch undermining of the old "social" idea that only the weak and afflicted require social assistance, the institutional ambitions of the social grant bureaucracy gradually creep toward a kind of universalistic, citizenship-based entitlement, in the process beginning to approach many of the goals of basic income via an incremental strategy. To be sure, the South African alphabet soup of different grant programs sorely lacks the simplicity and elegance of a basic income grant. But those who know the system best, working within the bowels of the distributive apparatus, are highly aware of the constraints of the political terrain and have developed a canny strategy that aims at achieving the BIG-like result of universal income support through the back door.[18]

On the ground, then, there may be more reasons for optimism than a simple assessment of the progress of the BIG movement might allow. Other national cases may tell a similar story. In Brazil, for instance, existing programs of distribution are dominated by traditionally familistic programs such as the Bolsa Familia, targeting mostly women and children. But a 2004 law commits the state to "an unconditional basic income" for every Brazilian citizen (or foreign resident of five years or more). This is meant to be realized in steps, with implementation going first to the poorest, but the law calls for the eventual creation of a truly universal system (Coêlho 2012; Lo Vuolo 2013). Iran shows a different sort of path. Here, a special-purpose cash transfer program was created to replace a very expensive and highly inefficient program of massive public subsidies of petroleum products, including gasoline. To relieve the sting of massive price rises, revenue from the new price structure was remitted to the public in the form of universal cash transfers to each individual citizen. Thus, again through a kind of back door, a de-facto national system of basic income has been established (Guillaume, Zytek, and Farzin 2011; Tabatabai 2011).

What is worth emphasizing here is not just a profusion of programs involving cash payments but also an explosion of new thinking suggesting that such payments are warranted as a kind of "rightful share," often rooted in arguments for the social origins of wealth. In the previous section, I noted new initiatives based on mineral "dividend" arguments from national ownership as well as proposed environmental payments based on such principles as climate justice or economic stewardship. Also worthy of note is an important feminist literature that sees practices of care (especially care for children, the old, and the sick) as a central, if undervalued, feature of societal membership and among the most important ways that citizens in fact contribute to society. Such contributions, disproportion-ately carried out by women, are often invisible to a view that sees "pull-ing one's weight" only in terms of paid labor. Expanded and de-familized programs of social transfers, in this view, are warranted as a way of ac-knowledging both the value and the universal societal importance of the work of care and of placing care within the domain of citizenship rather than the family.[19] Meanwhile, in philosophical discussions of justice, mate-rial distributions to the disadvantaged and the ethical reasoning that might ground them have become central to discussions of social justice in recent years, especially in the (Rawlsian) "distributive justice" tradition (discussed briefly below).

Even within Marxism (which as I have noted has often been dismissive of distributive approaches), we find new intellectual openings to distrib-utive arguments focused on things other than the claims of the wage la-borer. Michael Hardt (2000), for instance, has advocated the payment of a universal basic income based on the Kropotkinesque premise that "soci-ety" rather than "labor" is the real source of economic value (and that all members of society, rather than simply "workers," should therefore claim shares of that value).[20] From a very different branch of the Marxist tradi-tion, Erik Olin Wright also advocates basic income, seeing it as strength-ening the class position of labor (since it would give workers more choices and more leverage) but also as enabling the support of a range of different sorts of valuable "productive activity which is not oriented towards the market," including caregiving, artistic activity, politics, and community service (Wright 2006, 95). Kathi Weeks (2011) has thoughtfully reviewed the Marxist feminist tradition, critiquing the persistently "productivist" strain that runs through it and seeking to revitalize the feminist critique of wage labor by linking it to an ambitious agenda for a "postwork soci-ety," within which a program of state-supplied basic income would be central. And finally, perhaps the best indicator of all of a new opening to issues of distribution among Marx's descendants is a recent surge of interest in the work of Paul Lafargue, the multiracial, Haitian-descended, Cuban-born son-in-law of Karl Marx—evidenced by the recent republica-tion of his 1880 assault on the proletarian work ethic ("The Right to Be Lazy"), a delightfully heterodox text that remains one of the most radical challenges to the still largely hegemonic idea that the only "progressive" politics can be one that demands "jobs for all" (Lafargue 2011).

Of course, many on the traditional Left see nothing radical about any of this. They see no "real" or "structural" changes at stake here (often presuming, as noted in chapter 1, that only production counts as real and structural) and complain that even the most far-reaching schemes for basic income "remain within capitalism" (Žižek 2010, 236).[21] They see in the sorts of new distributive schemes I have discussed here only, at best, a way of ameliorating the most extreme of capitalism's social costs. At worst, they worry that (as Patrick Bond [2014] suggests) "social" transfers such as pensions and grants remain merely "tokenistic" gestures justifying capitalism as usual or that (as Du Toit and Neves [2009b] have put it) social protection may end up offering only "a kind of 'sustainable poverty,' mitigating its worst effects and heading off political challenges to the legitimacy of the established order."

But advocates for comprehensive forms of distribution such as basic income counter these arguments. In addressing those excluded from the world of wage labor, they propose, programs of direct distribution may engage precisely the people that Marxism has never known what to do with, the infamous "lumpen." Giving them a positive relation to the state, making them into rightful claimants, provides a new ground for mobilization and opens up a new kind of politics. And where, they ask, is the evidence that this "heads off political challenges"? Certainly that does not seem like a good account of the South African case, where expectations for "service delivery" do not head off political challenges so much as proliferate them (Alexander 2010). In India and Brazil, too, a wide range of new "social" programs have been sites of political contestation and provided the grounds for new forms of mobilization (including a campaign for basic income in Brazil and a push for a national "Right to Food" law in India). To be sure, the programs have been beset by a myriad of problems and failings, but it is far from obvious that their effects have in fact been depoliticizing.[22] Might the contrary, in fact, be the case: that we are now witnessing the beginnings of a new kind of politics—a distributive politics—that is potentially quite a radical one?

The fact is we do not know where all of this is headed. As I argued in the book's introduction, this is a time of possibilities, not certainties; a time for experiments, not conclusions. But, as I suggested in chapter 6, the combination of distributive demands rooted in things other than labor with emergent state apparatuses of direct distribution may be allowing us to at least begin to imagine how more radical and universalistic demands might emerge out of contemporary forms of direct distribution, and perhaps even (as I suggested in chapter 4) how one might see in these programs the elements of an emergent new conception of socialism] Such a development, if it occurs, will not be a revival of the socialism of old. It will not be led by a new vanguard class (whether "precariat," "multitude," or any other) that might take over the role of mystical protagonist long played by the proletariat in Leftist imaginings, nor will it be founded on the centrality or universality of wage labor. But neither will it have much to do with the "welfare" of old, with its breadwinners and dependents, its safety nets and insurance mechanisms. What it will look like is up for grabs. But it does seem possible, given the developments I have traced in this book, that it just may restore to relevance that much-maligned founding principle of "African socialism" long ago articulated by Julius Nyerere (1968, 3): "Socialism is essentially distributive."[23]

The Limits of Distributive Politics: The Nation-State and Other Horizons

The sorts of claims I have discussed here, from the most modest sorts of entitlements to social assistance to the boldest demands for citizens' ownership of a common national societal wealth, have in common that they have almost always been linked to one particular sort of "imagined community": the nation-state. This raises two problems.

First, while the nation form may provide an admirable basis for solidarities within its membership boundaries (Calhoun 2007), it inevitably implies a certain exclusion of those who lie beyond those boundaries, as is only too visible in the service-providing modern state's endless battles with xenophobia and the problem of the foreigner. Indeed, as Peter Geschiere has recently pointed out (2009), Africa and Europe have this experience in common. Southern Africa, with a recent history of ugly violence against real and perceived foreigners, is perhaps especially sensitive on this point. (A surge of xenophobic rioting across South Africa in 2008 killed scores, while smaller-scale episodes of violence and harassment are an only-too-familiar part of the social scene across the region.)[24] Other world regions may illuminate the dangers of political and social exclusion of "the foreigner" even more sharply.[25]

The second problem is that any distributive politics operating at the level of the nation is only as good as the institutional and fiscal capacities of the nation-state—a fact of considerable relevance in many of the poorest parts of the world (and most of all in Africa). Indeed, it is difficult to imagine the implementation of a South African sort of system of direct distribution in states that fail to raise significant tax revenues or to provide reliable social services, or that stand in a relation of more or less open predation to the populations they ostensibly govern. It is clear that the strongest distributive claims have been established via durably institutionalized state programs in "middle-income" countries with democratic politics and administratively capable states. But what about the rest? What is more, when we are speaking not of middle-income countries like South Africa and Brazil but instead of the very poorest nation-states, national citizenship cannot provide an appropriate frame for distributive remedies, since so many of the inequalities that one would wish to see addressed by distributive processes are global rather than national in scale.

One response to these issues is simply to note that all states that provide social ("welfare") benefits face practical problems in defining and bounding their membership groups. The fact that welfare states inevitably encounter such problems is hardly an argument against having welfare states. Similarly, one might respond to the second set of issues by noting that just because a goal such as basic income may not look viable in the contemporary Central African Republic is no reason not to fight for it in Namibia or India.

Yet other responses may be able to go further than this. Many thinkers today are engaged with the challenge of conceiving of schemes of social distribution (and, indeed, social responsibility) beyond the nation-state, at a level variously conceptualized as international, global, or supranational. From a historical vantage, Frederick Cooper has recently reminded us that the idea that the locus of "social" rights or "social" solidarity must be the nation-state is in fact a very recent piece of common sense—and, he suggests, "not, perhaps, a durable one." In the era of decolonization, he reminds us, "both the question of sovereignty and the question of social justice were debated in terms that transcended locality and specific political configurations," while "the relationship of the social and sovereignty" was revealed as more open-ended than it might appear from a presentist, nation-state-centered perspective (Cooper 2013, 476–77).

Perhaps we have entered into another such moment. It is striking, for instance, that contemporary philosophical discussions of topics such as justice, inequality, and responsibility often attempt to apply these ideals precisely to supra- or transnational conceptions of community or society.

Thomas Pogge, for instance, has argued that justice requires a view that would be both longer (in terms of history) and broader (in terms of geography) than has been typical of philosophical treatments of the topic. Only such a view, on his account, can grasp the relations of force that have been constitutive of the global inequalities that we today encounter as given. The highly advantaged position in the world occupied by the richest countries, he observes, is the product of a long and violent history involving enslavement, colonialism, and even genocide. Given this starting point, he proceeds to apply the concept of inheritance in a way that recalls the passages from Kropotkin cited earlier in this book: "The rich are quick to point out that they cannot inherit their ancestors' sins. Indeed. But how can they then be entitled to the fruits of these sins: to their huge inherited advantage in power and wealth over the rest of the world?"[26] As practical remedy, Pogge suggests a range of possible equalizing measures, including a "global resources dividend" to be paid on a worldwide basis (2008). Philippe van Parijs, writing from a similarly Rawlsian position, arrives at a different set of arguments for what he terms "international distributive justice" (2007) but also concludes with concretely distributive policy proposals (in his case, a global basic income). Ayelet Shachar (2009) has proposed that birthright citizenship in a wealthy nation-state can be thought of as a form of property inheritance and that redistributive measures are warranted by the self-evidently arbitrary (lottery-like) way in which this initial allocation is produced (the accident of where one happens to be born). Robin Blackburn (2011) has developed a detailed and well-conceived proposal for a universal and non-means-tested global old age pension, arguing that the globalization of the world economy means that social protection must be re-institutionalized on a global, rather than national, level.

Funding for global distribution schemes, in these accounts, might come from a variety of sources (concrete suggestions include levies on mineral extraction, development of a global currency within which seigniorage might provide a basic global taxation method, a "birthright privilege levy" collected by the governments of rich states, or a "Tobin Tax"—

that is, a tax on international currency exchanges, international financial transactions, or both). But the theorists' task here is less to develop detailed policy proposals than to insist that it cannot be beyond the bounds of human ingenuity to devise ways of raising revenue on a global scale that might be applied to meet the distributive demands of global justice.

Such proposals, it may be objected, remain at quite some distance from any prospect of immediate political realization. But even if we grant that current political realities leave slim chances (at least in the short term) for actually creating the sorts of comprehensive new transnational institutions of distribution that are implied in these more ambitious programs, a quieter sort of global distributism may be emerging from within the nation-state system itself. In recent years, the International Labour Office (ILO) has led a United Nations–backed international campaign for what they term a worldwide "Social Protection Floor." The "core idea" of the Social Protection Floor (SPF) is (according to an authoritative 2011 report) "that no one should live below a certain income level and everyone should at least have access to basic social services" (ILO 2011, xxiv). The campaign urges that all states implement a set of "basic social security guarantees" that would include access to health care as well as "basic income security," not only for children and older people but also for "persons in active age who are unable to earn sufficient income" (ILO 2012, 10). This is, significantly, not conceived as a "safety net" (that old circus image of insurance-based "social" care for those who "fall") but instead as a "floor"—a universal citizenship right that provides all with some minimal place to stand. The ILO argues that the recent social protection successes in middle-income countries such as Brazil and South Africa can and should be expanded and universalized. Cost, they note, is in most cases not the principal obstacle, citing a number of studies showing the extension of minimal measures of income security to be "affordable even in the poorest countries" (2011, 43) and asserting that even a scheme with the broad impact of Brazil's Bolsa Familia (covering 26 percent of the population) can be started "at a cost equivalent to less than 0.5 percent of GDP" (2011, 47). In the poorest states, they note, foreign aid revenues may also play a role.

Because we are not used to thinking of income maintenance as the sort of core service that one might reasonably expect even the poorest states to provide, such a proposal may sound like just so much unrealistic "pie in the sky" dreaming. But from the ILO's perspective, establishing global norms around social protection is not very different from its earlier campaigns that helped to establish other worldwide norms, such as that all states should prevent slavery and child labor or that they should all provide their citizens with primary education. We today take for granted the substantial success of these earlier programs for worldwide standards (even if we recognize their limits). Is it not conceivable that a modest state-guaranteed minimum income might become just as globally normal as a free, state-provided primary education? Put in these terms, the scheme seems less an unrealizable utopia than the sort of pragmatic reformist goal around which energies might quite realistically be organized. Indeed, there is already some momentum in that direction. As I pointed out in the introduction, we are already seeing a kind of demonstration effect, as the positive attention drawn by social protection schemes in countries such as South Africa, Namibia, and Botswana has led to "copycat" programs even in neighboring countries that are less well-resourced (e.g., the introduction of an old age pension and now even a child support grant in Lesotho) as well as modest new schemes in other African countries with little history of state social protection.[27] Taking a longer-term historical view, in fact, suggests that the force of global norms may shape public policy in surprisingly powerful ways, as has been argued by Frederick Cooper (2013) in the context of worldwide campaigns around slavery and humanitarianism and by the distinguished sociologist of "world society" John Meyer with reference to education and other now-standard social policies (see Krücken and Drori 2009).

As for the restricted horizon of national membership that makes citizenship and foreignness such a problem for programs of social distribution, here too things are in flux. Traditionally, welfare states have grounded their benefits in national citizenship and relied on nationalist forms of solidarity that have entailed, as their flip side, xenophobic forms of exclusion. Yet there is no inevitability in that particular way of defining eligibility for services, and in contemporary contexts of high population mobility across national boundaries, states around the world are feeling their way toward new ways of thinking about the relationship between citizenship and belonging. In Europe and the United States, lively debates are unfolding about which services should be provided and which withheld from unauthorized migrants (education for children? driver's licenses? health care?), and some have suggested that expanding the rights of denizens (rather than simply serving "citizens") should be the top priority (see, e.g., Standing 2011). In South Africa, I was struck that most of those with whom I discussed the matter within the Department of Social Development were in fact quite eager to dispense with the complications of national citizenship and much preferred to link service provision (including the payment of grants) simply to residence. This was the case both because sorting citizen from non-citizen was a logistical headache and because they were not eager to feed an already-existing social division within poor communities plagued by xenophobia. From their point of view, the real obstacle to linking service provisioning to residence rather than citizenship was not a practical one but a political one. This is perhaps a useful reminder that focusing social provisioning on actual residents rather than citizens is hardly a utopian or impractical move—indeed, in purely technical terms, providing services to residents is often *more* practical than trying to sort out who "belongs" where.

In truth, however, the experiments and new developments I have reviewed here can only take us so far. The fact is that, even with the clues that I have tried to harvest here, we can hardly imagine what a practical politics of distribution might look like on a global level. But surely it is time to start trying. In a time of momentous transformations, we cannot remain tethered to boundaries of the "realistic" that belong to the past. And, as I have suggested elsewhere (Ferguson 2010), contemporary progressives badly need to move beyond "the politics of the anti-" by focusing on *advocating* and *advancing* innovative new programs and not just *opposing* them. A truly global distributive politics might provide us with such a focus.

If we are really to push beyond the horizons of the nation-state in our thinking about distribution, we will need new ideas and new ways of reasoning. Where will these come from? Perhaps here we might turn at last to Lewis Henry Morgan, in whose honor these lectures have been presented. For Morgan was not only one of the founding figures of the discipline of anthropology, he was also among the first to see in the noncapitalist social forms that anthropologists have so often studied not only historical data but concrete forms of political inspiration. In the long history of the human species, he insisted, modern horizons of state and private property could not be understood as anything more than passing forms. "A mere property career," in his enduring words, "is not the final destiny of mankind" (1877, 552). And while he understood non-capitalist social formations (in characteristic nineteenth-century fashion) as belonging to the past ("ancient"), he also suggested that in important ways they might point to the future (notably in their exemplary embrace of "liberty, equality and fraternity").

In a similar spirit, perhaps we might return to the claim developed in the previous chapter (chapter 6) that direct distribution may, in certain contexts, be coming to be conceived as neither a market exchange nor a gift but rather as a share. As I noted there, anthropological work on sharing, within foraging bands and elsewhere, has underlined the importance of what is known as "demand sharing," in which distribution is organized around neither gifts nor exchanges but rather the aggressive demands of those who are understood to be in a position to rightfully receive shares. Such sharing is not based on citizenship nor indeed on abstract membership at all. It is, instead, based on what Widlok (2012) terms "presence." When a hunter returns to camp with a carcass, who is entitled to receive a share? The principle of demand sharing provides the answer: whoever is there. The morality is straightforward and compelling. To eat one's fill while hungry others stand by is plainly unacceptable. Instead, the force of the "demand," in such contexts, comes from a non-negotiable principle that presence itself brings with it a distributive entitlement. Those who are here among us must eat and may therefore rightfully demand a share. Anything else would be shameful.

There was perhaps a similar sentiment at work in the attitudes I mentioned earlier of the South African Department of Social Development staff when they contemplated the social protection needs of immigrants. Legalities aside, one official asked, "simply from a social services standpoint," who should receive services? She answered her own question: "Isn't it obvious? Those who are here! Those who are in need!" Neither being in need nor being "here" would count for much if the claims of "foreigners" were reckoned according to a strict logic of citizenship, but in this official's account it was neither citizenship nor legality but something more like presence that warranted service provision. Anne-Maria Makhulu (2012) has recently underlined the importance of claims based in just such presence, as South African squatters and others have asserted themselves via "informal home building, land invasion, . . . acts of 'staying put' and occupation, and myriad other practices of the everyday" (2012, 795). I have elsewhere suggested that a similar politics of presence is at work in the widespread illegal immigration of contemporary Africans who, through their spatial transgressions of the nation-state system, seek not only new kinds of economic opportunities but also new sorts of membership and recognition in an imagined modern, global world (Ferguson 2006). Asef Bayat (2009) has made a related argument about forms of "non-movement" politics that proceed via what he calls "the art of presence."

The figure of "biopolitics" has sometimes been invoked in understanding new forms of distribution that provision people not as workers or consumers but as mere members of a population. Tania Li has proposed an understanding of new forms of welfare as a kind of Foucauldian "making live," where some minimal support is provided to "surplus populations" in a way that is based less on economic contribution or political status than on "the intrinsic value of life" (2010, 68). But what is visible in the conceptions I have discussed above is not, in fact, a biological conception ("bare life" or what have you) but the more specific condition of *presence*—the specifically social (not biological) fact of being not only alive but also here and among us in a way that implicitly demands at least minimal forms of both recognition and obligation.

Here, then, is a different figure of "the social"—not the abstract membership, citizenship, and social contract of the nation-state but a concrete and embodied presence and the obligation it implies. This is an obligation that is neither a matter of charitable giving nor even of exchanging but rather of *sharing*—sharing within a community of responsibility that is not formed by free association, that is in fact involuntary, and within which co-presence, with all of its entailments, is not a political choice but simply the most elementary sort of social fact.

Clearly this raises more questions than it answers. It is obvious that the physical, face-to-face relations of presence that one finds in classically anthropological accounts of demand sharing can have no literal application in conceiving national- and supranational-scale relations of obligation. Some considerable conceptual and political invention, in fact, would be required to arrive at a plausible and useable modern analogue of presence. At the same time, simply expanding the nation-state ideal of citizenship to "the global level" is not, in the absence of a world state, a real solution (as if we could solve the problem while still keeping all our categories intact if we were only to make "society" big enough). Instead we need new ways of figuring membership, creating systems of inclusion and obligation that go beyond the abstractions of a global humanity to offer concrete forms of recognition and practical mechanisms of distribution.

To say as much is to invoke a politics yet to be invented, it is true. But Lewis Henry Morgan would not have been daunted by such a proposition. Finding in human history precisely an inexhaustible record of inventiveness, he remained confident in a future in which, as he put it, "human intelligence will rise to the mastery over property." And if my discussion here of distributive politics and its contemporary experimental possibilities does no more than scratch the surface of the topic, perhaps it is only right to conclude by quoting Morgan one last time: "Although the subject has been inadequately treated, its importance at least has been shown" (1877, 552).

Notes

Introduction. Cash Transfers and the New Welfare States

1. The "end of history" and "world is flat" arguments are associated with best-selling books by Francis Fukuyama and Thomas Friedman, respectively. The most influential critical accounts operating at the same "meta" level are perhaps David Harvey 2007, Mike Davis 2006, and (in a more popular vein) Naomi Klein 2008.

2. Even in Bangladesh (home of Muhammed Yunus's Grameen Bank and long the poster child for microcredit as anti-poverty remedy), Ananya Roy's revealing study (2010) has concluded that microcredit/microfinance programs there, successful as they have often been, have in fact been less about investment and interest than about public subsidies to the poor. "Despite the rhetoric of credit and entrepreneurship," she observes, "the Bangladesh institutions seem to be engaged in forms of social protection," following a "logic of development" that "fits much more comfortably in the 'social protection' family of programs and policies than in the 'micro-enterprises' family" (2010, 116, 117).

3. Hanlon, Barrientos, and Hulme 2010.

4. "Southern Africa" is both a conventional unit of scholarly specialization and a region that is meaningfully integrated both economically (insofar as it is oriented around the powerful industrial "core" economy of South Africa) and politically (via the Southern African Development Community, a regional grouping that began as an association of anti-apartheid "front line" states but today includes all the states in the region, including South Africa). Note that I will give special attention throughout to two states within the region, South Africa and Namibia, that have especially extensive and (from my point of view) interesting systems of social assistance, but I will also refer where appropriate to neighboring states where similar (if less extensive) programs have been

introduced or contemplated (including the two countries for which I have the most sustained direct research experience, Lesotho and Zambia).

5. Garcia and Moore 2012; for Zimbabwe, see UNICEF 2012.

6. On the theme of exclusion, see, for example, Wacquant 2009; Sassen 2010. More recently, scholars have paid more attention to the ways that new forms of inclusion-via-social-policy may also be part of the "neoliberal" story (see Collier 2011; Muehlebach 2012).

7. See Bond 2000 and Marais 2001 for accounts of this "neoliberal" turn.

8. The most recent official unemployment rate was reported as 25.2 percent, with an "expanded" definition (including all those desiring employment regardless of whether they are actively seeking it) at 35.1 percent. Youth unemployment was reported at 66 percent. "Employment Down for First Quarter of 2014," *Mail and Guardian*, May 5, 2014.

9. While not directly concerned with questions of social assistance, Hart (2008) has provided a related assessment of the limits of dominant neoliberalism narratives, insisting that understanding the specific political dynamics of concrete points of local political struggle in South Africa will require a more complex political and analytic strategy than simply "exposing neoliberal class power." See also Parnell and Robinson 2012.

10. The newly founded EFF (Economic Freedom Fighters) led by Julius Malema (treated in chapter 6) may prove an exception to this, for better or worse. It is also worth noting the recent emergence of two small alternative Left parties, the Democratic Left Front (DLF) and the Workers and Socialist Party (WASP), though clearly neither can at this point be termed major political parties.

11. For an overview of the development of social pensions in the region, see Devereux 2007; on the South African Child Support Grant program, see Lund 2008 and DSD, SASSA, and UNICEF 2012.

12. See National Treasury 2012 (85). Other grants include the War Veterans Grant, the Disability Grant, the Foster Care Grant, and the Care Dependency Grant.

13. Bond (2014) has disputed the reliability of these figures, claiming that many of the toilets, taps, and other new facilities tallied in the survey are in fact functioning imperfectly or not at all. This is likely true, but the same must have been true of the counts from earlier years (i.e., not all the counted infrastructural assets would have been functional). It is hard to see how considerations of this kind can stand in the way of acknowledging such a marked improvement over only a few years—a trend that is consistent with other difficult-to-dismiss data, such as the self-reported hunger figures cited above, as well as the extensive field studies reviewed in the authoritative report of Neves et al. 2009.

14. "Impressive Shift in Living Standards Trends," press release, South African Institute of Race Relations, August 28, 2012.

15. Dubbeld (2013) has recently reported that some rural recipients (in South Africa's KwaZulu-Natal province) condemn the proliferation of grants as corrosive of "tradition" and contrast the current world of grants unfavorably with a remembered past where men could earn more adequate incomes via wage labor. A yearning for wage labor and the social structure that it supported, however, should not be mistaken for a

desire to reduce or eliminate grants, which Dubbeld's informants estimated to be the primary source of income for 70 percent of the population of the village under study.

16. For an excellent account of exactly how such policymaking emerged in one specific case, see Francie Lund's exposition (2008) of the process that led to the creation of the South African Child Support Grant program.

17. The classic statement of this position is Wolpe 1972.

18. None of the several social policy experts to whom I have told this anecdote has disagreed—indeed, several registered their grim suspicion that the JSE would actually rise substantially on the news. One suggested that the experiment had in some sense already been performed, since the HIV/AIDS epidemic had in fact eliminated millions from the supposed "reserve army of the unemployed" with (she claimed) little impact on either industry or the national GDP.

19. On the emergence of "the poor" as local category of considerable political significance, see Ashwin Desai 2002.

20. Here and elsewhere, I use the term *progressive* not as a synonym for what we have come to know as the Left but in a broader sense (one closer to the word's literal meaning) that references simply a political commitment to altering or reforming the social and political status quo in such a way as to improve it. Some interesting forms of progressive politics today, I will suggest, may be more distorted than clarified by placing them within a traditional Left-Right grid.

21. Seekings (2008c), for instance, has argued that Esping-Andersen's (1990) typology of welfare states (which has become a kind of standard reference for cross-national comparative work) is based on analytical categories not appropriate for the new welfare states of the South. See also Sandbrook et al. 2007; Gough et al. 2008; and Haggard and Kaufman 2008.

22. This is, of course, a highly simplified account. Extensive scholarship has analyzed the significant differences among "first-world" welfare states, with perhaps the most influential account being Esping-Andersen's (1990) contrast between what he termed "liberal," "corporatist," and "social democratic" types of system. Since systems of the "social democratic" type (such as the well-known Swedish case) rely more on "universalistic" benefits (which benefit all or most of the population and not only the poor or the unfortunate who "fall"), they may appear closer to some of the southern African schemes discussed here than the "safety net" model that is more characteristic of Esping-Andersen's "liberal" model. But even the benefits offered by the most universalistic "social democratic" systems are (unlike the southern African social grants) normally graduated according to accustomed income, and they remain premised on a "normal" state of universal wage labor. Indeed, Esping-Andersen claims that of the three basic types of welfare state, it is the "social democratic" type that is most dependent on universal wage employment, "at once genuinely committed to a full-employment guarantee, and entirely dependent on its attainment" (1990, 28).

23. South Africa also has contributory systems for formal-sector workers. These work more like typical social insurance systems and are not part of the system of grants that is treated here.

24. A critical literature on this is reviewed in chapters 1 and 2.

25. These issues are discussed at greater length in chapter 2. See also Lund 2008 (80) on how and why it was decided to move away from older models of assistance that presumed "the nuclear family."

26. "Idea of Jobs for All Blinds Us to Need for Welfare," *Business Day*, July 26, 2013. I am grateful to Jess Auerbach for first bringing this column to my attention.

27. "Idea of Jobs for All Blinds Us to Need for Welfare," *Business Day*.

28. "Grants Encourage Liberation, Not Dependence," *Business Day*, August 23, 2013.

29. United States Bureau of Labor Statistics, "Labor Force Statistics from the Current Population Survey: 35. Persons not in the labor force by desire and availability for work, age, and sex," accessed December 4, 2013, http://www.bls.gov/cps/cpsaat35.htm.

30. United States Bureau of Labor Statistics, "Labor Force Statistics from the Current Population Survey: 1. Employment status of the civilian noninstitutional population, 1942 to date," accessed December 4, 2013, http://www.bls.gov/cps/cpsaat01.htm.

31. United States Bureau of Labor Statistics, "Labor Force Statistics from the Current Population Survey: 35. Persons not in the labor force by desire and availability for work, age, and sex."

32. United States Bureau of Labor Statistics, "Labor Force Statistics from the Current Population Survey: Frequently Asked Questions," accessed June 26, 2013, http://www.bls.gov/cps/faq.htm. Note that this does not include the self-employed, who are here reckoned as both "in the labor force" and "employed."

33. David Leonhardt, "Men, Unemployment, and Disability," *New York Times*, April 8, 2011, accessed December 4, 2013, http://economix.blogs.nytimes.com/2011/04/08/men-unemployment-and-disability/?_r=0.

34. United States Food and Drug Administration, Food Nutrition Service, "Supplemental Nutrition Assistance Program (SNAP)," accessed June 26, 2013, http://www.fns.usda.gov/pd/34SNAPmonthly.htm.

35. It is also perhaps worth remarking that even for those who *are* in wage employment, the distributive stream of wages is often supplemented with other (often extralegal) transfers of resources within the workplace (informal "perks" or privileges, "tolerated theft," etc.). As Lisa Dodson has recently pointed out for the United States (2011) prevailing ideas of "fairness" often allow such transfers to be justified within the workplace as "bending the rules" rather than theft, a phenomenon that is often noted to be a feature of southern African workplaces as well. Notable, too, is the extent of popular support in the United States for more formal sorts of direct redistribution, which is considerably greater than mainstream political discourse might suggest. A recent Gallup survey found that 52 percent of Americans (including 34 percent of self-described "conservatives") agreed that "our government should redistribute wealth by heavy taxes on the rich" and noted "a broad trend over time" suggesting that Americans have become "more rather than less in favor of active government involvement in redistributing wealth" ("Majority in U.S. Want Wealth More Evenly Distributed," accessed February 8, 2014, http://www.gallup.com/poll/161927/majority-wealth-evenly-distributed.aspx).

36. White 2001; Ngwane 2004; Niehaus 2010; White 2010; Barchiesi 2011; and Dubbeld 2013.

1. Give a Man a Fish

1. For a thoughtful reflection on the problematic use of "teach a man to fish" reasoning in the contemporary development fad for "sustainability," see Swidler and Watkins 2009.

2. "ANC Has Tough Job Rallying West Coast's Frustrated Fishermen," *Business Day*, February 24, 2006. A comprehensive study exploring the difficulties the post-apartheid South African fishing industry has faced in seeking to expand access to historically excluded groups concluded by pointing to the global industry trends referenced above, noting that "small-scale bona fide fishers are up against heavy odds, all over the world" (Hersoug 2002, 223).

3. "Mpulungu Job Hunt Kills 9," *Zambia Daily Mail*, May 29, 2012, accessed June 4, 2012, http://www.daily-mail.co.zm/?p=4484.

4. See discussion later in this chapter as well as chapter 6; cf. Ferguson 2013.

5. This history has recently been insightfully reviewed by Weeks (2011).

6. As Brian Turner has usefully pointed out in a discussion of T. H. Marshall's English context, citizenship has historically been associated with (typically male) participation in the formal labor market, sometimes supplemented with (again male) military service (thus the "worker-citizen" and the "soldier-citizen"). Women have historically been granted social rights not as individuals but as parts of "families," within which they have enjoyed certain entitlements "as fertile adults who are replenishing the nation" (Turner 2010, 70).

7. On the related association of the domestic domain with humanitarian practice, see Malkki 2015.

8. "Alan Simpson Calls Social Security 'Cow with 310 Million Tits,' Causes Uproar," *Talking Points Memo*, August 25, 2010, accessed September 27, 2013, http://talkingpoints memo.com/dc/alan-simspon-calls-social-security-cow-with-310-million-tits-causes -uproar.

9. In the *Communist Manifesto*, they famously described the lumpenproletariat as "the social scum, that passively rotting mass thrown off by the layers of the old society" ([1848] 1998, 48); as late as 1870 Engels described it as "this scum of depraved elements from all classes . . . the worst of all possible allies" (Engels [1870] 1968, 229). Elsewhere, Marx suggested such a class acted as an "industrial reserve army" whose function under capitalism was keeping wages low. For a critical account of the limitations of such Marxian functionalism in the context of massive labor surplus, see Li 2010 and cf. this book's conclusion. On Marx's concept of the lumpenproletariat, see also Stallybrass 1990 and the discussion in chapter 3.

10. "Any distribution whatever of the means of consumption," he later wrote, "is only a consequence of the distribution of the conditions of production themselves," and for a given arrangement of the elements of production, the distribution of the

means of consumption "results automatically." For this reason, Marx argued that it had been a mistake for the Gotha Programme to "make a fuss about so-called distribution" (Marx 1977, 569–70). Marx is of course famous for having proclaimed, in the same text, a certain distributive ideal as the ultimate endpoint of communism: "From each according to his ability, to each according to his need." But it must be remembered that in his vision such a distributive outcome was conceivable only as the culmination of a total transformation of the mode of production; until such a time, distribution could proceed only as an exchange for labor, a formula that Stalin would later famously render as "From each according to his ability, to each according to his work" and Lenin even more succinctly as "He who does not work shall not eat" (Lenin 1968, 223), a phrase that eventually found its way into the constitution of the USSR.

11. The primacy of production over distribution has been affirmed in a new form, for instance, in the influential work of Postone (1996). Hardt and Negri (2001), while giving welcome attention to distributive political strategies such as basic income, insist on seeing many of the practices that I describe as "distributive" as forms of what they call "immaterial labor," thus unintentionally reproducing the old oppositions between a production imagined as "real" and "material" and a distribution that is relegated to the realm of the immaterial. Chapter 3 presents an extended argument for both the materiality and the importance of distributive practices in the regional political economy.

12. See Macpherson (1962) 2011 on the Lockean roots of modern liberal conceptions that link rights and property in this way, a construction Macpherson termed "possessive individualism."

13. This is the translation offered by Balibar (2009) of the original French, "la part des sans-part." The phrase has also been rendered more literally (but, I think, more opaquely) as "the part of those without part" (e.g., in Rancière 2010).

14. This, at any rate, was the theory, even if things worked out rather differently in practice; cf. Ferguson 2006, 69–88; 2013.

15. On suffering as a ground for belonging and ownership, see Moore 2005. On the "negative heritage" of injury and harm, see Meskell 2011.

16. See, e.g., Hardt and Negri 2009; Hardt 2000, 2009.

17. Such as Philippe van Parijs, well-known proponent of basic income and advocate of what he once called a "capitalist road to communism" (van der Veen and van Parijs 1986; van Parijs 2013).

18. This is a theme of a number of recent publications from the Center for Global Development. See, for instance, Moss and Majerowicz 2013.

19. This is an issue I discuss at some length in this book's conclusion. For discussion of these issues in the regional context (where xenophobic passions have sometimes reached a murderous intensity), see Nyamnjoh 2006; Geschiere 2009; Sichone 2008; Landau 2012.

20. See this book's conclusion for a fuller discussion of these emergent new forms of thought.

21. For a critical analysis of the failings of public works schemes in Africa, see McCord 2012. For South Africa in particular, McCord 2003 and Seekings 2006 both point

to inefficiencies and high costs for such schemes as compared to programs of direct distribution. For a more sanguine account of South Africa's current Expanded Public Works Programme (especially the Community Work Programme component of it) see Philip 2013; for a more skeptical view, see Meth 2011.

22. This argument has recently been forcefully presented, in the South African context, by Franco Barchiesi 2011, 2012; see also Tribe of Moles 2011.

2. What Comes after the Social?

1. See also Davie 2005; Posel 2005; Seekings 2008b; Barchiesi 2011. Many have traced the turn to social welfare to the 1932 Carnegie Commission's analysis of the predicament of "poor whites," but Seekings (2007, 2008b) has convincingly refuted that view, arguing that the main developments predated the Carnegie Commission, which in any case constituted not an impetus toward modern welfare-state institutions but something more like a conservative backlash against them. On "poor whites," see Beinart, Delius, and Trapido 1986; Iliffe 1987; Morell 1992.

2. See Lund 2008 (80) for a thoughtful discussion of how and why policymakers moved away from policies based on "an outmoded model of family life . . . based on the model of the nuclear family."

3. The humanitarian and the medical also appear to be key sites—but that is another discussion. See the dissertation of Ramah McKay (2010).

3. Distributed Livelihoods

1. This devalorization of the nonproductive is perhaps the reason why Marxist analysts in southern Africa sometimes seem (in John Saul's phrase [2011]) "to label urban resisters as 'proletarian' almost by definition," thereby preserving the virtuous position of "worker" even for those whose actual social position is defined by not having work. On this point, see Barchiesi 2011.

2. Bourgois and Schonberg (2009) have recently attempted to retool the "lumpen" concept for contemporary circumstances. Other recent writers have attempted to remedy the failings of the traditional Marxist approach to the "lumpenproletariat" by developing an idea of "the precariat" as a new class position that might be the source of a new radical politics (see, e.g., Saul 2011; Standing 2011). This approach is briefly discussed in this book's conclusion.

3. Indeed, Guyer has suggested that, across what she terms "Atlantic Africa," economic formalization has always been a precarious project of carving out "islands" of formality amidst a sea of "informal" practices with their own logics. See Guyer 2004; cf. Ferguson 2007.

4. The broad literature is ably reviewed in Meagher 2010 (11–26). In southern Africa, see van der Waal and Sharp 1988; Hansen and Vaa 2004; Du Toit and Neves 2007; Hull and James 2012; Valodia and Devey 2012.

5. Note that this theme of improvisation has also been emphasized in AbdouMalik Simone's (2004) vivid writings on African urbanism.

6. As Meagher rightly emphasizes, social networks are crucial to such processes, but here I emphasize not simply the presence of networks (which are after all coextensive with sociality itself) but two more specific elements: (a) the precarious and improvised nature of livelihood activities and (b) the way social relations are made and tended in order to access resources in a fundamentally distributive process.

7. A vividly dark fictional account of this is provided in Ousmane Sembene's story "The Money-Order" (1997).

8. This has been discussed at some length in Ferguson 1999 for the Zambian Copperbelt and Swidler and Watkins 2007 for Malawi. For an anthropological account from South Africa, see Leclerc-Madlala 2004, and compare Cole 2010 on Madagascar.

9. Bähre's work, discussed later in this chapter, is exceptional in providing ethnographic case material on actual distributive practices; see also Lee 2011 for a rich historical account.

10. A later article (Bähre 2012) explores the increasing role of commercial insurance companies in selling funeral policies even to poor township customers and shows how even the brokers for these commercial firms find themselves entangled in the kinds of social reciprocities discussed below.

11. "Julius Malema: 'I live on handouts,'" *Mail and Guardian*, March 26, 2010, accessed July 4, 2013, http://mg.co.za/article/2010–03–26-julius-malema-i-live-on-handouts.

12. This phrase, now in common use in South Africa, refers to a politically connected businessperson who acquires riches through securing government contracts, or "tenders."

13. A recent survey found that some 26 percent of young South Africans would break with the ANC to vote for a political party led by Malema ("One in Four Youths Would Support Malema Party," *Mail and Guardian*, June 26, 2013, accessed July 4, 2013, http://mg.co.za/article/2013–06–26-survey-one-in-four-youths-would-support-malema-party).

14. As discussed in chapter 6, Malema equivocates on whether his "we" group is national (we South Africans) or racial (we Africans), sometimes voicing a nationalist universalism (in which the nation's wealth properly belongs to "all South Africans") while at other times articulating a politics of racial resentment (in which the riches of a country that originally and properly belonged to black South Africans have been illegitimately taken by white intruders).

4. The Social Life of Cash Payments

1. "Welcome to Welfare 2.0 for the World's Poor," *Newsweek*, August 10, 2010, accessed November 7, 2010, http://www.newsweek.com/welfare-developing-worlds-poor-68857.

2. Marx himself seems to have imagined that money would not be necessary in a post-revolutionary society. In a not-very-developed discussion in his *Critique of the Gotha Programme*, he refers instead to "certificates" that "society" would provide to laborers. Armed

with these certificates showing the number of hours they had worked, workers would then "draw from the social stock of means of consumption as much as costs the same amount of labour" (1977, 568). (He does not explain how, or according to what principle, distributions would be made to those unable to labour.) In our own era, Massimo De Angelis, a key recent theorist of "the commons," continues the traditional Marxist suspicion of money and markets, arguing that "the more we depend on money and markets to satisfy our needs and follow our desires, the more we are exposed to a vicious circle of dependence that pits livelihoods against each other" (De Angelis 2006, 151). Indeed, it is striking that a key strategy of many on the radical Left, even in recent years, has been to establish "prefigurative" social spaces (from countercultural communes and autonomist squats to the most recent Occupy encampments) whose "anticapitalist" character is imagined to be secured precisely by expelling the polluting presence of money.

3. One wonders whether Mauss's own background (a Jewish family—his father was a drapery salesman and his mother the daughter of a livestock merchant who ran a small embroidery business) may have sensitized him to the anti-Semitism that so often was entangled with anti-market/anti-money sentiment at this time in Europe (Fournier 2006, 10–13). Certainly, the southern African material would have much to say about how easily a hatred of "the market" may come to be entangled with an ethnicized or racialized hatred of the merchant.

4. Note that Mauss's critique of statism and defense of markets did not simply express the familiar liberal imperative to guard the rights of "the individual" against "the state." Indeed, both those forms, for Mauss, had to bow to the greater glory of intermediate-level forms of association and cooperation. "Collective appropriation," he wrote, "does not necessarily mean appropriation by the state, or state tyranny." "Smaller collectivities" also have their rights, including the right to participate in markets; for this reason, "the terms 'freedom' and 'collective control' are not contradictory" ([1924] 1983, 355).

5. This is a concept recently elaborated by Gudeman (2008), though it should be noted that I use the term here in a slightly different way.

6. Such observations have led Sylvia Yanagisako (2002), for instance, to suggest that we need an understanding of capitalism that would treat sentiments as just as central to economic action as interests, while Latour and Lépinay (2009) have recently urged a return to Gabriel Tarde's old insight that economics is first of all about "the passions" rather than rational calculation. See also Ho 2009 and Zaloom 2010.

7. I am grateful to Robert Frank for introducing me to this example and explaining its relevance to the topic at hand.

8. See, for example, Peppiatt, Mitchell, and Holzmann 2001; and Harvey and Holmes 2007.

9. Accounts of a few projects that have implemented such policies in contexts of food deficit, emergencies, or both are referenced in Ferguson 2010.

10. I am indebted to Patrick Bond for pointing this out to me in a stimulating discussion.

11. The literature has been ably summarized by Maurer (2006). See also Comaroff and Comaroff 1992 and Guyer 2004.

12. Especially relevant to my purposes here is a stimulating cluster of recent work from South Africa: see Bank and Minkley 2005; du Toit and Neves 2007; Seekings 2008a; du Toit and Neves 2009a, 2009b; Neves et al. 2009; Harper and Seekings 2010; Hunter 2010; Ross 2010; and Neves and du Toit 2012.

13. Even outside of marriage transactions, money can be semantically set aside from ordinary commodity exchange in ways that mark its specific sociality. Dlamani, for instance, has recently discussed the way that, in his own family history, an envelope of cash to be loaned among friends and family was never described as money but always as a "package" (in isiZulu, *impahla*), whose transfer was hedged in with rules of politeness and indirection (2009, 98–103).

14. Nicole Johnston, "Oxfam's Cash Trickle Goes a Long Way in Malawi," *Mail and Guardian*, May 21, 2011.

5. Declarations of Dependence

1. A lively debate has focused on the question of how this period should be named and understood. Older accounts tended to identify the period as "the *mfecane*" and understood it as a violent regional eruption that followed the founding of a highly militarized, centralized state by the Zulu kings Dingiswayo and Shaka. A controversial 1988 article by Julian Cobbing (1988) attacked the "mfecane mythology" and argued that the conflicts of the period were due instead to the European slave trade. Later research has mostly rejected Cobbing's specific arguments (especially regarding the role of the Delagoa Bay slave trade) but has also turned away from the idea of a singular eruption of violence, instead situating the period in a longer (and less Zulu-centric) history of state-making, within which warfare, raiding, and migration were fundamental features. See Omer-Cooper 1966; Cobbing 1988; Hamilton 1995; Wright 1995; and Etherington 2001. Delius (2010) has recently reviewed the entire literature with an eye to the central importance of the incorporation of captives, a theme not much developed in the "mfecane debate" but absolutely central to the argument I make later in this chapter.

2. Such voluntary submission to the fearsome Ngoni is also documented by Wiese ([1891] 1983, 58), who noted "entire settlements" fleeing to present themselves to the Ngoni even though the latter "are known for their savagery" and described (239) "thousands of wretched people" fleeing to the Ngoni chief Mpezeni to escape the taxation and violence meted out by a Portuguese-appointed chief, "preferring serfdom under a savage to the slavery of the ostensibly civilized African."

3. As Lucy Allais has recently pointed out, the foundational Enlightenment thinker Immanuel Kant was bothered by the spectacle of a man begging (and felt such practices should be restricted by the state) precisely because "a poor man who begs . . . *makes his existence dependent on other people*." A man is obliged, he claims, "to exert himself to the utmost to remain a free and independent being in relations to others, but as a beggar he depends upon the whims of other, and sacrifices his self-sufficiency." In shamelessly exhibiting such dependence, the beggar is demeaning himself and "de-

preciating his personhood"; indeed, he is displaying "the highest degree of contempt for himself" (Allais 2012, 2).

4. Barnes's account is in some respects dated, but more recent scholarship has confirmed the fundamental dynamic of incorporation that he described. Gordon (2009, 929), for instance, has noted that Ngoni captives and their children were incorporated into lineages and could even become chiefs; Phiri (1988, 21) notes the social mobility and full social participation that captives enjoyed. A contemporary observer, Wiese ([1891] 1983, 155) described the Ngoni as terrifyingly cruel in battle but noted that once captives were brought back to the village they were treated "with humanity" and mentioned specifically that he knew many former captives who had risen to positions of influence and wealth. See Delius (2010) for an excellent regional overview of the theme of incorporation of captives during the period together with a thoughtful reflection on the reasons for the relative neglect of the topic in the scholarly literature.

5. Some recent reinterpretations of "the mfecane" have suggested that a key dynamic motivating the accumulation of such "wealth in people" was an interest in the onward sale of captives as slaves (e.g., Cobbing 1988). Certainly, captives were sometimes sold, and the Ngoni did have dealings with Arab slavers. But Langworthy (in his editorial comments in Wiese [1891] 1983 [155]) insists that while Europeans often assumed that the endless Ngoni appetite for fresh captives must have been directed to supplying external slave markets, in fact "relatively few captives were sold," and "most captives remained within the Ngoni state." Wiese himself noted ([1891] 1983, 191) that "Mpezeni [the principal Ngoni chief] buys people but never sells them." As Delius (2010, 11) has pointed out, the astonishingly rapid expansion of the raiding states' populations alone points to the massive role of social incorporation of captives (and not their simple export). In the Ndebele case, he notes, it is estimated that Mzilikazi left northern Natal with a party of some 300; within a decade his followers numbered at least 20,000 (and perhaps many more). Barnes (1967) reckons that the Ngoni started in the early 1820s as a founding group of some 1,000; only three generations later there were perhaps half a million "Ngoni," almost all of whom could trace quasi-agnatic descent back to the chief (Zwangendaba) who led the original migration north (1967, 61).

6. See, for example, Radcliffe-Brown 1965; Fortes 1987; LaFontaine 1985; Piot 1991; and Englund 1996. For an insightful review of the issue of personhood from a specifically southern African perspective, see Comaroff and Comaroff 2001.

7. The literature I refer to is broadly Marxist in its inspiration, but it is hardly monolithic, neither at the level of theoretical models nor at that of empirical findings. Indeed, there has been a stimulating multiplicity of different ways of telling the story of the rise of industrial capitalism in the region and an impressive range of positions regarding how the transformation is to be understood (an industrial revolution? a case of internal colonialism? racial capitalism? the articulation of modes of production? uneven development?) as well as how, in historical terms, it proceeded (from the tidy periodizations of an orthodox Marxism to the messy, variegated landscape sketched by the social historians). It is a remarkably rich and nuanced literature far too vast to be reviewed here. All I want to say in this very crude overview is that, as different as

these stories have been, they have all been stories *about* the same thing: the transition from a pre-capitalist to a capitalist social order and the associated emergence of a proletariat. There is no doubt that such a transition is indeed a crucial feature of Southern African history, and debates about different ways to narrate it have rightly been central to the best scholarship in the region for many decades now. My point is not that this focus has been mistaken but only that the understandable dominance of (different versions of) what we might call the industrial capitalism story has made it harder to see certain continuities across "eras" (notably, what I describe as a social dynamic of competition over people) as well as breaks that would require a different periodization (notably, what I term a shift from a people-scarce social order to a people-surplus one).

8. Julia Livingston has recently noted the continuing relevance of such conceptions, in the context of physical disability in Botswana. While Western culture, in her terms, "fetishizes independence," Tswana, while valuing autonomy "also stress the relationships—or *dependencies*—that sustain personhood" (Livingston 2006, 121; emphasis in original).

9. To be sure, paternalistic and clientelistic attachments took significantly different forms in different industries, just as different kinds of social relationships often implied quite different idioms and practices of patron-client alliance (thus a white farmer might be a patron-protector to a landless laborer in a very different way than a black foreman to a fellow mineworker). My intent here is not to deny such differences but instead to identify, across a surprising range of social and institutional sites, an underlying commonality: a pervasive sociopolitical logic of social attachment via dependence.

10. Donham, for instance, relates stories told by black mineworkers that described white mine officials making sacrifices to a mystical snake in ways that "analogically transferred" to the officials the role of a kinsman making sacrifices to the ancestors (2011, 70–71). By the 1990s, with paternalistic solidarities being dishonored and discarded, Donham notes (following Niehaus) that the sacrificial scenario was being inverted to transform management "from a benevolent father figure who sacrifices to the ancestors into a horrible bloodsucker."

11. Indeed, Sylvia Yanagisako has noted that familial and paternalistic forms of authority have remained key features of capitalist production in Europe as well (Yanagisako 2002, 2012).

12. That what is at stake is not only employment but also an implicit social bond and the mutual responsibilities long understood to come with it is nicely revealed in the experience of one progressive white South African I met. Determined to treat the man he employed in his garden as a dignified professional engaged in a business transaction between equals, he reported that instead, to his dismay, the man "keeps going feudal on me!"—by seeking, that is, to replace the contractual relations of a business exchange with the intensely personalistic and intimate bonds of unequal dependence and care.

13. It is not a point I am able to develop here (lacking as I do both the space and the scholarly expertise to treat it properly), but it may also be worth considering whether

this sort of dynamic might not shed light on the very strong contemporary appeal of evangelical Christian churches across southern Africa and indeed much of the rest of the world as well. Like the NGO referenced above, these expanding collectivities "collect people"—and ascribe value to them not for their labor but for themselves. And like the old Ngoni state, the Kingdom of Heaven has the potential to incorporate anyone and everyone, offering a robust membership even to the lowest. Via a simple act of submission to a lord, one may acquire a form of social belonging, and a rightful place in something significant. In this sense, indeed, subordinating oneself to God might be considered the ultimate "declaration of dependence." It would not be wise, of course, to seek to reduce religious experience here to some sort of social "function" or symptom, but it would be well worth exploring (even if it is not my purpose here) how the apparently surging appeal of certain forms of Christian belonging might be understood as a response to the historical shedding of social relations of dependence that I have traced here. The issue is complex, however, since Christianity itself offers not only a form of belonging but sometimes also ways of refusing or escaping other ties of belonging and mutual obligation (such as those of kinship), as was pointed out nearly half a century ago by Norman Long (1968).

14. For a stimulating genealogy of the "dependency" concept, with special reference to its ideological uses in the context of U.S. welfare politics, see Fraser and Gordon 1994.

15. This observation should be put in the context of what Devereux and Lund (2010, 168–69) have termed "a perplexing dormancy of civil society in much of Africa with regard to mass mobilization and participation around welfare rights." The discussion here seeks to make that dormancy more intelligible; that of chapter 6 traces some ways in which it may be challenged as social payments come to be linked to a broader distributive politics.

16. Respondents chose this sentiment over an alternative that read "Government is like an employee; the people should be the bosses who control the government."

6. A Rightful Share

1. The Freedom Charter is a key statement of the core principles driving the ANC's long struggle against apartheid, originally declared by the South African Congress Alliance (an umbrella group that included the ANC) in 1955 and now a revered historical document and political touchstone.

2. For a recent articulation of this (traditional nationalist) reading, see ANCYL 2011.

3. Norway's oil industry, for instance, often cited as a model for responsible resource extraction, is dominated by a single state-owned company (Statoil), while Chile, even during its Pinochet-era tenure as poster child for neoliberalism, has preserved state ownership of its lucrative copper mines. See World Bank 2011 for an overview of state ownership models worldwide.

4. An anti-nationalization line was recently and forcefully reiterated at the ANC's 2012 party congress in Mangaung.

5. I am grateful to John Friedman (personal communication) for pointing to the importance of this issue in the Namibian context.

6. The one case of extensive land reform, Zimbabwe, is reviewed in Matondi 2012. For an overview of the land situation across the region, see Chigara 2012. On the South African land reform program and its manifold frustrations and limitations, see Deborah James 2007; Cherryl Walker 2008; O'Laughlin et al. 2013; and the many excellent publications of the Institute for Poverty, Land, and Agrarian Studies (PLAAS) at the University of the Western Cape (http:\\plaas.org.za).

7. See "Economic Justice? Piece of Cake, Says Juju," *Mail and Guardian*, January 6, 2012; "Blood for Land, Says Malema," *Mail and Guardian*, October 16, 2012; "Marches Will Restore Dignity, Says Malema," *Mail and Guardian*, October 19, 2012.

8. "What the Future May Look Like: Supplement—Transformation in Focus," *Mail and Guardian*, June 24, 2011.

9. "Blood for Land, Says Malema"; "Malema Stands Firm on Mineral Wealth Distribution," *Mail and Guardian*, October 23, 2011.

10. "They Really Are Out to Get Us, Says Julius," *Mail and Guardian*, October 25, 2011.

11. "Malema Stands Firm on Mineral Wealth Distribution."

12. "Malema's Latest 'Economic War' Heads to JSE," *Mail and Guardian*, September 10, 2011.

13. "Malema Stands Firm on Mineral Wealth Distribution."

14. " 'Because He Cares': Malema Sticks His Ore In," *Mail and Guardian*, February 29, 2012.

15. "Nationalisation Will Unite SA, Says Malema," *Mail and Guardian*, August 5, 2011.

16. "Ministers Fight Back on Nationalisation," *Mail and Guardian*, August 7, 2011.

17. "Malema Hogs the Limelight in Mangaung," *Mail and Guardian*, January 6, 2012.

18. "What the Future May Look Like: Supplement—Transformation in Focus"; " 'Because He Cares': Malema Sticks His Ore In."

19. " 'Because He Cares': Malema Sticks His Ore In."

20. Note that such worries are not only found on the political Right. Discussion documents of the COSATU labor federation have warned starkly of the dangers of the that corrupt state elites may come not only to demand bribes but to "systematically leverage their power to control large chunks of the economy," leading to "a predator state" that "will ultimately eat away and consume the whole of society" (COSATU 2010, 2, 11). The South African Communist Party, meanwhile, in the sort of political irony with which South Africans have become familiar in recent years, has become a vigorous and vocal opponent of nationalization for similar reasons ("Communists Slam Calls to Nationalize S. Africa Mines," Reuters, June 29, 2011, accessed March 12, 2013, http://www.reuters.com/article/2011/06/28/ozatp-safrica-nationalisation-idAFJOE75R07A20110628).

21. On the mixed record of South Africa's public employment schemes, see McCord 2003, 2012; Seekings 2006; Meth 2011; Philip 2013.

22. Woodburn's focus is particularly on what he calls "immediate-return hunter-gatherer sharing."

23. It is worth remembering that the corporate form has no intrinsic identity with capitalism. Indeed, "market socialists" like John Roemer see corporate shares precisely as a route to socialism ("coupon socialism"). (For a stimulating discussion, see Roemer 1996.) That is clearly not the direction things are taking in southern Africa, but it does open our eyes to some of the ways that sharing not only can be, but is already, central to the economic organization of our society, albeit in a highly particular and exclusionary form.

24. One could also, of course, deploy an anthropological language of redistribution (see Polanyi [1944] 2001; Sahlins 1974) to describe social payments, and indeed this has sometimes been done. But the ethnographic analogy of sharing, and especially demand sharing, poses the issues more sharply, since it entails not just a process of nonreciprocal apportionment (as does redistribution) but also an active role for the bearer of the "demand," the recipient of a rightful share.

25. Woodburn suggests this is in fact already the case with existing systems of social payments, in which (as in demand sharing) those who fund the system face compulsory demands (in the form of taxation) while "those who receive the benefits regard them as entitlements which do not have to be earned or even acknowledged" (1998, 63). This seems overoptimistic, since (whether in Southern welfare climes like South Africa or Northern ones like the United States) payments so often continue to be linked to ideas of generosity, charity, and desert. But the statement serves well as a kind of anticipation of the strong "demand sharing" claim that, I suggest below, may be starting to replace older ideas of "aid" and "assistance" driven by generosity or compassion for the unfortunate. For a recent discussion of how indigenous Australian systems of demand sharing articulate with contemporary social welfare regimes, see Peterson 2013.

26. A report from the Eastern Cape (Maistry and Vasi 2010) contains an impressive compilation of press accounts of instances in which grant-recipients have complained or protested about failings in the delivery system, also suggesting that transfers are received with at least some sense of rightful expectation rather than simply gratitude.

27. This amount was equal to about US$16 at the time it was originally proposed. Today, thanks to changes in the currency exchange rates, it is worth about US$10.

28. It should be noted, though, that similar invocations of the nation as a family, and of the country as the nation's common "house," have long been central to the legitimacy of European welfare states (Esping-Andersen 1990), while appeals to kinship as a model for broader duties to others are also well attested in "the West"—both within the nation (as in appeals to father- and motherlands, "fraternity" as a principle of solidarity, and so on) and occasionally beyond it (as in the nineteenth-century abolitionist medallion that, as Frederick Cooper [2013] has recently reminded us, pictured an enslaved African with the words "Am I not a man and a brother?"). The hierarchical possibilities of such familistic solidarity, of course, are also highly visible in Africa, where heads of state are often granted the symbolic and affective attributes of a father (see White 2012 for a thoughtful reflection on the way ideas of "love" help bind follower to leader in the case of South African president Jacob Zuma).

29. In an anthropological context, Widlok (2012, 188) has discussed the theme of sharing as a virtue (rather than as a gift animated by expectations of reciprocation).

30. Letter to the editor from Petrus Kariseb, *The Namibian*, May 13, 2011.

31. Letter to the editor from K. W. Shimwafeni, *The Namibian*, March 25, 2011.

32. Letter to the editor from T. Itembu, *The Namibian*, April 1, 2011.

33. Letter to the editor from D. Aluteni and T. Itembu, *The Namibian*, April 4, 2014.

34. "SADC Basic Income Grant," Studies in Poverty and Inequality Institute (Johannesburg), accessed February 23, 2014, http://takuspii.wordpress.com/projects /ser-programme-2/sadc-big. See also "SADC-Wide Basic Income Grant: Campaign Strategy Workshop Report, 18–19 November, 2013," Studies in Poverty and Inequality Institute and Open Society Initiative for Southern Africa, accessed February 23, 2014, http://spii.org.za/wp-content/uploads/2014/02/SADC-WIDE-BIG-REPORT.pdf. The organizing coalition is composed of NGOs from across the region and partly funded by the Open Society Initiative for Southern Africa. The SADC region comprises the following countries: South Africa, Lesotho, Swaziland, Botswana, Namibia, Angola, Mozambique, Zimbabwe, Zambia, Malawi, and the Democratic Republic of the Congo.

35. It is no accident that the most developed existing example of universal cash payment understood as an ownership share is a distribution of oil revenues—the Alaska Permanent Fund. Other examples, such as the Namibian BIG scheme discussed here and the new Iranian system of cash grants (discussed in the conclusion) are also tightly linked to ideas of a distribution of a national mineral wealth.

36. See Nash 1979; Taussig 1980; and Coronil 1997.

37. As Marxist philosopher Slavoj Žižek has recently acknowledged, a labor theory of value cannot provide a satisfactory account of the issue of mineral wealth: "We cannot have it both ways: something has to go, either Marx's labor theory of value or the notion of exploitation of the developing countries through robbing them of their natural resources" (2010, 242).

38. Kropotkin provides another example, even closer to the southern African bone, when he discusses mining: "The shafts of the mine still bear on their rocky walls the marks made by the pick of the workman who toiled to excavate them. The space between each prop in the underground galleries might be marked as a miner's grave; and who can tell what each of these graves has cost, in tears, in privations, in unspeakable wretchedness, to the family who depended on the scanty wage of the worker cut off in his prime by fire-damp, rockfall, or flood" ([1892] 1995, 14).

39. In fact, Hardt's break with a productionist logic here is only a partial one. He still seems to accept (2000, 29) that "the right to citizenship is founded on production for the nation," adding only the radical twist that such production is collective and universal. In fact, as suggested in chapter 1, Kropotkin's turn to inheritance was arguably more radical in dismissing productionist bias altogether and styling the entire productive apparatus as a common inheritance. The idea of "immaterial labor" (Hardt and Negri 2001), meanwhile, seems deeply wrongheaded, ignoring as it does the profound materiality of both the productive and the distributive practices that constitute

the lifeways of the poor, even as it analytically merges such lifeways with those of (sociologically entirely distinct) others such as highly paid software consultants and the like. (The related error of trying to create a collective subject "the precariat" that could replace "the proletariat" is briefly discussed in this book's conclusion.)

40. Kropotkin's highly unrealistic ideas about how distribution would be organized in a postrevolutionary society are briefly cited in this book's conclusion.

Conclusion. What Next for Distributive Politics?

1. See, e.g., Tania Li (2010) for a parallel discussion of related issues in Asia.

2. In this context, it is noteworthy that the rather anguished conversations about "jobs" that take place in so much of the world today turn not on the role of labor in production but precisely its role in distribution. This is increasingly as true in the global North as it is in the South. Indeed, to listen to contemporary American politicians, one would think the chief "output" of capitalist enterprises to be jobs rather than valuable goods and services (thus entrepreneurs and corporate CEOs are hailed as "job creators," not "product creators"). The owner of a factory that produces pins, in this logic, is valorized and rewarded not (as Adam Smith would have had it) as an efficient producer of a useful good (pins) but as a cherished creator of something far more precious: jobs. As this suggests, what is really scarce here is not economic goods (pins) but distributive entitlements (jobs).

3. The long history of the idea of basic income is reviewed in Van Parijs 1995; an impressive anthology of writings addressing basic income from a huge variety of perspectives has recently been published by Widerquist et al. (2013).

4. Of special interest are the experiences in the Netherlands, where a substantial political debate around basic income occurred already in the 1970s, and in Denmark, where a serious set of policy discussions in the early 1990s have been analyzed by Christensen (2008).

5. "GiveDirectly's Breakthrough 'Free Money' Program Grows as Evidence Builds," *Forbes*, February 10, 2014, accessed February 12, 2014, http://www.forbes.com/sites/hollieslade/2014/02/10/give-directlys-breakthrough-free-money-model-grows-as-evidence-mounts/?ss=social-impact/.

6. Pope Francis I, Apostolic Exhortation *Evangelii Gaudium*, Vatican City: Libreria Editrice Vaticana, 2013.

7. See also Gillies 2010 and Moss and Majerowicz 2013.

8. "Cap and Fade," *New York Times*, December 6, 2009, accessed February 8, 2014, http://www.nytimes.com/2009/12/07/opinion/07hansen.html?_r=0. See also http://citizensclimatelobby.org/carbon-tax.

9. Ideas of precarity and the precariat emerged out of Italian autonomist Marxism and have been disseminated into the English-speaking world largely through the writings of Paulo Virno (2004), Antonio Negri (see, e.g., 2008), and Michael Hardt (Hardt and Negri 2001, 2009). More recently, the idea of the precariat has become central to the work of basic income pioneer Guy Standing (2011).

10. Hardt, for instance, makes an admirable argument for a universal basic income but justifies such a payment precisely as a reward for production—all should receive payment because "labor is collective and social" and "global society as a whole produces wealth collectively" (2000, 27, 29).

11. On this view, recently articulated in the lively South African Left periodical *Amandla!*, the precariat is simply a class waiting to be organized. Once the unemployed and the "casualized and informalized" are organized, all that remains is to bring them into alliance with the organized labor movement ("With Friends Like These Who Needs Enemies?" *Amandla!* 25 [July 2012], 2–3).

12. While a social class is characterized by social relations that bound and reproduce it as such, distributed livelihoods work by crossing political boundaries and fragmenting social unities, as Marx recognized in his treatment of "lumpen" no-goods who are only too happy to attach themselves to whomever will provide them with sausages (see discussion in chapter 3).

13. In Kropotkin's improbable account, "the people" (in the form of "bands of volunteers") would spontaneously seize all warehouses, stores, and markets, with the happy result (he imagines) that a just system of universal public provisioning, including quite elaborate procedures of accounting and distributing goods, would simply "spring up spontaneously" out of the "admirable spirit of organization inherent in the people" ([1892] 1995, 60–61). Kropotkin's practical politics here seem to have been informed by his conviction (elaborated most fully in his treatise *Mutual Aid* [[1902] 2008]) that processes of cooperation lay at the heart of biological evolution. The effective inversion of Darwin's theme of competition resulted in an approach that was less a refutation of social Darwinian "survival of the fittest" than a mirror image of it and consequently led to a politics rooted in an essentialized idea of (cooperative) human nature.

14. Seekings and Matisonn 2010; cf. Meth 2008.

15. "Grants Encourage Liberation, Not Dependence," *Business Day*, August 23, 2013. Emphasis added.

16. Steven Friedman, "The Importance of Giving the Poor Some Choice," *Business Day*, September 4, 2013.

17. This was briefly proposed at a 2012 ANC Policy Conference but eventually passed over in favor of a controversial youth employment subsidy scheme ("Little Clarity on Zuma's Jobs Grant," *Mail and Guardian*, July 6, 2012). But given the prevailing anguished discussions about "the youth" as well as electoral pressure on that front coming from the newly formed Economic Freedom Fighters (EFF) party, one suspects that we may not have heard the last of the job-seekers' grant.

18. Standing (2008) has forcefully argued that even *conditional* cash transfer programs (whose limits he has long argued against) in the end help to promote the case for basic income and are ultimately likely to help to move policy in that direction.

19. On the idea of an "ethic of care," see Sevenhuijsen 1998. For an application of the concept to the South African social protection system, see Sevenhuijsen et al. 2003; for reflection on its relevance to anthropology, see Spiegel 2005.

20. As I observed in an earlier note, however, there remains a lingering productivism in Hardt's formulation, since "society" is seen as entirely composed of "workers" who (even when their work is "immaterial" or when they are not employed in any traditional sense) are busily "producing."

21. Žižek here appears to contradict himself, having asserted on just the previous page that Philippe van Parijs's proposal for universal basic income "offers a real 'Third Way' beyond capitalism and socialism" (2010, 235).

22. On Brazil, see Gledhill and Hita 2009 and Coêlho 2012; for India, see Corbridge et al. 2005 and Li 2010. See also Ballard 2013.

23. To be sure, Nyerere was aligned with other twentieth-century socialists in understanding rightful distribution to be firmly grounded in labor, such that "those who sow reap a fair share of what they sow." But he also held that a foundational principle of African socialism (past and future) was that any member of the society "could depend on the wealth possessed by the community of which he was a member" (1968, 2–4).

24. On xenophobia and xenophobic violence in the region, see Nyamnjoh 2006; Sichone 2008; and Landau 2012. More generally, John and Jean Comaroff (2009) have discussed the way that the proliferation of new forms of property has been associated with a similar proliferation of property-holding corporate groups, including those ostensibly based in ethnicity.

25. The oil-rich states of the Persian Gulf, for instance, may perhaps be regarded as cautionary examples here, insofar as the limitation of "welfare" provisioning to national citizens may mean in fact excluding the majority of the population, composed as it often is of "migrants." See, for example, Ahmed Kanna's (2011) account of Dubai.

26. "Ethics Matters: A Conversation with Thomas Pogge," Carnegie Council for Ethics in International Affairs, New York, accessed February 14, 2014, http://www .carnegiecouncil.org/calendar/data/0304.html.

27. In the previous chapter, I noted the recent inauguration of a southern Africa–wide basic income grant campaign aiming to institutionalize a system of universal cash transfers based on mineral extraction within the framework of the Southern African Development Community (SADC). It should also be noted that, already in 2006, representatives of thirteen African nations met in Livingstone, Zambia, and signed an agreement to expand social protection programs (including social transfers) in what was termed "The Livingstone Call to Action." Since that time, the African Union has sponsored a series of regular international conferences on social protection in Africa.

References

Afrobarometer. 2009. *Are Democratic Citizens Emerging in Africa? Evidence from the Afrobarometer.* Afrobarometer Briefing Paper 70, Institute for Democracy in South Africa, Pretoria.

Alexander, Peter. 2010. "Rebellion of the Poor: South Africa's Service Delivery Protests—A Preliminary Analysis." *Review of African Political Economy* 37 (123): 123–40.

Aliber, Michael, Cobus de Swardt, Andries du Toit, Themba Mbhele, and Themba Mthethwa. 2005. *Trends and Policy Challenges in the Rural Economy: Four Provincial Case Studies.* Cape Town: Human Sciences Research Council (HSRC) Press.

Allais, Lucy. 2012. "Kant on Giving to Beggars." Paper presented to the WISER Seminar, Wits Institute for Social and Economic Research, University of the Witwatersrand, South Africa, May 2012.

Ally, Shireen. 2009. *From Servants to Workers: South African Domestic Workers and the Democratic State.* Ithaca, NY: Cornell University Press.

ANCYL (African National Congress Youth League). 2011. "ANC Youth League and CONTRALESA Joint Media Statement after a Bi-Lateral Meeting," October 20.

Anderson, Perry. 2011. "Lula's Brazil." *London Review of Books* 33 (7): 3–12.

Bähre, Erik. 2007a. "Reluctant Solidarity: Death, Urban Poverty, and Neighbourly Assistance in South Africa." *Ethnography* 8 (1): 33–59.

———. 2007b. *Money and Violence: Financial Self-Help Groups in a South African Township.* Leiden: Brill.

———. 2012. "The Janus Face of Insurance in South Africa: From Costs to Risk, from Networks to Bureaucracies." *Africa* 82 (1): 150–67.

Balibar, Etienne. 2009. "What Is Political Philosophy? Contextual Notes." In *Rancière: History, Politics, Aesthetics,* ed. Gabriel Rockhill and Philip Watts. Durham, NC: Duke University Press.

Ballard, Richard. 2013. "Geographies of Development II: Cash Transfers and the Reinvention of Development for the Poor." *Progress in Human Geography* 37 (6): 811–21.

Bank, Leslie, and Gary Minkley. 2005. "Going Nowhere Slowly? Land, Livelihoods and Rural Development in the Eastern Cape." *Social Dynamics* 31 (1): 1–38.

Barchiesi, Franco. 2011. *Precarious Liberation: Workers, the State, and Contested Social Citizenship in Postapartheid South Africa*. Albany: State University of New York Press.

———. 2012. "Liberation of, through, or from Work? Postcolonial Africa and the Problem with 'Job Creation' in the Global Crisis." *Interface: A Journal for and about Social Movements* 4 (2): 230–53.

Barnes, J. A. 1967. *Politics in a Changing Society: A Political History of the Fort Jameson Ngoni*. Manchester, UK: Manchester University Press.

Barnett, Michael. 2013. *Empire of Humanity: A History of Humanitarianism*. Ithaca, NY: Cornell University Press.

Bayart, Jean-François. 1993. *The State in Africa: The Politics of the Belly*. London: Longman.

———. 2000. "Africa in the World: A History of Extraversion." *African Affairs* 99:217–67.

Bayat, Asef. 2009. *Life as Politics: How Ordinary People Change the Middle East*. Palo Alto, CA: Stanford University Press.

BBC (British Broadcasting Corporation). 2006. "Zimbabwe Jail over Bread Prices." BBC *News*, December 1.

Beinart, William, Peter Delius, and Stanley Trapido, eds. 1986. *Putting a Plough to the Ground: Accumulation and Dispossession in Rural South Africa, 1850–1930*. Johannesburg: Ravan Press.

Berman, Bruce. 1998. "Ethnicity, Patronage, and the African State: The Politics of Uncivil Nationalism." *African Affairs* 97:305–41.

Beveridge, William Henry. 1942. *Social Insurance and Allied Services: Report by Sir William Beveridge*. New York: Macmillan.

Biko, Steve. 1979. *I Write What I Like: A Selection of His Writings*. London: Heinemann.

Blackburn, Robin. 2011. "The Case for a Global Pension and Youth Grant." *Basic Income Studies* 6 (1): 1–12.

Bond, Patrick. 2000. *Elite Transition: From Apartheid to Neoliberalism in South Africa*. London: Pluto.

———. 2005. "South Africa's Left Critiques." *Africa Review of Books* 1 (20): 6–8.

———. 2012. "South Africa's 'Rights Culture' of Water Consumption." In *Water, Cultural Diversity and Global Environmental Change: Emerging Trends, Sustainable Futures?* ed. Barbara Johnston, Lisa Hiwasaki, Irene Klaver, A. Ramos Castillo, and Vernonica Strong. Paris: UNESCO.

———. 2013. "Water Rights, Commons, and Advocacy Narratives." *South African Journal on Human Rights* 29 (1): 125–43.

———. 2014. " 'Talk Left, Walk Right,' in South African Social Policy: Tokenistic Extension of State Welfare, or Bottom-up Commoning of Services." Paper presented to the seminar on social policy at the School of Development Studies, University of KwaZulu-Natal, February 19, 2014. Accessed March 30, 2014. http://ccs.ukzn.ac.za/files/Bond%20SA's%20tokenistic%20social%20policy.pdf.

Bornstein, Erica, and Peter Redfield, eds. 2011. *Forces of Compassion: Humanitarianism between Ethics and Politics.* Santa Fe, NM: School for Advanced Research Press.

Bourgois, Philipe, and Jeffery Schonberg. 2009. *Righteous Dopefiend.* Berkeley: University of California Press.

Breckenridge, Keith. 2005. "The Biometric State: The Promise and Peril of Digital Government in the New South Africa." *Journal of Southern African Studies* 31 (2): 267–82.

———. 2010. "The World's First Biometric Money: Ghana's E-Zwich and the Contemporary Influence of South African Biometrics." *Africa* 80 (4): 642–62.

Brokensha, David. 2007. *Brokie's Way: An Anthropologist's Story.* Fish Hoek, South Africa: Amani Press.

Busby, Helen. 2004. "Reassessing the 'Gift Relationship': The Meaning and Ethics of Blood Donation for Genetic Research in the UK." PhD dissertation, School of Sociology and Social Policy, University of Nottingham.

Calhoun, Craig. 2007. *Nations Matter: Culture, History and the Cosmopolitan Dream.* New York: Routledge.

Carlyle, Thomas. 1840. *Chartism.* London: James Fraser.

Case, Anne, Anu Garrib, Alicia Menendez, and Analia Olgiati. 2008. "Paying the Piper: The High Cost of Funerals in South Africa." Working Paper 14456, National Bureau of Economic Research, Washington, DC.

Chesterton, Gilbert K. 1912. *What's Wrong with the World.* New York: Dodd, Mead, and Company.

Chigara, Ben, ed. 2012. *Southern African Development Community Land Issues.* Vol. I, *Towards a New Sustainable Land Relations Policy.* London: Routledge.

Christensen, Erik. 2008. *The Heretical Political Discourse: A Discourse Analysis of the Danish Debate on Basic Income.* Aalborg, Denmark: Aalborg University Press.

Clarke, John. 2007. "What Is 'The Social' in Social Justice?" Paper presented at the annual meetings of the American Anthropological Association, Washington, DC, November 28–December 2.

Cobbing, Julian. 1988. "The Mfecane as Alibi: Thoughts on Dthakong and Mbolompo." *Journal of African History* 29 (3): 487–519.

Cock, Jacklyn. 1990. *Maids and Madams: Domestic Workers under Apartheid.* London: Women's Press.

Coêlho, Denilson Bandeira. 2012. "Brazil: Basic Income—A New Model of Innovation Diffusion." In *Basic Income Worldwide: Horizons of Reform,* ed. Matthew C. Murray and Carole Pateman, 59–80. New York: Palgrave Macmillan.

Cohen, G. A. 2009. *Why Not Socialism?* Princeton, NJ: Princeton University Press.

Cohen, Lawrence. Forthcoming. "Biometrics against the Social: De-duplication, Abject Matter, and the Future Government of the Indian Poor." Article manuscript.

Cole, Jennifer. 2010. *Sex and Salvation: Imagining the Future in Madagascar.* Chicago: University of Chicago Press.

Collier, Stephen J. 2011. *Post-Soviet Social: Neoliberalism, Social Modernity, Biopolitics.* Princeton, NJ: Princeton University Press.

———. 2012. "Neoliberalism as Big Leviathan, or . . . ? A Response to Wacquant and Hilgers." *Social Anthropology* 20 (2): 186–95.

Collins, Daryl, Jonathan Morduch, Stuart Rutherford, and Orlanda Ruthven. 2009. *Portfolios of the Poor: How the World's Poor Live on $2 a Day*. Princeton, NJ: Princeton University Press.

Comaroff, Jean, and John L. Comaroff. 2000. "Millennial Capitalism: First Thoughts on a Second Coming." *Public Culture* 12 (2): 291–343.

———. 2011. *Theory from the South: Or, How Euro-America is Evolving toward Africa*. Boulder, CO: Paradigm Publishers.

Comaroff, John L., and Jean Comaroff. 1992. *Ethnography and the Historical Imagination*. Boulder, CO: Westview Press.

———. 2001. "On Personhood: An Anthropological Perspective from Africa." *Social Identities: Journal for the Study of Race, Nation and Culture* 7 (2): 267–83.

———. 2009. *Ethnicity, Inc.* Chicago: University of Chicago Press.

Cooper, Frederick. 1996. *Decolonization and African Society: The Labor Question in French and British Africa*. New York: Cambridge University Press.

———. 2013. "Afterword: Social Rights and Human Rights in the Time of Decolonization." *Humanity* 3 (3): 473–92.

Corbridge, Stuart, Glyn Williams, Manoj Srivastava, and René Véron. 2005. *Seeing the State: Governance and Governmentality in India*. New York: Cambridge University Press.

Coronil, Fernando. 1997. *The Magical State: Nature, Money, and Modernity in Venezuela*. Chicago: University of Chicago Press.

COSATU. 2010. *COSATU CEC Political Discussion Paper: The Alliance at a Crossroads: The Battle against a Predatory Elite and Political Paralysis*. September 2010. Johannesburg: Congress of South African Trade Unions.

Crush, Jonathan, and Charles Ambler, eds. 1992. *Liquor and Labor in Southern Africa*. Athens: Ohio University Press.

Dagger, Richard. 1989. "Rights." In *Political Innovation and Conceptual Change*, ed. Terence Ball, James Farr, and Russell L. Hanson. New York: Cambridge University Press.

Dahl, Bianca. 2009. "The 'Failures of Culture': Christianity, Kinship, and Moral Discourses about Orphans during Botswana's AIDS Crisis." *Africa Today* 56 (1): 23–43.

Davie, Grace. 2005. "Poverty Knowledge in South Africa: The Everyday Life of Social Science Expertise in the Twentieth Century." PhD thesis, Department of History, University of Michigan.

Davis, Mike. 2006. *Planet of Slums*. New York: Verso.

Dean, Mitchell. 1992. "A Genealogy of the Government of Poverty." *Economy and Society* 21 (3): 215–51.

De Angelis, Massimo. 2006. *The Beginning of History: Value Struggles and Global Capital*. London: Pluto.

Defert, Daniel. 1991. "'Popular Life' and Insurance Technology." In *The Foucault Effect: Studies in Governmentality*, ed. Graham Burchell, Colin Gordon, and Peter Miller. Chicago: University of Chicago Press.

Delius, Peter. 2010. "Recapturing Captives and Conversations with 'Cannibals': In Pursuit of a Neglected Stratum in South African History." *Journal of Southern African Studies* 36 (1): 7–23.

Denning, Michael. 2010. "Wageless Life." *New Left Review* 66:79–97.

Desai, Ashwin. 2002. *We Are the Poors: Community Struggles in Post-Apartheid South Africa.* New York: Monthly Review Press.

de Soto, Hernando. 2003. *The Mystery of Capital: Why Capitalism Triumphs in the West and Fails Everywhere Else.* New York: Basic Books.

Devarajan, Shanta, and Marcelo Giugale. 2013. *The Case for Direct Transfers of Resource Revenues in Africa.* Working Paper 333, Center for Global Development, Washington, DC, July.

Devereux, Stephen. 2001. *Social Pensions in Namibia and South Africa.* Discussion Paper 379, Institute of Development Studies, Sussex.

———. 2007. "Social Pensions in Southern Africa in the Twentieth Century." *Journal of Southern African Studies* 33 (3): 539–60.

Devereux, Stephen, and Francie Lund. 2010. "Democratising Social Welfare in Africa." In *The Political Economy of Africa,* ed. Vishun Padayachee. New York: Routledge.

DFID (Department for International Development). 2011. *Cash Transfers: Literature Review.* Policy Division, UK Department for International Development, April 2011.

Dlamini, Jacob. 2009. *Native Nostalgia.* Auckland Park, South Africa: Jacana Media.

Dodson, Lisa. 2011. *The Moral Underground: How Ordinary Americans Subvert an Unfair Economy.* New York: The New Press.

Donham, Donald. 2011. *Violence in a Time of Liberation: Murder and Ethnicity at a South African Gold Mine, 1994.* Durham, NC: Duke University Press.

Donzelot, Jacques. 1979. *The Policing of Families.* New York: Pantheon Books.

———. 1984. *L'invention du social.* Paris: Vrin.

Douglas, Mary. 1971. "Review of Richard M. Titmuss, *The Gift Relationship: From Human Blood to Social Policy.*" *Man* (n.s.) 6 (3): 499–500.

Drèze, Jean, and Amartya Sen. 1991. *Hunger and Public Action.* New York: Oxford University Press.

DSD (Department of Social Development). 2002. *Transforming the Present—Protecting the Future: Report of the Committee of Inquiry into a Comprehensive System of Social Security for South Africa.* Pretoria: Government Printer.

———. 2008. *Creating Our Future: Strategic Considerations for a Comprehensive System of Social Security.* Pretoria: Department of Social Development.

DSD (Department of Social Development), SASSA (South Africa Social Security Agency), and UNICEF (United Nations Children's Fund). 2012. *The South African Child Support Grant Impact Assessment: Evidence from a Survey of Children, Adolescents and Their Households.* Pretoria: UNICEF South Africa.

Dubbeld, Bernard. 2013. "How Social Security Becomes Social Insecurity: Fluid Households, Crisis Talk and the Value of Grants in a KwaZulu-Natal Village." Seminar Paper, Wits Institute for Social and Economic Research, Johannesburg, University of the Witwatersrand, September 9.

Du Toit, Andries. 1993. "The Micro-politics of Paternalism: The Discourses of Management and Resistance on South African Fruit and Wine Farms." *Journal of Southern African Studies* 19 (2): 314–36.

———. 2007. "Poverty Measurement Blues: Some Reflections on the Space for Understanding 'Chronic' and 'Structural' Poverty in South Africa." Paper presented at the conference Workshop on Concepts and Methods for Analysing Poverty Dynamics and Chronic Poverty, Manchester.

———. 2012. *The Trouble with Poverty: Reflections on South Africa's Post-apartheid Anti-poverty Consensus*. Working Paper 22, Institute for Poverty, Land and Agrarian Studies (PLAAS), Bellville, University of the Western Cape.

Du Toit, Andries, and Joachim Ewert. 2002. "Myths of Globalization: Private Regulation and Farm Worker Livelihoods on Western Cape Farms." *Transformation* 50:77–104.

Du Toit, Andries, and David Neves. 2007. *In Search of South Africa's 'Second Economy': Chronic Poverty, Economic Marginalisation and Adverse Incorporation in Mt Frere and Khayelitsha*. Working Paper 1, Programme for Land and Agrarian Studies (PLAAS), University of the Western Cape, South Africa.

———. 2009a. *Informal Social Protection in Post-apartheid Migrant Networks*. Working Paper 2, Programme for Land and Agrarian Studies (PLAAS), University of the Western Cape, South Africa.

———. 2009b. *Trading on a Grant: Integrating Formal and Informal Social Protection in Post-apartheid Migrant Networks*. Working Paper 3, Programme for Land and Agrarian Studies (PLAAS), University of the Western Cape, South Africa.

Ellis, Frank, Stephen Devereux, and Philip White. 2009. *Social Protection in Africa*. Northampton, Massachusetts: Edward Elgar.

Elmslie, Walter Angus. 1899. *Among the Wild Ngoni: Being Some Chapters in the History of the Livingstonia Mission in British Central Africa*. New York: Fleming H. Revell Company.

Engels, Friedrich. (1870) 1968. "Preface to the Peasant War in Germany." In *Marx and Engels: Selected Works*, 224–36. London: Lawrence and Wishart.

Englund, Harri. 1996. "Witchcraft, Modernity and the Person: The Morality of Accumulation in Central Malawi." *Critique of Anthropology* 16:257–79.

———. 2006. *Prisoners of Freedom: Human Rights and the African Poor*. Berkeley: University of California Press.

———. 2008. "Extreme Poverty and Existential Obligations: Beyond Morality in the Anthropology of Africa?" *Social Analysis* 52:3, 33–50.

———. 2011. *Human Rights and African Airwaves: Mediating Equality on the Chichewa Radio*. Bloomington: Indiana University Press.

Esping-Andersen, Gøsta. 1990. *The Three Worlds of Welfare Capitalism*. Princeton: Princeton University Press.

Etherington, Norman. 2001. *The Great Treks: The Transformation of Southern Africa, 1815–1854*. London: Longman.

Evans, Peter. 2008. "Is an Alternative Globalization Possible?" *Politics and Society* 36 (2): 271–305.

Everatt, David, and Geetesh Solanki. 2008. "A Nation of Givers? Results from a National Survey of Social Giving." In *Giving and Solidarity: Resource Flows for Poverty Alleviation and Development in South Africa*, ed. Adam Habib and Brij Maharaj. Pretoria: Human Sciences Research Council (HSRC) Press.

Ewald, François. 1986. *L'Etat providence*. Paris: Grasset.

Fanon, Franz. (1961) 2005. *The Wretched of the Earth*. New York: Grove Press.

FAO (Food and Agricultural Organization of the United Nations). 2010. *The State of World Fisheries and Aquaculture 2010*. Rome: Food and Agriculture Organization of the United Nations, Fisheries and Aquaculture Department.

———. 2012. *The State of World Fisheries and Aquaculture 2012*. Rome: Food and Agriculture Organization of the United Nations, Fisheries and Aquaculture Department.

Fassin, Didier. 2011. *Humanitarian Reason: A Moral History of the Present*. Berkeley: University of California Press.

Feldman, Ilana, and Miriam Ticktin, eds. 2010. *In the Name of Humanity: The Government of Threat and Care*. Durham, NC: Duke University Press.

Ferguson, James. 1985. "The Bovine Mystique: Power, Property and Livestock in Rural Lesotho." *Man* (n.s.) 20 (4): 647–74.

———. 1990. *The Anti-Politics Machine: "Development," Depoliticization, and Bureaucratic Power in Lesotho*. New York: Cambridge University Press.

———. 1999. *Expectations of Modernity: Myths and Meanings of Urban Life on the Zambian Copperbelt*. Berkeley: University of California Press.

———. 2006. *Global Shadows: Africa in the Neoliberal World Order*. Durham: Duke University Press.

———. 2007. "Formalities of Poverty: Thinking about Social Assistance in Neoliberal South Africa." *African Studies Review* 50 (2): 71–86.

———. 2010. "The Uses of Neoliberalism." *Antipode* 41 (S1): 166–84.

———. 2013. "Invisible Humanism: An African 1968 and Its Aftermaths." In *The Long 1968: Revisions and New Perspectives*, ed. Jasmine Alinder, Aneesh Aneesh, Daniel J. Sherman, and Ruud van Dijk. Bloomington: Indiana University Press.

Fine, Ben. 2000. *Social Capital versus Social Theory: Political Economy and Social Science at the Turn of the Millennium*. New York: Routledge.

Fortes, Meyer. 1987. "The Concept of the Person." In *Religion, Morality and the Person: Essays on Tallensi Religion*, 247–86. New York: Cambridge University Press.

Foucault, Michel. 1988. *Politics, Philosophy, Culture: Interviews and Other Writings, 1977–1984*. New York: Routledge.

———. 2003. *"Society Must Be Defended": Lectures at the Collège de France, 1975–1976*. New York: Picador.

———. 2008. *The Birth of Biopolitics: Lectures at the Collège de France, 1978–1979*. Translated by Graham Burchell. New York: Palgrave MacMillan.

Fourcade, Marion, and Kieran Healy. 2007. "Moral Views of Market Society." *Annual Review of Sociology* 33:285–311.

Fournier, Marcel. 2006. *Marcel Mauss: A Biography*. Princeton: Princeton University Press.

Fraser, Nancy. 2013. *Fortunes of Feminism: From State-Managed Capitalism to Neoliberal Crisis.* New York: Verso.

Fraser, Nancy, and Linda Gordon. 1994. "A Genealogy of Dependency: Tracing a Keyword of the U.S. Welfare State." *Signs* 19 (2): 309–36.

Frassanito Network. 2005. "Precarious, Precarization, Precariat?" *Understanding Precarity* (blog). Accessed August 10, 2011. http://precariousunderstanding.blogsome .com/2007/01/05/precarious-precarization-precariat/.

Friedman, John. 2011. *Imagining the Post-apartheid State: An Ethnographic Account of Namibia.* London: Berghahn Books.

Garcia, Marito, and Charity M. T. Moore. 2012. *The Cash Dividend: The Rise of Cash Transfer Programs in Sub-Saharan Africa.* Washington, DC: The World Bank.

Gelb, Alan, and Caroline Decker. 2011. *Cash at Your Fingertips: Biometric Technology for Transfers in Resource-Rich Countries.* Working Paper 253, Center for Global Development, Washington, DC.

Geschiere, Peter. 2009. *The Perils of Belonging: Autochthony, Citizenship, and Exclusion in Africa and Europe.* Chicago: University of Chicago Press.

Gibson-Graham, J. K. 2006. *The End of Capitalism (As We Knew It): A Feminist Critique of Political Economy.* Minneapolis: University of Minnesota Press.

Gillies, Alexandra. 2010. *Giving Money Away? The Politics of Direct Distribution in Resource-Rich States.* Working Paper 231, Center for Global Development, Washington, DC.

Gledhill, John, and Maria Gabriela Hita. 2009. *New Actors, New Political Spaces, Same Divided City? Reflections on Poverty and the Politics of Urban Development in Salvador, Bahia.* Working Paper 102, Brooks World Poverty Institute, University of Manchester.

Gorden, Kea. 2008. "Conjuring Power: The Politics of Culture and Democratization in Post-apartheid South Africa." PhD dissertation, Department of Politics, University of California, Santa Cruz.

Gordon, David M. 2009. "The Abolition of the Slave Trade and the Transformation of the South-Central African Interior during the Nineteenth Century." *William and Mary Quarterly Third Series* 66 (4): 915–38.

Gough, Ian, Geof Wood, Armando Barrientos, Philippa Bevan, Peter Davis, and Graham Room. 2008. *Insecurity and Welfare Regimes in Asia, Africa and Latin America: Social Policy in Development Contexts.* New York: Cambridge University Press.

Graeber, David. 2004. *Fragments of an Anarchist Anthropology.* Chicago: Prickly Paradigm Press.

Grinker, Roy Richard. 1994. *Houses in the Rainforest: Ethnicity and Inequality among Farmers and Foragers in Central Africa.* Berkeley: University of California Press.

Gudeman, Stephen. 2008. *Economy's Tension: The Dialectics of Community and Market.* New York: Berghahn Books.

Guillaume, Dominique, Roman Zytek, and Mohammed Reza Farzin. 2011. *Iran—The Chronicles of the Subsidy Reform.* Working Paper WP/11/167, International Monetary Fund, Washington, DC.

Gupta, Akhil. 2012. *Red Tape: Bureaucracy, Structural Violence, and Poverty in India.* Durham, NC: Duke University Press.

Guyer, Jane L. 1993. "Wealth in People and Self-Realization in Equatorial Africa." *Man* (n.s.) 28 (2): 243–65.

———. 2004. *Marginal Gains: Monetary Transactions in Atlantic Africa.* Chicago: University of Chicago Press.

Haarmann, Claudia, Dirk Haarmann, Herbert Jauch, Hilma Shindondola-Mote, Nicoli Nattrass, Ingrid van Niekirk, and Michael Sampson. 2009. *Making the Difference! The* BIG *in Namibia, Basic Income Grant Pilot Project Assessment Report.* Windhoek: BIG (Basic Income Grant) Coalition.

Habib, Adam, and Brij Maharaj. 2008. *Giving and Solidarity: Resource Flows for Poverty Alleviation and Development in South Africa.* Pretoria: Human Sciences Research Council (HSRC) Press.

Hacking, Ian. 1990. *The Taming of Chance.* New York: Cambridge University Press.

Haggard, Stephan, and Robert R. Kaufman. 2008. *Development, Democracy, and Welfare States: Latin America, East Asia, and Eastern Europe.* Princeton, NJ: Princeton University Press.

Hamilton, Carolyn, ed. 1995. *The Mfecane Aftermath: Reconstructive Debates in Southern African History.* Johannesburg: Witwatersrand University Press.

Han, Clara. 2011. "Symptoms of Another Life: Time, Possibility, and Domestic Relations in Chile's Credit Economy." *Cultural Anthropology* 26 (1): 7–32.

Hanlon, Joseph, Armando Barrientos, and David Hulme. 2010. *Just Give Money to the Poor: The Development Revolution from the Global South.* Sterling: Kumarian Press.

Hansen, Karen Tranberg, and Mariken Vaa, eds. 2004. *Reconsidering Informality: Perspectives from Urban Africa.* Uppsala: Nordic Africa Institute.

Hardt, Michael. 2000. "Guaranteed Income: Or, the Separation of Labor from Income." *Hybrid* 5:21–31.

———. 2009. "The Politics of the Common." Z-Net document. Accessed August 10, 2011. http://www.zcommunications.org/politics-of-the-common-by-michael-hardt.

Hardt, Michael, and Antonio Negri. 2001. *Empire.* Cambridge, MA: Harvard University Press.

———. 2009. *Commonwealth.* Cambridge, MA: Belknap Press of Harvard University Press.

Harper, Sarah, and Jeremy Seekings. 2010. *Claims on and Obligations to Kin in Cape Town, South Africa.* Working Paper 272, Center for Social Science Research, University of Cape Town.

Hart, Gillian. 2008. "The Provocations of Neoliberalism: Contesting the Nation and Liberation after Apartheid." *Antipode* 40 (4): 678–704.

Hart, Keith. 2005. "Notes toward an Anthropology of Money." *Kritikos* 2 (June).

———. 2007a. "Marcel Mauss: In Pursuit of the Whole. A Review Essay." *Comparative Studies in Society and History* 49 (2): 473–85.

———. 2007b. "Bureaucratic Form and the Informal Economy." In *Linking the Formal and Informal Economy: Concepts and Policies,* ed. Basudeb Guha-Khasnobis, Ravi Kanbur, and Elinor Ostrom. New York: Oxford University Press.

Hart, Keith, Jean-Louis Laville, and Antonio David Cattani. 2010. *The Human Economy: A Citizen's Guide.* Cambridge: Polity Press.

Harvey, David. 2005. *The New Imperialism*. New York: Oxford University Press.

———. 2007. *A Brief History of Neoliberalism*. New York: Oxford University Press.

Harvey, Paul, and Rebecca Holmes. 2007. *The Potential for Joint Programmes for Long-Term Cash Transfers in Unstable Situations: A Report Commissioned by the Fragile States Team and the Equity and Rights Team of the UK Department for International Development*. London: Humanitarian Policy Group, Overseas Development Institute.

Henderson, Ian. 1972. "White Populism in Southern Rhodesia." *Comparative Studies in Society and History* 14 (4): 387–99.

Henderson, Patricia C. 2012. *AIDS, Intimacy and Care in Rural KwaZulu-Natal: A Kinship of Bones*. Amsterdam: Amsterdam University Press.

Hersoug, Bjørn. 2002. *Fishing in a Sea of Sharks: Reconstruction and Development in the South African Fishing Industry*. Delft: Eburon.

Higginson, John. 1989. *A Working Class in the Making: Belgian Colonial Labor Policy, Private Enterprise, and the African Mineworker, 1907–1951*. Madison: University of Wisconsin Press.

Ho, Karen. 2009. *Liquidated: An Ethnography of Wall Street*. Durham, NC: Duke University Press.

Horn, David G. 1994. *Social Bodies: Science, Reproduction, and Italian Modernity*. Princeton, NJ: Princeton University Press.

Hull, Elizabeth, and Deborah James. 2012. "Introduction: Popular Economies in South Africa." *Africa* 82 (1): 1–19.

Hunt, Nancy Rose. 1999. *A Colonial Lexicon: Of Birth Ritual, Medicalization, and Mobility in the Congo*. Durham, NC: Duke University Press.

Hunter, Mark. 2010. *Love in the Time of AIDS: Inequality, Gender, and Rights in South Africa*. Bloomington: Indiana University Press.

Iliffe, John. 1987. *The African Poor: A History*. New York: Cambridge University Press.

ILO (International Labour Organization). 2011. *Social Protection Floor for a Fair and Inclusive Globalization*. Report of the Advisory Group chaired by Michelle Bachelet, convened by the ILO with the collaboration of the WHO. Geneva: International Labour Office.

———. 2012. *Social Protection Floors for Social Justice and a Fair Globalization*. Report IV (2B). International Labour Conference, 101st Session, 2012. Geneva: International Labour Office.

James, Deborah. 2007. *Gaining Ground? Rights and Property in South African Land Reform*. London: Routledge-Cavendish.

———. 2012. "Money-Go-Round: Personal Economies of Wealth, Aspiration, and Indebtedness." *Africa* 82 (1): 20–40.

Kanna, Ahmed. 2011. *Dubai: The City as Corporation*. Minneapolis: University of Minnesota Press.

Kaseke, Edwin. 2002. "Zimbabwe." In *The State of Social Welfare: The Twentieth Century in Cross-national Review*, ed. John Dixon and Robert P. Scheurell. Westport, CT: Praeger.

Kepe, Thembela, Ruth Hall, and Ben Cousins. 2008. "Land." In *New South African Keywords*, ed. Nick Shepherd and Steven Robins. Athens: Ohio University Press.

King, Martin Luther, Jr. 1967. *Where Do We Go From Here: Chaos or Community?* New York: Harper and Row.

Klein, Naomi. 2008. *The Shock Doctrine: The Rise of Disaster Capitalism.* New York: Picador.

Koopman, Colin, and Tomas Matza. 2013. "Putting Foucault to Work." *Critical Inquiry* 39 (4): 817–40.

Kropotkin, Peter. (1892) 1995. *The Conquest of Bread and Other Writings.* Ed. Marshall S. Shatz. New York: Cambridge University Press.

———. (1902) 2008. *Mutual Aid: A Factor of Evolution.* Charleston, SC: Forgotten Books.

Krucken, Georg, and Gili S. Drori, eds. 2009. *World Society: The Writings of John W. Meyer.* New York: Oxford University Press.

Kumchulesi, Grace. 2011. "Determinants of Women's Marriage Decisions in South Africa." Paper presented at the annual meeting of the Population Association of America (PAA), Washington, DC.

Lafargue, Paul. 2011. *The Right to Be Lazy: Essays by Paul Lafargue.* Ed. Bernard Marszalek. Oakland, California: AK Press.

LaFontaine, Joan. 1985. "Person and Individual: Some Anthropological Reflections." In *The Category of the Person*, ed. Michael Carrithers, Steven Collins, and Steven Lukes, 123–41. New York: Cambridge University Press.

Lakshmi, Rama. 2010. "Biometric Identity Project in India Aims to Provide for Poor, End Corruption." *Washington Post*, March 28.

Landau, Loren B., ed. 2012. *Exorcising the Demons Within: Xenophobia, Violence and Statecraft in Contemporary South Africa.* Tokyo: United Nations University Press.

Landless People's Movement. 2001. "The Landless People's Charter." Durban, South Africa: Landless People's Movement.

Latour, Bruno, and Vincent Antonin Lépinay. 2009. *The Science of Passionate Interests: An Introduction to Gabriel Tarde's Economic Anthropology.* Chicago: Prickly Paradigm Press.

Leach, Edmund. 1971. "The Heart of the Matter." *New Society* 21 (January).

Leclerc-Madlala, Suzanne. 2004. *Transactional Sex and the Pursuit of Modernity.* Working Paper 68, Centre for Social Science Research, University of Cape Town.

Lee, Rebekah. 2011. "Death 'on the Move': Funerals, Entrepreneurs and the Rural-Urban Nexus in South Africa." *Africa: The Journal of the International African Institute* 81 (2): 226–47.

Lenin, V. I. 1968. *Lenin on Politics and Revolution: Selected Writings.* Ed. James E. Connor. New York: Pegasus.

Levine, Sebastian, Servaas van der Berg, and Derek Yu. 2009. *Measuring the Impact of Social Cash Transfers on Poverty and Inequality in Namibia.* Economic Working Papers 25/09, Department of Economics and the Bureau for Economic Research, University of Stellenbosch.

Lévi-Strauss, Claude. 1976. "Race and History." In *Structural Anthropology*, vol. 2. Chicago: University of Chicago Press.

Li, Tania. 2010. "To Make Live or Let Die? Rural Dispossession and the Protection of Surplus Populations." *Antipode* 41 (supplement S1): 66–93.

Livingston, Julia. 2006. "Insights from an African History of Disability." *Radical History Review* 94:111–26.

Lo Vuolo, Rubén M. 2013. *Citizen's Income and Welfare Regimes in Latin America: From Cash Transfers to Rights*. New York: Palgrave Macmillan.

Long, Norman. 1968. *Social Change and the Individual: A Study of the Social and Religious Responses to Innovation in a Zambian Rural Community*. Manchester: Manchester University Press.

Lund, Francie. 2008. *Changing Social Policy: The Child Support Grant in South Africa*. Cape Town: Human Sciences Research Council (HSRC) Press.

Macleod, Catriona, and Tiffany Tracey. 2009. *Review of South African Research and Interventions in the Development of a Policy Strategy on Teen-Aged Pregnancy*. Grahamstown, South Africa: Rhodes University (for Department of Health, Republic of South Africa, and the World Health Organization).

Macpherson, C. B. (1962) 2011. *The Political Theory of Possessive Individualism: Hobbes to Locke*. New York: Oxford University Press.

Mahmood, Saba. 2005. *Politics of Piety: The Islamic Revival and the Feminist Subject*. Princeton, NJ: Princeton University Press.

Maistry, Margie, and Shirlee Vasi. 2010. "Social Development, including Social Grants." The Eastern Cape Basic Services Delivery and Socio-economic Trends Series, Number 12. Fort Hare, South Africa: Fort Hare Institute of Social and Economic Research.

Makhulu, Anne-Maria. 2012. "The Conditions for After Work: Financialization and Informalization in Posttransition South Africa." PMLA 127 (4): 782–99.

Malinowski, Bronislaw. (1922) 1984. *Argonauts of the Western Pacific: An Account of Native Enterprise and Adventure in the Archipelagoes of Melanisian New Guinea*. Long Grove, IL: Waveland Press.

Malkki, Liisa H. 2015. *The Need to Help: The Domestic Arts of International Humanitarianism*. Durham, NC: Duke University Press.

Mamdani, Mahmood. 2002. "Amnesty or Impunity? A Preliminary Critique of the Report of the Truth and Reconciliation Commission of South Africa (TRC)." *Diacritics* 32 (3–4): 33–59.

Marais, Hein. 2001. *South Africa: Limits to Change*. London: Zed.

———. 2011. *South Africa Pushed to the Limit: The Political Economy of Change*. London: Zed.

Marshall, T. H. (1949) 1987. "Citizenship and Social Class." In *Citizenship and Social Class*, ed. Trevor Marshall and Tom Bottomore. London: Pluto Press.

Marx, Karl. (1850) 1964. *Class Struggles in France*. New York: International Publishers.

———. (1852) 1978. *The Eighteenth Brumaire of Louis Bonaparte*. Peking: Foreign Languages Press.

———. (1857) 1973. *Grundrisse: Foundations of the Critique of Political Economy*. Trans. Martin Nicolaus. New York: Vintage.

———. 1977. *Karl Marx: Selected Writings*. Ed. David McLellan. Oxford: Oxford University Press.

Marx, Karl, and Frederick Engels. (1848) 1998. *The Communist Manifesto: A Modern Edition*. New York: Verso.

Matondi, Prosper B. 2012. *Zimbabwe's Fast Track Land Reform*. London: Zed.

Maurer, Bill. 2006. "The Anthropology of Money." *Annual Review of Anthropology* 35:15–36.

Mauss, Marcel. (1924) 1983. "A Sociological Assessment of Bolshevism (1924–25)." Trans. Ben Brewster. *Economy and Society* 13 (3): 331–74.

———. (1924) 2000. *The Gift: The Form and Reason for Exchange in Archaic Societies*. Trans. W. D. Halls. New York: W. W. Norton.

McCloskey, Deirdre N. 2006. *The Bourgeois Virtues: Ethics for an Age of Commerce*. Chicago: University of Chicago Press.

McCord, Anna Gabriele. 2003. *An Overview of the Performance and Potential of Public Works Programmes in South Africa*. Working Paper 49, Centre for Social Science Research, University of Cape Town.

———. 2012. *Public Works and Social Protection in Sub-Saharan Africa: Do Public Works Work for the Poor?* Tokyo: United Nations University Press.

McIntosh, Mary. 2006. "Feminism and Social Policy." In *The Welfare State Reader*, ed. Christopher Pierson and Francis G. Castles. Malden, MA: Polity Press.

McKay, Ramah. 2010. "Post-social Prescriptions: Medical Welfare in Mozambique." PhD dissertation, Department of Anthropology, Stanford University.

———. 2012. "Afterlives: Humanitarian Histories and Critical Subjects in Mozambique." *Cultural Anthropology* 27:286–309.

McLean, Iain. 2010. "The Gift Relationship." The Policy Network. Accessed June 2, 2011. http://www.policy-network.net/articles_detail.aspx?ID=3872.

Meagher, Kate. 2010. *Identity Economics: Social Networks and the Informal Economy in Nigeria*. London: James Currey.

Meskell, Lynn. 2011. *The Nature of Heritage: The New South Africa*. Malden, MA: Wiley-Blackwell.

Meth, Charles. 2004. "Ideology and Social Policy: 'Handouts' and the Spectre of 'Dependency.'" *Transformation* 56:1–30.

———. 2008. *Basic Income Grant: There Is No Alternative! (BIG TINA!)*. Working Paper 54, School of Development Studies, University of KwaZulu-Natal, October.

———. 2011. *Employer of Last Resort? South Africa's Expanded Public Works Programme (EPWP)*. Working Paper 58, South African Labour and Development Research Unit, University of Cape Town.

Miers, Suzanne, and Igor Kopytoff, eds. 1977. *Slavery in Africa: Historical and Anthropological Perspectives*. Madison: University of Wisconsin Press.

Miller, Peter, and Nikolas Rose. 2008. *Governing the Present: Administering Economic, Social and Personal Life*. Cambridge: Polity Press.

Molyneux, Maxine. 2007a. *Change and Continuity in Social Protection: Mothers at the Service of the State?* Gender and Development Program Paper 1, United Nations Research Institute for Social Development. Accessed October 1, 2013. http://www.unrisd.org/80256B3C005BCCF9/%28httpAuxPages%29/BF80E0A84BE41896C12573240033C541/$file/Molyneux-paper.pdf.

——. 2007b. "Two Cheers for CCTs." *IDS Bulletin* 38 (3): 69–74.

Moodie, T. Dunbar, with Vivian Ndatshe. 1994. *Going for Gold: Men, Mines, and Migration.* Berkeley: University of California Press.

Moore, Donald. 2005. *Suffering for Territory: Race, Place, and Power in Zimbabwe.* Durham, NC: Duke University Press.

Moore, Henrietta L., and Megan Vaughan. 1994. *Cutting Down Trees: Gender, Nutrition, and Agricultural Change in the Northern Province of Zambia, 1890–1990.* London: Heinemann.

Morgan, Kimberly J. 2013. "America's Misguided Approach to Social Welfare: How the Country Could Get More for Less." *Foreign Affairs* 92 (1): 153–64.

Morgan, Lewis Henry. 1877. *Ancient Society: Or, Researches in the Lines of Human Progress from Savagery, Through Barbarism to Civilization.* New York: Henry Holt.

Morrell, Robert. 1992. *White but Poor: Essays on the History of Poor Whites in Southern Africa, 1880–1940.* Pretoria: University of South Africa.

Moss, Todd. 2012. "How to Turn Citizens into Owners of National Wealth." Center for Global Development, Washington, DC. Accessed February 13, 2014. http://www .cgdev.org/blog/how-turn-citizens-owners-national-wealth.

Moss, Todd, and Stephanie Majerowicz. 2013. *Oil-to-Cash Won't Work Here! Ten Common Objections.* Policy Paper 024, Center for Global Development, Washington, DC.

Mudhara, Maxwell. 2010. "Agrarian Transformation in Smallholder Agriculture in South Africa: A Diagnosis of Bottlenecks and Public Policy Options." Paper presented at the conference Overcoming Inequality and Structural Poverty in South Africa: Towards Inclusive Growth and Development, September 2010. Accessed July 6, 2012. http://www.plaas.org.za/sites/default/files/publications-pdf/Mudhara.pdf.

Muehlebach, Andrea. 2012. *The Moral Neoliberal: Welfare and Citizenship in Italy.* Chicago: University of Chicago Press.

Murray, Colin. 1981. *Families Divided: The Impact of Migrant Labour in Lesotho.* New York: Cambridge University Press.

Murray, Matthew C., and Carole Pateman, eds. 2012. *Basic Income Worldwide: Horizons of Reform.* New York: Palgrave Macmillan.

Nash, June. 1979. *We Eat the Mines and the Mines Eat Us: Dependency and Exploitation in Bolivian Tin Mines.* New York: Columbia University Press.

National Treasury. 2012. *Budget Review 2012.* Pretoria: Department of National Treasury, South African Ministry of Finance.

——. 2013. *Budget Review 2013.* Pretoria: Department of National Treasury, South African Ministry of Finance.

Negri, Antonio. 2008. *Goodbye Mr. Socialism.* New York: Seven Stories Press.

Neves, David, and Andries du Toit. 2012. "Money and Sociality in South Africa's Informal Economy." *Africa* 82 (1): 131–49.

Neves, David, Michael Samson, Ingrid van Niekirk, Sandile Hlatshwayo, and Andries du Toit. 2009. *The Use and Effectiveness of Social Grants in South Africa.* Cape Town: Institute for Poverty, Land and Agrarian Studies (PLAAS), University of Western Cape; Economic Policy Research Institute (EPRI), University of Cape Town; and FinMark Trust.

Ngwane, Zolani. 2004. " 'Real Men Reawaken Their Father's Homesteads, the Educated Leave Them in Ruins.' " In *Producing African Futures: Ritual and Reproduction in a Neoliberal Age*, ed. Brad Weiss. New York: Brill.

Niehaus, Isak. 2010. "Maternal Incest as Moral Panic: Envisioning Futures without Fathers in the south African Lowveld." *Journal of Southern African Studies* 36 (4): 833–49.

Nyamnjoh, Francis B. 2006. *Insiders and Outsiders: Citizenship and Xenophobia in Contemporary Southern Africa*. London: Zed.

Nyerere, Julius K. 1968. *Ujamaa: Essays on Socialism*. Dar es Salaam: Oxford University Press.

O'Laughlin, Bridget, Henry Bernstein, Ben Cousins, and Pauline E. Peters. 2013. Special Issue: "Agrarian Change, Rural Poverty and Land Reform in South Africa since 1994." *Journal of Agrarian Change* 13 (1): 1–196.

O'Malley, Pat. 1996. "Risk and Responsibility." In *Foucault and Political Reason: Liberalism, Neo-liberalism, and Rationalities of Government*, ed. Andrew Barry, Thomas Osborne, and Nikolas S. Rose. London: UCL Press.

Omer-Cooper, John D. 1966. *The Zulu Aftermath: A Nineteenth-Century Revolution in Bantu Africa*. London: Longmans.

Owen, Robert. (1813) 2004. *A New View of Society: Or, Essays on the Formation of the Human Character and the Application of the Principle to Practice*. Whitefish, MT: Kessinger Publishing.

Paine, Thomas. 1830. *The Political Writings of Thomas Paine*, vol. 2. New York: Solomon King.

Parnell, Susan, and Jennifer Robinson. 2012. "(Re)theorizing Cities from the Global South: Looking Beyond Neoliberalism." *Urban Geography* 33 (4): 593–617.

Pateman, Carole. 1989. *The Disorder of Women: Democracy, Feminism, and Political Theory*. Palo Alto, CA: Stanford University Press.

Peppiatt, David, John Mitchell, and Penny Holzmann. 2001. *Cash Transfers in Emergencies: Evaluating Benefits and Assessing Risks*. Network Paper 35, Humanitarian Practice Network, Overseas Development Institute, London.

Perrings, Charles. 1979. *Black Mineworkers in Central Africa: Industrial Strategies and the Evolution of an African Proletariat in the Copperbelt, 1911–1941*. London: Holmes and Meier.

Peterson, Nicolas. 1993. "Demand Sharing: Reciprocity and the Pressure for Generosity among Foragers." *American Anthropologist* 95 (4): 860–74.

———. 2013. "On the Persistence of Sharing: Personhood, Asymmetrical Reciprocity, and Demand Sharing in the Indigenous Australian Domestic Moral Economy." *Australian Journal of Anthropology* 24:166–76.

Philip, Kate. 2013. *The Transformative Potential of Public Employment Programmes*. Occasional Paper Series 1/2013, Graduate School of Development Policy and Practice, University of Cape Town.

Phiri, Kings M. 1988. "Pre-colonial States of Central Malawi: Towards a Reconstruction of Their History." *Society of Malawi Journal* 41 (1): 1–29.

Piot, Charles. 1991. "Of Persons and Things: Some Reflections on African Spheres of Exchange." *Man* (n.s.) 26:405–24.

Pitcher, M. Anne. 2007. "What Has Happened to Organized Labor in Southern Africa?" *International Labor and Working-Class History* 72 (1): 134–60.

Piven, Frances Fox, and Richard Cloward. 1993. *Regulating the Poor: The Functions of Public Welfare*. New York: Vintage.

Platzky, Laurine, and Cherryl Walker. 1985. *The Surplus People: Forced Removals in South Africa*. Johannesburg: Ravan Press.

Pogge, Thomas W. 2008. *World Poverty and Human Rights: Cosmopolitan Responsibilities and Reforms*, 2nd ed. Malden, MA: Polity Press.

Polanyi, Karl. (1944) 2001. *The Great Transformation: The Political and Economic Origins of Our Time*. Boston: Beacon Press.

Posel, Deborah. 2005. "The Case for a Welfare State: Poverty and the Politics of the Urban African Family in the 1930s and 1940s." In *South Africa's 1940s: Worlds of Possibilities*, ed. Saul Dubow and Alan Jeeves. Cape Town: Double Storey Books.

Postone, Moishe. 1996. *Time, Labor, and Social Domination: A Reinterpretation of Marx's Critical Theory*. New York: Cambridge University Press.

Povinelli, Elizabeth A. 2006. *The Empire of Love: Toward a Theory of Intimacy, Genealogy, and Carnality*. Durham, NC: Duke University Press.

Radcliffe-Brown, A. R. 1965. "On Social Structure." In *Structure and Function in Primitive Society*, 188–204. New York: Free Press.

Rancière, Jacques. 2010. *Dissensus: On Politics and Aesthetics*. London: Bloomsbury Academic.

Rees, Tobias. 2014. "Humanity/Plan; or, On the 'Stateless' Today (Also Being an Anthropology of Global Health)." *Cultural Anthropology* 29 (3): 457–78.

Robins, Steven. 2003. "Grounding 'Globalisation from Below': 'Global Citizens' in Local Spaces." In *What Holds Us Together: Social Cohesion in South Africa*, ed. David Chidester, Phillip Dexter, and Wilmot Godfrey James. Pretoria: Human Sciences Research Council (HSRC) Press.

———. 2008. *From Revolution to Rights: Social Movements, NGOs, and Popular Politics after Apartheid*. New York: James Currey.

Roelen, Keetie, and Stephen Devereux. 2013. *Promoting Inclusive Social Protection in the Post-2015 Framework*. Policy Briefing 39, Institute of Development Studies, Brighton, UK.

Roemer, John E. 1996. *Equal Shares: Making Market Socialism Work*. New York: Verso.

Rogerson, Christian M. 1996. "Urban Poverty and the Informal Economy in South Africa's Economic Heartland." *Environment and Urbanization* 8 (1): 167–79.

Rosaldo, Michelle Zimbalist. 1974. "Woman, Culture, and Society: A Theoretical Overview." In *Woman, Culture, and Society*, ed. Michelle Zimbalist Rosaldo and Louise Lamphere. Palo Alto, CA: Stanford University Press.

Rose, Nikolas. 1999. *Powers of Freedom: Reframing Political Thought*. New York: Cambridge University Press.

Ross, Fiona C. 2010. *Raw Life, New Hope: Decency, Housing and Everyday Life in a Postapartheid Community*. Cape Town: Juta Academic.

Roy, Ananya. 2010. *Poverty Capital: Microfinance and the Making of Development*. New York: Routledge.

Russell, Bertrand. (1918) 2008. *Proposed Roads to Freedom: Socialism, Anarchism, and Syndicalism.* Rockville, Maryland: Arc Manor.

Rutherford, Blair. 2008. "Conditional Belonging: Farm Workers and the Cultural Politics of Recognition in Zimbabwe." *Development and Change* 39 (1): 73–99.

Sahlins, Marshall. 1974. *Stone Age Economics.* Chicago: Aldine.

Sandbrook, Richard, Marc Edelman, Patrick Heller, and Judith Teichman. 2007. *Social Democracy in the Global Periphery: Origins, Challenges, Prospects.* New York: Cambridge University Press.

Sansom, Basil. 1976. "A Signal Transaction and Its Currency." In *Transaction and Meaning: Directions in the Anthropology of Exchange and Symbolic Behavior,* ed. Bruce Kapferer. Philadelphia: Institute for the Study of Human Issues.

Sassen, Saskia. 2010. "A Savage Sorting of Winners and Losers: Contemporary Versions of Primitive Accumulation." *Globalizations* 7 (1–2): 23–50.

Saul, John. 2011. "Proletariat and Precariat: Non-transformative Global Capitalism and the African Case." Paper presented at the conference Beyond Precarious Labor: Rethinking Socialist Strategies, CUNY Graduate Center, New York, May 12–13.

Schmitt, John, Kris Warner, and Sarika Gupta. 2010. *The High Budgetary Cost of Incarceration.* Washington, DC: Center for Economic and Policy Research.

Seekings, Jeremy. 2005. "Visions, Hopes and Views about the Future: The Radical Moment of South African Welfare Reform." In *South Africa's 1940s: Worlds of Possibilities,* ed. Saul Dubow and Alan Jeeves. Cape Town: Double Storey Books.

———. 2006. "Employment Guarantee or Minimum Income? Workfare and Welfare in Developing Countries." Paper presented at the Fifth Congress of the US Basic Income Guarantee Network, Philadelphia, February 2006.

———. 2007. " 'Not a Single White Person Should Be Allowed to Go Under': Swartgevaar and the Origins of South Africa's Welfare State, 1924–1929." *Journal of African History* 48 (3): 375–94.

———. 2008a. *Beyond 'Fluidity': Kinship and Households as Social Projects.* Working Paper 237, Center for Social Science Research, University of Cape Town.

———. 2008b. "The Carnegie Commission and the Backlash against Welfare State-Building in South Africa, 1931–1937." *Journal of Southern African Studies* 34 (3): 515–37.

———. 2008c. " 'Just Deserts': Race, Class and Distributive Justice in Post-apartheid South Africa." *Journal of Southern African Studies* 34 (1): 39–60.

———. 2008d. "Welfare Regimes and Redistribution in the South." In *Divide and Deal: The Politics of Distribution in Democracies,* ed. Ian Shapiro, Peter A. Swenson, and Daniela Donno Panayides. New York: NYU Press.

Seekings, Jeremy, and Heidi Matisonn. 2010. *The Continuing Politics of Basic Income in South Africa.* Working Paper 286, Center for Social Science Research, University of Cape Town.

Seekings, Jeremy, and Nicoli Nattrass. 2005. *Class, Race, and Inequality in South Africa.* New Haven, CT: Yale University Press.

Sembene, Ousmane. 1997. *The Money-Order with White Genesis: Two Novellas.* London: Heinemann.

Sen, Amartya. 1983. *Poverty and Famines: An Essay on Entitlement and Deprivation.* Oxford: Oxford University Press.

———. 1997. "Equality of What?" In *Choice, Welfare and Measurement.* Cambridge, MA: Harvard University Press.

———. 1999. *Development as Freedom.* New York: Anchor Books.

Sevenhuijsen, Selma. 1998. *Citizenship and the Ethics of Care: Feminist Considerations on Justice, Morality and Politics.* New York: Routledge.

Sevenhuijsen, Selma, Vivienne Bozalek, Amanda Bouws, and Marie Minnaar-McDonald. 2003. "South African Social Welfare Policy: An Analysis Using the Ethic of Care." *Critical Social Policy* 23 (3): 299–321.

Shachar, Ayelet. 2009. *The Birthright Lottery: Citizenship and Global Inequality.* Cambridge, MA: Harvard University Press.

Sharife, Khadija, and Patrick Bond. 2013. "Payment for Ecosystem Services versus Ecological Reparations: The 'Green Economy,' Litigation and a Redistributive Eco-debt Grant." *South African Journal of Human Rights* 29 (1): 144–69.

Sichone, Owen. 2008. "Xenophobia." In *New South African Keywords,* ed. Nick Shepherd and Steven Robins, 255–63. Athens: Ohio University Press.

Simon, Julian L. 1994. "The Airline Oversales Auction Plan: The Results." *Journal of Transport Economics and Policy* 28 (3): 319–23.

Simone, AbdouMaliq. 2004. *For the City Yet to Come: Changing African Life in Four Cities.* Durham, NC: Duke University Press.

Smith, Daniel Jordan. 2008. *A Culture of Corruption: Everyday Deception and Popular Discontent in Nigeria.* Princeton, NJ: Princeton University Press.

Soares, Fábio Veras, Rafael Perez Ribas, and Rafael Guerreiro Osório. 2010. "Evaluating the Impact of Brazil's Bolsa Família: Cash Transfer Programs in Comparative Perspective." *Latin American Research Review* 45 (2): 173–90.

South Africa. 2011. "About SA—Social Development." South Africa Government Online. Accessed October 13, 2011. http://www.info.gov.za/aboutsa/socialdev.htm.

Spiegel, Andrew. 2005. "From Exposé to Care: Preliminary Thoughts about Shifting the Ethical Concerns of South African Social Anthropology." *Anthropology Southern Africa* 28 (3–4): 133–41.

Stallybrass, Peter. 1990. "Marx and Heterogeneity: Thinking the Lumpenproletariat." *Representations* 31 (1): 69–95.

Standing, Guy. 2002. *Beyond the New Paternalism: Basic Security as Equality.* New York: Verso.

———. 2008. "How Cash Transfers Promote the Case for Basic Income." *Basic Income Studies* 3 (1): 1–30.

———. 2011. *The Precariat: The New Dangerous Class.* London: Bloomsbury Academic.

———. 2013. "India's Experiment in Basic Income." *Global Dialogue: Newsletter for the International Sociological Association* 3 (5): 24–26.

Standing, Guy, and Michael Samson. 2003. *A Basic Income Grant for South Africa.* Lansdowne: University of Cape Town Press.

Statistics South Africa. 2013. *General Household Survey, 2012.* Statistical Release P0318. Pretoria: Statistics South Africa.

Strange, Susan. 1997. *Casino Capitalism*. Manchester, UK: Manchester University Press.

Strathern, Marilyn, ed. 2000. *Audit Cultures: Anthropological Studies in Accountability, Ethics and the Academy*. London: Taylor and Francis.

Swidler, Ann, and Susan Cotts Watkins. 2007. "Ties of Dependence: AIDS and Transactional Sex in Rural Malawi." *Studies in Family Planning* 38 (3): 147–62.

———. 2009. "Teach a Man to Fish: The Sustainability Doctrine and Its Social Consequences." *World Development* 37 (7): 1182–96.

Tabatabai, Hamid. 2011. "The Basic Income Road to Reforming Iran's Price Subsidies." *Basic Income Studies* 6 (1): 1–24.

Taussig, Michael T. 1980. *The Devil and Commodity Fetishism in South America*. Chapel Hill: University of North Carolina Press.

Thompson, T. Jack. 1995. *Christianity in Northern Malawi: Donald Fraser's Missionary Methods and Ngoni Culture*. New York: Brill.

Tilton, Doug. 2005. "BIG Fact Sheet #1." BIG Coalition website. Accessed September 11, 2005. http://www.big.org.za/index.php?option=articles&task=viewarticle&artid=5.

Titmuss, Richard M. (1970) 1997. *The Gift Relationship: From Human Blood to Social Policy*. London: The New Press.

Tribe of Moles. 2011. "Work, Production and the Common: A Provocation." Accessed February 27, 2013. http://tribeofmoles.wordpress.com/a-provocation/.

Turner, Bryan S. 2010. "T. H. Marshall, Social Rights and English National Identity." *Citizenship Studies* 13 (1): 65–73.

Turner, Stephen J. 2005. *Livelihoods and Sharing: Trends in a Lesotho Village, 1976–2004*. Research Report 22, Program for Land and Agrarian Studies (PLAAS), University of the Western Cape, South Africa.

UNICEF (United Nations Children's Fund). 2012. *Zimbabwe Harmonized Social Cash Transfer Programme (HSCT): Analysis of the Process and Results of Targeting Labour Constrained Food Poor Households in the First 10 Districts*. Harare: UNICEF Zimbabwe.

USBLS (United States Bureau of Labor Statistics). 2013. *Women in the Labor Force: A Databook*. Washington, DC: United States Bureau of Labor Statistics.

Valodia, Imraan, and Richard Devey. 2012. "The Informal Economy in South Africa: Debates, Issues and Policies." *Margin: The Journal of Applied Economic Research* 6:133.

van der Veen, Robert J., and Philippe van Parijs. 1986. "A Capitalist Road to Communism." *Theory and Society* 15 (5): 635–55.

van der Waal, Kees, and John Sharp. 1988. "The Informal Sector: A New Resource." In *South African Keywords: The Uses and Abuses of Political Concepts*, ed. Emile Boonzaier and John Sharp. Cape Town: David Philip.

van Onselen, Charles. 1976. "Randlords and Rotgut 1886–1903: An Essay on the Role of Alcohol in the Development of European Imperialism and Southern African Capitalism, with Special Reference to Black Mineworkers in the Transvaal Republic." *History Workshop* 2:33–89.

———. 1986. *Chibaro: African Mine Labour in Southern Rhodesia, 1900–1933*. London: Pluto.

———. 1992. "The Social and Economic Underpinning of Paternalism and Violence on the Maize Farms of the South-Western Transvaal, 1900–1950." *Journal of Historical Sociology* 5 (2): 127–60.

———. 1996. *The Seed Is Mine: The Life of Kas Maine, a South African Sharecropper, 1894–1985.* New York: Hill and Wang.

van Parijs, Philippe. 1993. *Marxism Recycled.* New York: Cambridge University Press.

———. 1995. *Real Freedom for All: What (If Anything) Can Justify Capitalism?* New York: Oxford University Press.

———. 2007. "International Distributive Justice." In *A Companion to Contemporary Political Philosophy,* vol. 2, ed. Robert E. Goodin, Philip Pettit, and Thomas Pogge, 638–52. Oxford: Blackwell.

———. 2013. "The Universal Basic Income: Why Utopian Thinking Matters, and How Sociologists Can Contribute to It." *Politics and Society* 41 (2): 171–82.

Vansina, Jan. 1990. *Paths in the Rainforests: Toward a History of Political Tradition in Equatorial Africa.* Madison: University of Wisconsin Press.

Virno, Paolo. 2004. *A Grammar of the Multitude: For an Analysis of Contemporary Forms of Life.* New York: Semiotext(e).

von Schnitzler, Antina. 2008. "Citizenship Prepaid: Water, Calculability, and Techno-Politics in South Africa." *Journal of Southern African Studies* 34 (4): 899–917.

Wacquant, Loïc. 2001. "The Penalization of Poverty and the Rise of Neo-liberalism." *European Journal of Criminology Policy Research* 9 (4): 401–12.

———. 2009. *Punishing the Poor: The Neoliberal Government of Social Insecurity.* Durham, NC: Duke University Press.

Walker, Cherryl. 2008. *Landmarked: Land Claims and Restitution in South Africa.* Athens: Ohio University Press.

Weeks, Kathi. 2011. *The Problem with Work: Feminism, Marxism, Antiwork Politics, and Post-work Imaginaries.* Durham, NC: Duke University Press.

White, Hylton. 2001. "Tempora et Mores: Family Values and the Possessions of a Post-apartheid Countryside." *Journal of Religion in Africa* 31 (4): 457–79.

———. 2004. "Ritual Haunts: The Timing of Estrangement in a Post-apartheid Countryside." In *Producing African Futures: Ritual and Politics in a Neoliberal Age,* ed. Brad Weiss. Leiden: Brill.

———. 2010. "Outside the Dwelling of Culture: Estrangement and Difference in Postcolonial Zululand." *Anthropological Quarterly* 83 (3): 497–518.

———. 2012. "A Post-Fordist Ethnicity: Insecurity, Authority, and Identity in South Africa." *Anthropological Quarterly* 85 (2): 397–428.

Widerquist, Karl, and Michael W. Howard, eds. 2012. *Exporting the Alaska Model: Adapting the Permanent Fund Dividend for Reform around the World.* New York: Palgrave Macmillan.

Widerquist, Karl, José A. Noguera, Yannick Vanderborght, Jurgen De Wispelaere, eds. 2013. *Basic Income: An Anthology of Contemporary Research.* Hoboken, NJ: Wiley-Blackwell.

Widlok, Thomas. 2012. "Virtue." In *A Companion to Moral Anthropology,* ed. Didier Fassin, 186–203. Hoboken, NJ: John Wiley and Sons.

Wiese, Carl. (1891) 1983. *Expedition in East-Central Africa, 1888–1891: A Report.* Ed. Harry W. Langworthy. Trans. Donald Ramos. Norman: University of Oklahoma Press.

Wilding, Paul. 1976. "Richard Titmuss and Social Welfare." *Social and Economic Administration* 10 (3): 147–66.

Wolpe, Harold. 1972. "Capitalism and Cheap Labour-Power in South Africa: From Segregation to Apartheid." *Economy and Society* 1 (4): 425–56.

Woodburn, James. 1998. " 'Sharing Is Not a Form of Exchange': An Analysis of Property-Sharing in Immediate-Return Hunter-Gatherer Societies." In *Property Relations: Renewing the Anthropological Tradition*, ed. C. M. Hann, 48–63. New York: Cambridge University Press.

World Bank. 2009. *Conditional Cash Transfers: Reducing Present and Future Poverty.* Washington, DC: The World Bank.

———. 2011. *Overview of State Ownership in the Global Minerals Industry.* Washington, DC: Raw Material Group, World Bank.

Wright, Eric Olin. 2006. "Basic Income, Stakeholder Grants, and Class Analysis." In *Redesigning Distribution: Basic Income and Stakeholder Grants as Cornerstones for an Egalitarian Capitalism*, ed. Bruce Ackerman, Anne Alstott, and Philippe Van Parijs, 91–100. New York: Verso.

Wright, John. 1995. "Mfecane Debates." *Southern African Review of Books*, 39–40.

Wright, Marcia. 1993. *Strategies of Slaves and Women: Life-Stories from East/Central Africa.* London: James Currey.

Yanagisako, Sylvia. 2002. *Producing Culture and Capital: Family Firms in Italy.* Princeton, NJ: Princeton University Press.

———. 2012. "Immaterial and Industrial Labor: On False Binaries in Hardt and Negri's Trilogy." *Focaal* 64:16–23

Zaloom, Caitlin. 2010. *Out of the Pits: Traders and Technology from Chicago to London.* Chicago: University of Chicago Press.

Zelizer, Viviana A. 2005. *The Purchase of Intimacy.* Princeton, NJ: Princeton University Press.

Zhang, Li. 2002. *Strangers in the City: Reconfigurations of Space, Power, and Social Networks within China's Floating Population.* Palo Alto, CA: Stanford University Press.

Žižek, Slavoj. 2010. *Living in the End Times.* New York: Verso.

Index